Pow

Power

Edited by STEVEN LUKES

NEW YORK UNIVERSITY PRESS
Washington Square, New York

NEW YORK UNIVERSITY PRESS
Washington Square, New York, N.Y. 10003

Library of Congress Cataloging-in-Publication Data
  Power.
    (Readings in social and political theory)
    Bibliography: p.
    Includes index.
    1. Power (Social sciences)   I. Lukes, Steven.
    II. Series.
    HM136.P82 1986   303.3   86-8511
    ISBN 0-8147-5030-3
    ISBN 0-8147-5031-1 (pbk.)

New York University Press books are printed on acid-free paper,
and their binding materials are chosen for strength and durability.

Manufactured in the United States of America.

Contents

Introduction

STEVEN LUKES

When we are interested in power – in studying, acquiring, maintaining, increasing, reducing or destroying it – what is it that we are interested in? Answering this question turns out to be far from simple, as this book demonstrates. Its chief aim is to show what divides and what unites the various plausible answers that can be given to it.

It is often suggested that the answer is simple, even self-evident. But such suggestions, once they are examined, reveal hidden assumptions and unanswered questions. Once these are raised, the views of power advanced seem by no means obvious.

Thus, for instance, Bertrand Russell defines power as 'the production of intended effects'. But is power the actual *production* of such effects or the *capacity* to produce them? Don't my resources – my strength, say, or personal magnetism or wealth or skill or organizational backing – give me power, even when I do not deploy them? And is it *necessary* that the effects be intended? Can't I have or exercise power without deliberately seeking to do so, in routine or unconsidered ways, without grasping the effects I can or do bring about, as when, by making investment decisions, I may deprive unknown people of work, or provide them with it? And is it *sufficient* that the results be intended? What if, even if they are, I produce them by luck or through factors entirely beyond my control, as when I win a game of chance? And, even if intended, how are such intentions to be ascertained: by accepting what I say in advance, or by interpreting what I do? (In the passage included here, Michel Foucault suggests that one should study power 'at the point where its intention, if it has one, is completely invested in its real and effective practices'.) And *which* effects are going to count? Surely not all intended effects? Am I powerful (as opposed to you) if the effects I intentionally produce are produced because you have threatened or induced me, or if I produce them because I know they are the effects you want me to produce? And am I powerful if I can only produce such effects at enormous cost, say by sacrificing my life or what gives it value, or if I produce nothing but trivial and unimportant effects (and how do we decide what is and what is not important)?

Max Weber's view of power was like Russell's in stressing the element of intention or 'will' but unlike it in stressing the capacity to realize it (rather than its actual realization) and in suggesting that resistance, actual or potential, is relevant to attributions of power. Weber variously defined power as 'the probability that an actor in a social relationship will be in a position to carry out his own will despite resistance, regardless of the basis on which this probability rests'[1] and as 'the chance of a man or a number of men to realize their own will even against the resistance of others who are participating in the action'.[2] But, first, we may ask Weber (and indeed Russell) whether the will or intention (as distinct from its realization) is actual or hypothetical. Am I powerful if I can only achieve what I actually want? What if, like the Stoics, I want only what I can get, or, like a conformist, only what others want, or, like a sycophant, only what (I think) others want me to want? Surely power is in part the power to achieve what I might plausibly but don't actually want? And, second, what is the relevance of *resistance*? Is the *presence* of conflict or resistance endemic to power? Surely not, for power can be used to avert or pre-empt it and can also, as we shall see, be co-operatively held and exercised. Perhaps rather, as Weber's second definition suggests, resistance is relevant in the sense that, *if* it is actualized, it provides the test by which one can measure relative power, where parties conflict over an issue. But even this can't be quite right, since I can have more power than you, indeed power over you, even though you can on particular occasions, perhaps at great cost to yourself, resist me successfully.

A different approach is suggested by Robert Dahl, for whom power amounts to the control of behaviour. His 'intuitive idea of power' is that '*A* has power over *B* to the extent that he can get *B* to do something that *B* would not otherwise do'.[3] But with this there are various problems. First, it is hard to see how the 'extent' in question can be uncontroversially measured, since what counts as changing *B*'s behaviour, and what counts as a lesser or greater change, depend both on context and on one's point of view. (Do I change your behaviour by getting you to do the same thing in a different way? If I get you to run or jump, which is the greater change?). Second, not every such change looks like an effect of *power*. What about, say, successful *requests* or persuasive *advice* or convincing *arguments*? And what about certain unintended consequences, as when *A* can get *B* to wait at the bus stop, just by being the last to get on the bus? And third, are there not many cases – say, when I beat you or imprison you or deprive you of desired resources – when, without changing your behaviour, I plainly seem not merely to have more power than you, but power *over* you?

Weber's and Dahl's approaches both focus on the idea of 'power over', but other approaches reject this focus as either misconceived or too narrow. Thus Hannah Arendt rejects the suggestion that the 'power question' is 'Who rules whom?' and the focus on the 'command–obedience relationship' and she speaks rather of political institutions as 'manifestations and materializations of power'. Power is 'not the property of an individual'; it 'corresponds to the human ability not just to act but to act in concert'. But, as Habermas's essay in this volume argues, this view relies on too narrow and nostalgic a view of the field of power (politics) as *praxis*, 'the speaking and acting together of individuals': it bans from consideration power's strategic uses, it isolates politics, thus conceived, from its economic and social context, and it cannot account, in terms of power, for all the ways in which genuine mutual understanding and consent, based on common convictions, are systematically blocked and given spurious form in actual political societies.

Talcott Parsons, like Arendt, rejects the Weberian view of power as 'highly selective' and serving to 'elevate a secondary and derived aspect of a total phenomenon into the central place'. Power for Parsons is a system resource, a 'generalized facility or resource in the society', analogous to money, which enables the achievement of collective goals through the agreement of members of a society to legitimize leadership positions whose incumbents further the goals of the system, if necessary by the use of 'negative sanctions'.[4] Parsons claims that his account presents power as a phenomenon both of coercion and of consensus because 'it is a phenomenon which integrates a plurality of factors and outputs of political effectiveness and is not to be identified with any one of them'. Power depends on 'the institutionalization of authority and hence the rights of collective agents to mobilize performances and define them as binding obligations'; this authority rests on a 'consensus' with respect to a system of norms legitimized by 'the values of the system'. But this is to make authority – authority based on the attaining of 'system goals' and recognized by an assumed 'value consensus' – not merely a basis, but the *only* basis of power. 'Illegitimate power' then becomes a self-contradiction and 'the threat of coercive measures, or of compulsion, without legitimation or justification, should not properly be called the use of power at all'. In this way much of what has preoccupied most students of power down the ages is filtered out.

Nicos Poulantzas is like Parsons in adopting a systemic (or, as he prefers to say, structural) perspective on power. Both treat it, in Parsons's words, as 'a *specific* mechanism operating to bring about changes in the action of other units, individual or collective, in the processes of social interaction'. Both refuse to apply it to 'inter-individual' relations or to social relations that are independent of the wider system as defined and explained by their respective theories. But for Poulantzas, power identifies the ways in which that system (the '*ensemble* of the structures') affects 'the relations of the practices of the various classes in conflict': it is 'the capacity of a class to realize its specific objective interests'. On this view class becomes not only a locus but the only locus of power operating through individuals (the 'bearers' or 'supports' of the structure) and its effects are understood solely in terms of the pursuit of class interests. On this view, classes, facing others in a field of struggle, extend their power as they extend their 'horizons of action'. To accept this account of power, you have to accept not merely the rejection of 'the problematic of the subject' (a 'problematic' well illustrated here by Russell, Weber and Dahl) but also Poulantzas's structuralist version of the marxist theory of class.

I have so far considered a number of answers to the question with which I began, selected partly because they have been influential and partly because they exhibit something of the range of views of power that exist and which this book seeks further to display. I have also suggested that they all fail satisfactorily to answer the question asked. *A fortiori*, none offers a generally satisfying and informative definition that excludes just what all can agree should be excluded and includes just what all can agree should be included.

On the other hand, each does say something true and relevant. The effects of power seem clearly to bear some relation to intention and will: someone whose actions regularly subvert his intentions and wants can scarcely be called powerful. The outcome of resist-ance is certainly relevant where comparisons of power are at issue. Affecting behaviour is certainly a centrally important form of power, though not all such affecting is power and not all power is such affecting. The co-operative and communicative aspect of empowerment certainly requires attention, as do the ways in which power maintains social systems and advances conflicting collective interests within them. Perhaps a generally satisfying definition can be devised by fitting these various insights together into a single picture?

Perhaps, but I doubt it. It is more likely that the very search for such a definition is a mistake. For the variations in what interests us when we are interested in power run deep, as I shall show, and what unites the various views of power is too thin and formal to provide a generally satisfying definition, applicable to all cases.

Let us begin with the following, very thin suggestion: that to have power is to be able to make a difference to the world. Those interested in power are interested in two questions: in the difference that is made, and in the making of that difference. Let us call the first an interest in the outcomes and the second an interest in the locus of power.

To begin with outcomes, it is clear that not all outcomes, or differences we make to the world, are going to qualify as resulting from power. They must, in the first place, stand in a certain relation to the desires and beliefs of the powerful. To develop further a point already made, we would not think of someone as powerful if his actions regularly subverted his wants and frustrated his expectations. So in what relation must the outcomes of power stand to the desires and beliefs of the powerful?

The simplest answer to this is one we have already considered: that the powerful must intend them, that is, specifically desire them and believe them to be the likely result of appropriate action undertaken to bring them about. This answer does of course cover many cases but, as we have also begun to see, it is too narrow to cover many other cases where power seems to be at work. Thus, for example, I may own some land, thereby prohibiting you from trespassing on it, yet I may not intend this outcome (never perhaps having even thought of it) nor do I do anything to bring it about. Again, party workers may advance a politician's cause, say by mobilizing votes in his favour, perhaps because they hope for his patronage, without his knowing, let alone intending, that they do so.

A better answer might be that the outcomes of power must serve the *interests* of the powerful. To assess this suggestion, we need some grasp of what interests are. Following Joel Feinberg, let us say that one's interests

> taken as a miscellaneous collection, consist of all those things in which one has a stake, whereas one's interest in the singular, one's personal interest or self-interest, consists in the harmonious advancement of all one's interests in the plural. These interests, or perhaps more accurately, the things these interests are *in*, are distinguishable components of a person's well-being: he flourishes or languishes as they flourish or languish. What promotes them is to his advantage or *in his interest*; what thwarts them is to his detriment or *against his interest*.[5]

Interests, thus defined, may be seen as falling into two categories: a person's 'more ultimate goals and aspirations'; and his interests 'in the necessary means to his more ultimate goals, whatever the latter may be, or later come to be'. The latter, which have been called 'welfare interests' are interests in 'conditions that are generalized means to a great variety of possible goals and whose joint realization, in the absence of very special circumstances, is necessary for the achievement of more ultimate aims'.[6]

How do interests, so defined and classified, relate to desires and beliefs? The answer is complex, but here a few points are worth stressing. First, it seems, on the face of it, odd for someone to believe that he or she has an interest in something but not want it. On the other hand, second, one can fail to want something that is in one's interests, either because one does not know it is in one's interest(s), or because one does not know it is causally related to what is in one's interest(s), or because one may have other overriding wants, principles or passions.

As regards welfare interests, as Feinberg says, 'we are inclined to say that what promotes them is good for a person *in any case*, whatever his beliefs or wants may be'. For instance,

> A person's interest in health . . . would in fact be one of his interests, even if he mistakenly believed the contrary, and even if he wanted ill health and decay instead of good health and vitality. In regard to this particular interest, at least, there may be a correspondence between interest and want, but the existence of the former is not dependent upon, nor derivative from, the existence of the latter.[7]

As regards ulterior interests, by contrast, 'wants seem to have an essential role to play', for 'I seem to have a stake in them because I desire their fulfilment, rather than the other way round. In these instances, if my wants changed, my interests would too'.[8] On the other hand, not every want, however strong or urgent, is sufficient to create such interests: it must be linked to longer-range purposes and, Feinberg suggests, have at least these features: that it is 'a relatively deep-rooted and stable want whose fulfilment (can) both be reasonably hoped for and (usually) influenced by one's own efforts'. Our ultimate interests 'characteristically resemble what C. L. Stevenson has called "focal aims", ends (not *the* end) which are also means to many other divergent ends'. Indeed, 'their advancement or fulfilment invariably produces benefits of a great many kinds throughout the whole network of personal wants and interests':

Thus, building a dream house is a means to the entertainment of house guests, to the private pursuit of studies and pleasures, to hours of aesthetic contemplation, and so on; the achievement of political power is a means to the advancement of favourite causes and policies; and the solution to a scientific problem is a means to the further advance of knowledge and technology, to say nothing of personal glory.[9]

So perhaps the outcomes of power are such as to further the *interests* of the powerful (either their welfare interests or their ulterior interests, or their total interests taken together)? This suggestion certainly captures many types of case, including the two cited earlier: namely, the landlord's legally protected welfare interest in freedom from trespass, or exclusive possession and enjoyment of his land; and the politician's interdependent focal aims of gaining office and furthering his favoured causes. Yet it excludes other cases, such as the dictator who imprisons me on some arbitrary whim (which act may well be against his interests, both welfare and ulterior) and in general all cases where power realizes wants that do not constitute interests. It also fails to capture what we might call the 'service conception'[10] of power, according to which the powerful person merely serves the interests of others (either submitting his own interests to those of others or identifying his with theirs, or even with those of 'society' as a whole). Needless to say, this service conception is usually and especially favoured by the powerful and those employed in defending and promoting their power, though, as Arendt shows, it can also have a radical and critical edge. On the service conception, the interests, and thus by extension the wants and goals, that power outcomes exemplify are adopted and interpreted by the powerful on behalf of those they claim, or are claimed, to serve.

I have so far indicated various ways, direct and indirect, in which the outcomes of power relate to the desires and beliefs of those who hold or exercise it (or of those they are said to represent). They may be specifically desired via their intentions, they may be the generalized means or necessary conditions for realizing their ulterior wants and goals, they may directly contribute to realizing such wants and goals, or they may exhibit any of these features in surrogate form, in relation to the desires and beliefs of those the powerful represent. Can the class of possible outcomes of power be narrowed down any further?

Here a distinction needs to be drawn between power relative to an issue or an outcome, and power *simpliciter*. I take an issue to be a set of related outcomes. Issues can be 'partitioned' into outcomes in various ways (for instance, whether or not there will be a tax rise next April; or whether taxes will fall next April by $X_1, X_2, \ldots X_n$, remain unchanged or rise by $X_1, X_2, \ldots X_n$). To have power relative to an issue is to have power over one or more of its outcomes (and, *ceteris paribus*, the more of an issue's outcomes one has power over, the greater one's power relative to that issue). Power relative to an issue or an outcome can be studied relative to any issue or outcome, however big or small, the siting of nuclear weapons or of dustbins. The first four parts of Goldman's paper in this volume represent the most sophisticated attempt to date to analyse what such a study would involve – though Goldman's analysis is marred by the assumption, criticized above as over-simple, that 'the central idea in the concept of power . . . is concerned with *getting what one wants*'.

What, then, can be said of power *simpliciter*, where neither issues nor outcomes are specified? Goldman suggests that what we are here concerned with is 'overall power of individuals or groups' – how much power they have 'on the whole'. But, since he also rightly indicates that issues can be divided up in any way one chooses and thus cannot simply be *counted*, it is hard to see how any such summation or aggregation could be undertaken. Rather a judgement is made as to which are appropriate issues by which to assess which people have power and how much power they have. In trying to ascertain how much (unspecified) power individuals or groups or institutions have, we consider what Dahl calls the *scope* of their power – that is, what kinds of issues, and thus outcomes, they have power over. If they have power over certain kinds of issues, then they will be judged as having more power. 'A better answer to our question', Goldman writes, 'would appeal not to the number of issues over which we have power, but to their importance'. Thus

> I may have power with respect to what I eat for dinner tonight, what grades my students get, what sentences are written on my blackboard, etc. But Rockefeller has power with respect to 'really important' issues.[11]

How, then, is the *importance* of issues to be determined?

Here we have arrived at another major source of variation in conceptions of power. Different judgements of what is important yield different assessments of comparative (unspecified) power. Of course, within any given scope, or range of issues, one issue is likely to be more important than another if more people are affected. But this may not be true across scopes (compare the power of a pop star with that of a judge). What is crucial in deciding what is important is *how* people are affected by the outcomes of issues.

One apparently obvious answer to this question is to say that issues are important if they affect people's welfare. This is Goldman's answer. Goldman suggests that in deciding an issue's importance we must look not only at how many people are affected but also at 'how much difference in welfare the outcomes of the issue would cause', and that we should look at conjunctions of such welfare-affecting issues in assessing an agent's overall power. By welfare Goldman says he means ('for illustrative purposes') the satisfaction or non-satisfaction of desires. But a moment's reflection is enough to suggest that there are other more specific and other divergent ways of significantly and importantly affecting people, thus yielding other and divergent assessments of comparative power. These divergences are amply illustrated in the essays reprinted in this volume.

Maybe a useful way to think about these divergences is to distinguish various 'power questions' that people have in mind when they seek to locate and compare power. Different questions – and different interpretations of the same questions – arise out of different judgements about the importance of issues and outcomes: that is, about which issues and outcomes affect people significantly.

One such question is: 'Who can adversely affect the interests of whom?' This question, focusing on effects upon interests, can be interpreted in various ways, and indeed contending interpretations of it have generated one of the more lively debates about power in recent years, centring mainly around the literature of community power studies, beginning with Floyd Hunter's *Community Power Structure* and Dahl's study of New Haven, *Who Governs?* On what I have called the one-dimensional view of power,[12] interests are seen as equivalent to revealed preferences – revealed, that is, by political behaviour in decision-making; to exercise power is to prevail over the contrary preferences of others, with respect to 'key issues'. (This is the view that Dahl puts to work in *Who Governs?*, though it is only distantly related to his definition of power cited above.) On the two-dimensional view of power advanced by Peter Bachrach and Morton Baratz,[13] one exercises power in the manner the one-dimensionalists favour, but also by controlling the agenda, mobilizing the bias of the system, determining which issues are 'key' issues, indeed which issues come up for decision, and excluding those which threaten the interests of the powerful. Here interests adversely affected are shown by politically expressed preferences *and* extra-political or covertly expressed grievances and demands that are, in various ways, denied entry into the decision-making process. The three-dimensional view incorporates power of the first two kinds, but also allows that power may operate to shape and modify desires and beliefs in a manner contrary to people's interests. In consequence, neither revealed preferences nor grievances and inchoate demands will always express them. Our earlier discussion of interests helps clarify this possibility. Power, on this view, may encourage and sustain attitudes and expectations that work against people's 'welfare interests' or subvert and thwart their pursuit of their ulterior, focal aims, or both.

A second, different question is: 'Who can *control* whom?' This question can be seen as one that essentially concerns *freedom* and it can be interpreted as meaning 'Who can limit the freedom of whom?' (Of course, a certain range of freedoms can be seen as a central welfare interest, and this question can be seen as a sub-variant of the first.) The question, so interpreted, can point in a number of different directions, to different freedom-diminishing outcomes: to interferences with actual choices (as when I ban your preferred newspaper or political party or proscribe your religion); to structuring the available choices (by changing the price-tags, making some more attractive and others less so, as in all the varieties of inducement and coercion); to narrowing the 'feasible set' – the range of significant options that are available (precluding otherwise feasible choices); and to limiting the agent's capacity to make them. The topic of freedom is, of course, at least as complex as that of power (and one, as we are now seeing, closely interrelated with it), and we cannot here enter into the implications of these, and other, interpretations. Suffice it to point out (1) that *whether*, and if so *when*, inducement is freedom-restricting ('I made him an offer he couldn't refuse') and what constitutes coercion are matters of controversy, especially these days, with the present revival of laissez-faire liberalism; and (2) that in most of these postulated cases of freedom-diminishment, the actor whose *freedom* has, putatively, been restricted, can continue to act *freely*. This important point is clearly made in the extract included here by Georg Simmel, which focuses upon 'the spontaneity and co-efficiency of the subordinate subject'. Simmel argues that

> the super–subordination relationship destroys the subordinate's freedom only in the case of direct physical violation. In every other case this relationship only demands a price for the realization of freedom – a price, to be sure, which we are not willing to pay. It can narrow down more and more the sphere

of external conditions under which freedom is clearly realized, but, except for physical force, never to the point of the complete disappearance of freedom.

Nevertheless, the freedom-diminishing outcomes indicated plainly do significantly affect people's lives and thus determine attributions of power, as the passages reprinted here show. Thus Max Weber is here interested both in the power of monopolies 'acting upon the conduct of those dominated, who remain, however, formally free and are motivated simply by the pursuit of their own interests' and in 'the authoritative power of command' exacting obedience where the command is accepted as a 'valid norm'. In the first case the dominator structures the dominated's field of choice and in the second case (on Weber's view) narrows it, by imposing or appealing to 'a duty to obey'. And J. K. Galbraith, also interested in monopolistic or rather oligopolistic power, focuses here upon the realities of the corporate power of the modern business enterprise, only partially hidden behind the myths of the market and consumer sovereignty, seeking to condition people to believe that alternatives are not real. And finally Foucault treats of power, within a modern 'society of normalization', as a 'closely linked grid of disciplinary coercions' which involve an 'on-going subjugation' through 'continuous and uninterrupted processes which subject our bodies, govern our gestures, dictate our behaviours, etc.'. In this way, according to Foucault, 'subjects are gradually, progressively, really and materially constituted through a multiplicity of organisms, forces, energies, materials, desires, thoughts, etc.'. People thus become *subjects* in a double sense: subject to others 'by control and dependence' and tied to their 'own identity by consciousness and self-knowledge'.[14] In this way all the 'micro-mechanisms of power' – such as 'the apparatuses of surveillance, the medicalization of sexuality, of madness, of delinquency' – structure our field of action, rendering us both unfree and free.

The first two 'power questions' we have considered are versions of Lenin's famous question 'Who whom?', suggesting that power is held by some over others. The third question, now to be considered, does not necessarily carry this suggestion, though it does presuppose a background of competitive and conflictual social relations, and it may (but need not) require power of the other two kinds for its successful deployment. This is the distributive question: 'Who can get what?', where not all can get what they want or need. Here the significant effects of power are the securing of mutually recognized advantages (material or social), in a context of relative scarcity and competing claims. This is the notion of power typically used in sociological studies of stratification, and distributive discussions generally. Frank Parkin has isolated this way of thinking about power most clearly:

> To some extent, in fact, to conceive of stratification in terms of power may simply be another way of conceptualising the distribution of class and status advantages. That is, to speak of the distribution of power could be understood as another way of describing the flow of rewards; the very fact that the dominant class can successfully claim a disproportionate share of rewards *vis-à-vis* the subordinate class, is in a sense a measure of the former's power over the latter.[15]

It is in this sense that Weber, in another part of his work, spoke of 'classes', 'status groups' and 'parties' as 'phenomena of the distribution of power within a community'.[16] And it is in this sense that Gerhard Lenski, in the passage cited here, writes of power as 'the determinant of privilege' and of 'institutionalized forms of power' as 'the most useful resource in the struggle between individuals and groups for prestige and privilege'.

The 'power questions' so far considered all presuppose some kind of competition or conflict (even if only latent, as in the third dimension of interest-harming power) between those with more power and those with less. A further power question, that is familiar and well-embedded in our daily and scholarly discourse, makes no such assumption. It asks: 'Who can secure the achievement of collective goods?' Here the outcomes attributed to power are deemed important because of their significant effects on individuals *qua* members of some group, association or community: they advance goals or interests that they are held to share. Note that the first three power questions (and especially the first two) may seem to have a negative or pejorative implication, whereas this carries no such suggestion (from which it does not follow that combining the questions leads to greater objectivity or neutrality). It is with this question in mind that we may speak of the power that goes with political office and authority, and of the powers of delegates and representatives. This is the power question that is explored in this volume by Hannah Arendt and Talcott Parsons. Neither, however, explores the interconnections between the various power questions: when and to what extent advancing collective interests or the public interest requires acting against others' interests, diminishing their freedom, or benefiting at their expense. These interconnections are plainly presupposed (though not explored) in Poulantzas's specifically marxist account of power. Illustrating the tightly knit character of marxist class theory, he assumes that to advance a class's interests is to work against another's and that it involves social control and a struggle over the available surplus.

I have so far explored a number of divergences in our interests in the differences that power makes – in the outcomes in which, when concerned with power, we typically take an interest. Such outcomes, it seems, will be related to the desires and beliefs of the powerful, or those they represent, either (directly) through their intentions or (indirectly or directly) via their interests, and, unless otherwise specified, they will involve effects upon welfare, harm to interests, limits on freedom, distributive advantage or the securing of collective goods, or some combination of these.

It remains to consider our interest in *locating* power. What do we want to know when we want to know where power lies, and why do we want to know it?

One answer, which has, I suspect, wide intuitive appeal, invokes the link between power and responsibility – whether political, or legal, or moral. We want to know whom to hold responsible for the effects indicated above. Thus C. Wright Mills in his *The Power Elite* and elsewhere could write of calling the 'men of power' to account. Mills argued that power should be attributed to those in strategic positions who are able to initiate changes that are in the interests of broad segments of society but do not; he claimed that it is 'now sociologically realistic, morally fair and politically imperative to make demands upon men of power and to hold them responsible for specific courses of events'.[17] William Connolly and I have argued similarly.[18]

However, this unmediated view of the link between power and agency certainly seems, from various points of view, unduly simplistic. After all, the powerful typically only have and exercise their power by virtue of a web of causal relations over which they have scant control. Certainly from the standpoints both of Parsonian normative functionalism and of marxism (represented here by Habermas and Poulantzas) the direct attribution of responsibility, whether causal or moral, to individual power holders for the effects indicated will often make little sense. Indeed, Foucault argues, power 'is not to be taken to be a phenomenon of one individual's consolidated and homogeneous domination over others, or that of one group or class over others'. On the contrary, 'one should try to locate power at the extreme points of its exercise':

> It is never localised here or there, never in anybody's hands, never appropriated as a commodity or piece of wealth. Power is employed and exercised through a net-like organisation.

And not only do individuals circulate between its threads; they are always in the position of undergoing and exercising this power.[19]

Raymond Aron also doubts the sense of looking for elites of individual power holders, at least in contemporary Western democracies. He suggests, as against Wright Mills, that it is arguable that modern democracy disperses power: that conservatism and the maintenance of privilege are consequences of the dispersion of power in pluralistic societies and democratic regimes, not the result of a power elite at work that can be called to account. On the other hand, as Aron also persuasively argues, the kind of analysis that typically yields pluralist conclusions in such societies, focusing on decision-making in organizations and local communities, such as New Haven, will miss a crucially *political* dimension of power: after all, 'the decisions to be taken in New Haven are rarely of a kind to overturn individual habits or collective destiny'. For:

> At a certain level of social organization, what counts is not the number of decisions taken by one or another person, nor the number of cases in which A prevails over B, or B over C, or C over A. What counts is the person who takes the big decisions, those that are irreversible, whose consequences risk being prolonged indefinitely and being experienced by all of the collectivity's members.

Such decisions – whether taken individually or collegially and typically, though not always, in the field of strategy and diplomacy – are properly called historic and are perhaps a fit locus for the joint attribution of power and responsibility.

A second, familiar interest that guides our location of power is distributive. We ask: '*Cui bono?*' – who gains by bringing about, or helping to bring about, the outcomes indicated above? There must of course be a causal relationship. The mere fact that a person or elite or class may gain when others are significantly affected is not in itself significant: that I benefit from others' interests being harmed, or from their freedom being limited or from their gaining less than they might or from the securing of benefits accruing to all is not enough to show that I have power over others. But if my resources or my social position or my actions are causally related to such outcomes, *that* I so benefit, as compared to others, can often be the guiding reason for singling me (or my group or class) out as a powerholder. Others may be no less causally involved, but at cost or no benefit to their interests, in the short or long run. It is this that may lead us to see them as merely the accomplices or the instruments of those who in turn benefit at their expense. In a sense, we might say that they exercise a power that is not theirs. Power, thus conceived, lies where its benefits accrue. To conceive it thus is likely to lead us to locate it elsewhere than where a focus on fixing political or moral or legal responsibility would lead us to find it. It is, I suggest, this interest in locating power that underlies the complex notion of exploitation.

A third, no less familiar, interest in the location of power is more directly practical and political. It is the search for the sources of change – for the access points, the winning coalitions, the pivots, the levers, the bastions, the weak links (the metaphors reflect different social theories) by means of which desired social changes may be brought about, or prevented. Power lies where a certain proposed difference to significant outcomes can be made, or resisted. This is the intuition behind the maxim that power lies where the pressure groups go in a political system and behind Lenin's theory of the capitalist state and Antonio Gramsci's theory of hegemony, in which the state is compared to a series of fortifications demanding either a 'war of position' or a 'war of manoeuvre' (both these theories are replete with military metaphors). Interestingly, it is also present in Foucault's much more diffuse picture of power, when he stresses (though not in the passage here) the significance of recalcitrance and resistance in bringing power relations to light.

The problem is that the idea of 'making a difference' is by no means simple; indeed, it is highly controversial. One interesting attempt to make sense of it is to be found in a second article by Goldman (not reprinted here)[20] which develops the suggestion that '*S* has power over *e* just in case *S* is a nonredundant member of some set of persons such that, if all these persons wanted *e* to occur, then *e* would occur.'[21] I doubt that Goldman's attempt successfully captures all or even most plausible interpretations of the idea of 'making a difference', in the context of attributions of power. For one thing, as we have already seen, the focus on the relation between 'wanting' (even conditional wanting) and an outcome is, from various points of view, misleadingly narrow (and a view which requires joint wanting must be doubly so). You may have the power to advance my political career – say by supporting me on some issue or by merely letting me join your club – though you may not particularly want to do so, and may even be unaware of this outcome. Also, unwanted outcomes that nevertheless serve one's interests may be a basis for the attribution of power. Suppose that by standing in an election, I get you, not to vote for me, but to abstain from voting for my opponent? A whole (contestable) range of outcomes would seem to be includable within the ambit of power that, through chains of unintended consequences, fail to realize the wants of those who make a difference to their coming about.

More deeply, it will not be universally agreed that being able (nonredundantly) to make a difference even to wanted outcomes always counts as power. Consider the cases, referred to earlier, of *advice* and rational *argument*. These may be decisive in shaping indubitably significant outcomes, but do they constitute a form of *power*? Was Keynes powerful (rather than immensely influential) because of his impact on post-war economic policy (an impact he undoubtedly wanted)? The answer to this takes us back to the issue of power's relation to freedom. From some points of view, freely accepting advice and being convinced by arguments is incompatible with being subject to power (as control). Here the nature of the *link* between locus and outcome precludes an attribution of power (though we might well speak of the power of Keynes's arguments where we would not speak of the power of Keynes). From other points of view, however (for example, a concern with harm to interests or the pursuit of collective goods), or, indeed, from the same point of view if one classes economic 'advice' not as 'argument' but as 'ideology', an attribution of power could be perfectly in order.

I do, however, agree with Goldman that the 'possession of power ... depends on the truth of certain subjunctive conditionals',[22] most of them counterfactuals. The problem, in short, is to decide what to vary and what to hold constant when imagining alternative scenarios. This deep problem is no less endemic to the fourth, closely related interest we typically have in locating where power lies or lay. This is the historian's or social scientist's, or indeed plain human, interest in identifying points at which alternative arrangements or events *could have* made a significant difference. These points have been called 'branching points',[23] locations from which, it is arguable, alternative feasible paths could plausibly be envisaged. In fact we are interested, not merely in branching points, but in *turning* points – that is, points at which, we believe, individual or collective agency could have *made* a difference. Why we should be interested in identifying these – as, I suspect, we inescapably are – is itself an interesting question. Fortunately, perhaps, this is not the place to pursue it.

In this Introduction I have tried to answer the question 'What interests us when we are interested in power?' It turns out that there are various answers, all deeply familiar, which respond to our interests in both the outcomes and the location of power. Perhaps this explains why, in our ordinary unreflective judgements and comparisons of power, we normally know what we mean and have little difficulty in understanding one another, yet every attempt at a single general answer to the question has failed and seems likely to fail.

NOTES

1 Max Weber, *Economy and Society*, translated by G. Roth and C. Wittich (University of California Press, Berkeley and Los Angeles, 1978), p. 53.
2 Ibid., p. 926.
3 Robert Dahl, 'The concept of power', *Behavioral Science*, 2 (1957), pp. 201–15.
4 See also Parsons's critique of C. Wright Mills's *The Power Elite* in his 'The distribution of power in American society', *World Politics*, 10, (1957), pp. 123–43.
5 Joel Feinberg, *Harm to Others* (Oxford University Press, New York, 1984), p. 34.
6 Ibid., p. 37.
7 Ibid., p. 42.
8 Ibid. This is Feinberg's (and the present author's) view. On some ethical theories, of course, it would not be so. Feinberg's interpretation of how ulterior interests relate to wants derives from a certain meta-ethical position. An Aristotelian, say, would not agree with the last passage cited.
9 Ibid., pp. 45, 60, 45. Feinberg's idea of an 'interest network' is most illuminating.
10 I borrow this phrase from Joseph Raz who in a different context has defended the 'service conception of authority', which I have in turn criticized. See J. Raz, 'The justification of authority', *Philosophy and Public Affairs*, 14 (1), (Winter 1985), pp. 2–29; and S. Lukes, 'Perspectives on authority', *Nomos*, forthcoming.
11 A more thought-provoking contrast is made in the following joke: A man argues bitterly with his wife. Seeing this, a friend of the husband's reasons with him. 'I don't understand you', he says. 'In my household we never argue because everything is regulated once and for all. I make the important decisions and my wife looks after the details.' But how do you decide which is which?' asks the first. 'It's simple. My wife decides about the children's schooling, the doctor who treats them, where we take our holidays, what kind of car we have, and so on. . . . These are the details. And I decide how to solve the Northern Ireland

problem, whether to use sanctions against South Africa and how to bring peace to the Middle East.'

12 S. Lukes, *Power: A Radical View* (Macmillan, London, 1974).

13 See their *Power and Poverty: Theory and Practice* (Oxford University Press, New York, 1970).

14 Michael Foucault, 'Why study power? The question of the subject', translated as part of the Afterword to Hubert Drayfus and Paul Rabinow, *Michel Foucault: Beyond Structuralism and Hermeneutics*, 2nd edn, with an Afterword by, and an Interview with, Michel Foucault (University of Chicago Press, Chicago, 1983), p. 212.

15 Frank Parkin, *Class, Inequality and Political Order* (MacGibbon and Kee, London, 1971), p. 46. I think Parkin's last comment here is misleading. The fact indicated is not a measure of a dominant class's power *over* a subordinate class, but of its *greater* power. To see this, consider the situation of organized *vis-à-vis* unorganized workers. The former have *greater* power to secure rewards than the latter but need not have power *over* them.

16 *From Max Weber*, edited by H. H. Gerth and C. Wright Mills (Routledge and Kegan Paul, London, 1948), p. 181.

17 C. Wright Mills, *The Causes of World War Three* (Secker and Warburg, London, 1959), p. 100.

18 William Connolly, *The Terms of Political Discourse*, 2nd edn (Blackwell, Oxford, 1983), chapter 3 and my *Power: A Radical View*.

19 For a fascinating exploration of this last thought, in relation to contemporary Soviet-type societies, see the remarkable essay by Vaclav Havel, 'The power of the powerless' in Václav Havel et al., *The Power of the Powerless: Citizens against the State in Central-Eastern Europe*, with Introduction by Steven Lukes (Hutchinson, London, 1985). Havel speaks of what he calls 'the post-totalitarian system' in which the line of conflict between rulers and ruled 'runs *de facto* through each person, for everyone in his or her own way is both a victim and a supporter of the system' (p. 37).

20 Alvin Goldman, 'On the measurement of power', *Journal of Philosophy*, 71 (May 1974), pp. 231–52. Goldman's argument builds on and seeks to generalize that of L. S. Shapley and M. Shubik in their article 'A method for evaluating the distribution of power in a committee system', *American Political Science Review*, XLVIII (3), (September 1954), pp. 787–92.

21 Ibid., p. 233.

22 Ibid.

23 Jon Elster, *Logic and Society* (John Wiley, Chichester 1978), chapter 6.

1

The Forms of Power

BERTRAND RUSSELL

Power may be defined as the production of intended effects. It is thus a quantitative concept: given two men with similar desires, if one achieves all the desires that the other achieves, and also others, he has more power than the other. But there is no exact means of comparing the power of two men of whom one can achieve one group of desires, and another another; e.g. given two artists of whom each wishes to paint good pictures and become rich, and of whom one succeeds in painting good pictures and the other in becoming rich, there is no way of estimating which has the more power. Nevertheless, it is easy to say, roughly, that A has more power than B, if A achieves many intended effects and B only a few.

There are various ways of classifying the forms of power, each of which has its utility. In the first place, there is power over human beings and power over dead matter or non-human forms of life. I shall be concerned mainly with power over human beings, but it will be necessary to remember that the chief cause of change in the modern world is the increased power over matter that we owe to science.

Power over human beings may be classified by the manner of influencing individuals, or by the type of organization involved.

An individual may be influenced: (a) by direct physical power over his body, e.g. when he is imprisoned or killed; (b) by rewards and punishments as inducements, e.g. in giving or withholding employment; (c) by influence on opinion, i.e. propaganda in its broadest sense. Under this last head I should include the opportunity for creating desired habits in others, e.g. by military drill, the only difference being that in such cases action follows without any such mental intermediary as could be called opinion.

Reprinted with permission from Bertrand Russell, *Power: A New Social Analysis*, London: Allen and Unwin, 1938, Unwin paperbacks, 1975, chapter 3, pp. 25–34.

These forms of power are most nakedly and simply displayed in our dealings with animals, where disguises and pretences are not thought necessary. When a pig with a rope round its middle is hoisted squealing into a ship, it is subject to direct physical power over its body. On the other hand, when the proverbial donkey follows the proverbial carrot, we induce him to act as we wish by persuading him that it is to his interest to do so. Intermediate between these two cases is that of performing animals, in whom habits have been formed by rewards and punishments; also, in a different way, that of sheep induced to embark on a ship, when the leader has to be dragged across the gangway by force, and the rest then follow willingly.

All these forms of power are exemplified among human beings.

The case of the pig illustrates military and police power.

The donkey with the carrot typifies the power of propaganda.

Performing animals show the power of 'education'.

The sheep following their unwilling leader are illustrative of party politics, whenever, as is usual, a revered leader is in bondage to a clique or to party bosses.

Let us apply these Aesopian analogies to the rise of Hitler. The carrot was the Nazi programme (involving, e.g. the abolition of interest); the donkey was the lower middle class. The sheep and their leader were the Social Democrats and Hindenburg. The pigs (only so far as their misfortunes are concerned) were the victims in concentration camps, and the performing animals are the millions who make the Nazi salute.

The most important organizations are approximately distinguishable by the kind of power that they exert. The army and the police exercise coercive power over the body; economic organizations, in the main, use rewards and punishments as incentives and deterrents; schools, churches, and political parties aim at influencing opinion. But these distinctions are not very clear-cut, since every organization uses other forms of power in addition to the one which is most characteristic.

The power of the Law will illustrate these complexities. The ultimate power of the Law is the coercive power of the State. It is the characteristic of civilized communities that direct physical coercion is (with some limitations) the prerogative of the State, and the Law is a set of rules according to which the State exercises this prerogative in dealing with its own citizens. But the Law uses punishment, not only for the purpose of making undesired actions physically impossible, but also as an inducement; a fine, for example, does not make an action impossible, but only unattractive.

Moreover – and this is a much more important matter – the Law is almost powerless when it is not supported by public sentiment, as might be seen in the United States during Prohibition, or in Ireland in the eighties, when moonlighters had the sympathy of a majority of the population. Law, therefore, as an effective force, depends upon opinion and sentiment even more than upon the powers of the police. The degree of feeling in favour of Law is one of the most important characteristics of a community.

This brings us to a very necessary distinction, between traditional power and newly acquired power. Traditional power has on its side the force of habit; it does not have to justify itself at every moment, nor to prove continually that no opposition is strong enough to overthrow it. Moreover it is almost invariably associated with religious or quasi-religious beliefs purporting to show that resistance is wicked. It can, accordingly, rely upon public opinion to a much greater degree than is possible for revolutionary or usurped power. This has two more or less opposite consequences: on the one hand, traditional power, since it feels secure, is not on the look-out for traitors, and is likely to avoid much active political tyranny; on the other hand, where ancient institutions persist, the injustices to which holders of power are always prone have the sanction of immemorial custom, and can therefore be more glaring than would be possible under a new form of government which hoped to win popular support. The reign of terror in France illustrates the revolutionary kind of tyranny, the *corvée* the traditional kind.

Power not based on tradition or assent I call 'naked' power. Its characteristics differ greatly from those of traditional power. And where traditional power persists, the character of the regime depends, to an almost unlimited extent, upon its feeling of security or insecurity.

Naked power is usually military, and may take the form either of internal tyranny or of foreign conquest. Its importance, especially in the latter form, is very great indeed – greater, I think, than many modern 'scientific' historians are willing to admit. Alexander the Great and Julius Caesar altered the whole course of history by their battles. But for the former, the Gospels would not have been written in Greek, and Christianity could not have been preached throughout the Roman Empire. But for the latter, the French would not speak a language derived from Latin, and the Catholic Church could scarcely have existed. The military superiority of the white man to the American Indian is an even more undeniable example of the power of the sword. Conquest by force of arms has had more to do with the spread of civilization than any other single agency.

Nevertheless, military power is, in most cases, based upon some other form of power, such as wealth, or technical knowledge, or fanaticism. I do not suggest that this is always the case; for example, in the War of the Spanish Succession Marlborough's genius was essential to the result. But this is to be regarded as an exception to the general rule.

When a traditional form of power comes to an end, it may be succeeded, not by naked power, but by a revolutionary authority commanding the willing assent of the majority or a large minority of the population. So it was, for example, in America in the War of Independence. Washington's authority had none of the characteristics of naked power. Similarly, in the Reformation, new Churches were established to take the place of the Catholic Church, and their success was due much more to assent than to force. A revolutionary authority, if it is to succeed in establishing itself without much use of naked power, requires much more vigorous and active popular support than is needed by a traditional authority. When the Chinese Republic was proclaimed in 1911, the men of foreign education decreed a parliamentary Constitution, but the public was apathetic, and the regime quickly became one of naked power under warring Tuchuns (military governors). Such unity as was afterwards achieved by the Kuo-Min-Tang depended on nationalism, not parliamentarianism. The same sort of thing has happened frequently in Latin America. In all these cases, the authority of Parliament, if it had had sufficient popular support to succeed, would have been revolutionary; but the purely military power which was in fact victorious was naked.

The distinction between traditional, revolutionary, and naked power is psychological. I do not call power traditional merely because it has ancient forms: it must also command respect which is partly due to custom. As this respect decays, traditional power gradually passes over into naked power. The process was to be seen in Russia in the gradual growth of the revolutionary movement up to the moment of its victory in 1917.

I call power revolutionary when it depends upon a large group united by a new creed, programme, or sentiment, such as Protestantism, Communism, or desire for national independence. I call power naked when it results merely from the power-loving impulses of individuals or groups, and wins from its subjects only submission through fear, not active cooperation. It will be seen that the nakedness of power is a matter of degree. In a democratic country, the power of the government is not naked in relation to opposing political parties, but is naked in relation to a convinced anarchist. Similarly, where persecution exists, the power of the Church is naked in relation to heretics, but not in relation to orthodox sinners.

Another division of our subject is between the power of organizations and the power of individuals. The way in which an organization acquires power is one thing, and the way in which an individual acquires power within an organization is quite another. The two are, of course, interrelated: if you wish to be Prime Minister, you must acquire power in your Party, and your Party must acquire power in the nation. But if you had lived before the decay of the hereditary principle, you would have had to be the heir of a king in order to acquire political control of a nation; this would, however, not have enabled you to conquer other nations, for which you would have needed qualities that kings' sons often lack. In the present age, a similar situation still exists in the economic sphere, where the plutocracy is largely hereditary. Consider the two hundred plutocratic families in France against whom French Socialists agitate. But dynasties among the plutocracy have not the same degree of permanence as they formerly had on thrones, because they have failed to cause the widespread acceptance of the doctrine of Divine Right. No one thinks it impious for a rising financial magnate to impoverish one who is the son of his father, provided it is done according to the rules and without introducing subversive innovations.

Different types of organization bring different types of individuals to the top, and so do different states of society. An age appears in history through its prominent individuals, and derives its apparent character from the character of these men. As the qualities required for achieving prominence change, so the prominent men change. It is to be presumed that there were men like Lenin in the twelfth century, and that there are men like Richard Coeur de Lion at the present time; but history does not know of them. Let us consider for a moment the kinds of individuals produced by different types of power.

Hereditary power has given rise to our notion of a 'gentleman'. This is a somewhat degenerate form of a conception which has a long history, from magic properties of chiefs, through the divinity of kings, to knightly chivalry and the blue-blooded aristocrat. The qualities which are admired, where power is hereditary, are such as result from leisure and unquestioned superiority. Where power is aristocratic rather than monarchical, the best manners include courteous behaviour towards equals as an addition to bland self-assertion in dealing with inferiors. But whatever the prevalent conception of manners may be, it is only where power is (or lately was) hereditary that men will be judged by their manners. The *bourgeois gentilhomme* is only laughable when he intrudes into a society of men and women who have never had anything better to do than study social niceties. What survives in the way of admiration of the 'gentleman' depends upon inherited wealth, and must rapidly disappear if economic as well as political power ceases to pass from father to son.

A very different type of character comes to the fore where power is achieved through learning or wisdom, real or supposed. The two most important examples of this form of power are traditional China and the Catholic Church. There is less of it in the modern world than there has been at most times in the past; apart from the Church, in England, very little of this type of power remains. Oddly enough, the power of what passes for learning is greatest in the most savage communities, and steadily decreases as civilization advances. When I say 'learning' I include, of course, reputed learning, such as that of magicians and medicine men. Twenty years of study are required in order to obtain a Doctor's Degree at the University of Lhasa, which is necessary for all the higher posts except that of Dalai Lama. This position is much what it was in Europe in the year 1000, when Pope Silvester II was reputed a magician because he read books, and was consequently able to increase the power of the Church by inspiring metaphysical terrors.

The intellectual, as we know him, is a spiritual descendant of the priest; but the spread of education has robbed him of power. The power of the intellectual depends upon superstition: reverence for a traditional incantation or a sacred book. Of these, something survives in English-speaking countries, as is seen in the English attitude to the Coronation Service and the American reverence for the Constitution: accordingly, the Archbishop of Canterbury and the Supreme Court Judges still have some of the traditional power of learned men. But this is only a pale ghost of the power of Egyptian priests or Chinese Confucian scholars.

While the typical virtue of the gentleman is honour, that of the man who achieves power through learning is wisdom. To gain a reputation for wisdom a man must seem to have a store of recondite knowledge, a mastery over his passions, and a long experience of the ways of men. Age alone is thought to give something of these qualities; hence 'presbyter', 'seigneur', 'alderman', and 'elder' are terms of respect. A Chinese beggar addresses passers-by as 'great old sire'. But where the power of wise men is organized, there is a corporation of priests or literati, among whom all wisdom is held to be concentrated. The sage is a very different type of character from the knightly warrior, and produces, where he rules, a very different society. China and Japan illustrate the contrast.

We have already noted the curious fact that, although knowledge plays a larger part in civilization now than at any former time, there has not been any corresponding growth of power among those who possess the new knowledge. Although the electrician and the telephone man do strange things that minister to our comfort (or discomfort), we do not regard them as medicine-men, or imagine that they can cause thunderstorms if we annoy them. The reason for this is that scientific knowledge, though difficult, is not mysterious, but open to all who care to take the necessary trouble. The modern intellectual, therefore, inspires no awe, but remains a mere employee; except in a few cases, such as the Archbishop of Canterbury, he has failed to inherit the glamour which gave power to his predecessors.

The truth is that the respect accorded to men of learning was never bestowed for genuine knowledge, but for the supposed possession of magical powers. Science, in giving some real acquaintance with natural processes, has destroyed the belief in magic, and therefore the respect for the intellectual. Thus it has come about that, while men of science are the fundamental cause of the features which distinguish our time from former ages, and have, through their discoveries and inventions, an immeasurable influence upon the course of events, they have not, as individuals, as great a reputation for wisdom as may be enjoyed in India by a naked fakir or in Melanesia by a medicine-man. The intellectuals, finding their prestige slipping from them as a result of their own activities, become dissatisfied with the modern world. Those in whom the dissatisfaction is least take to Communism; those in whom it goes deeper shut themselves up in their ivory tower.

The growth of large economic organizations has produced a new type of powerful individual: the 'executive', as he is called in America. The typical 'executive' impresses others as a man of rapid decisions, quick insight into character, and iron will; he must have a firm jaw, tightly closed lips, and a habit of brief and incisive speech. He must be able to inspire respect in equals, and confidence in subordinates who are by no means nonentities. He must combine the qualities of a great general and a great diplomatist: ruthlessness in battle, but a capacity for skilful concession in negotiation. It is by such qualities that men acquire control of important economic organizations.

Political power, in a democracy, tends to belong to men of a type which differs considerably from the three that we have considered hitherto. A politician, if he is to succeed, must be able to win the confidence of his machine, and then to arouse some degree of enthusiasm in a majority of the electorate. The qualities required for these two stages on the road to power are by no means identical, and many men possess the one without the other. Candidates for the Presidency in the United States are not infrequently men who cannot stir the imagination of the general public, though they possess the art of ingratiating themselves with party managers. Such men are, as a rule, defeated, but the party managers do not foresee their defeat. Sometimes, however, the machine is able to secure the victory of a man without 'magnetism'; in such cases, it dominates him after his election, and he never achieves real power. Sometimes, on the contrary, a man is able to create his own machine; Napoleon III, Mussolini, and Hitler are examples of this. More commonly, a really successful politician, though he uses an already existing machine, is able ultimately to dominate it and make it subservient to his will.

The qualities which make a successful politician in a democracy vary according to the character of the times; they are not the same in quiet times as they are during war or revolution. In quiet times, a man may succeed by giving an impression of solidity and sound judgement, but in times of excitement something more is needed. At such times, it is necessary to be an impressive speaker – not necessarily eloquent in the conventional sense, for Robespierre and Lenin were not eloquent, but determined, passionate, and bold. The passion may be cold and controlled, but must exist and be felt. In excited times, a politican needs no power of reasoning, no apprehension of impersonal facts, and no shred of wisdom. What he must have is the capacity of persuading the multitude that what they passionately desire is attainable, and that he, through his ruthless determination, is the man to attain it.

The most successful democratic politicians are those who succeed in abolishing democracy and becoming dictators. This, of course, is only possible in certain circumstances; no one could have achieved it in nineteenth-century England. But when it is possible, it requires only a high degree of the same qualities as are required by democratic politicians in general, at any rate in excited times. Lenin, Mussolini, and Hitler owed their rise to democracy.

When once a dictatorship has been established, the qualities by which a man succeeds a dead dictator are totally different from those by which the dictatorship was originally created. Wire-pulling, intrigue, and Court favour are the most important methods when heredity is discarded. For this reason, a dictatorship is sure to change its character very considerably after the death of its founder. And since the qualities by which a man succeeds to a dictatorship are less generally impressive than those by which the regime was created, there is a likelihood of instability, palace revolutions, and ultimate reversion to some different system. It is hoped, however, that modern methods of propaganda may successfully counteract this tendency, by creating popularity for the Head of the State without the need for any display of popular qualities on his part. How far such methods can succeed it is as yet impossible to say.

There is one form of the power of individuals which we have not yet considered, namely, power behind the scenes: the power of courtiers, intriguers, spies, and wire-pullers. In every large organization, where the men in control have considerable power, there are other less prominent men (or women) who acquire influence over the leaders by personal methods. Wire-pullers and party bosses belong to the same type, though their technique is different. They put their friends, quietly, into key positions, and so, in time, control the organization. In a dictatorship which is not hereditary, such men may hope to succeed to the dictator when he dies; but in general they prefer not to take the front of the stage. They are men who love power more than glory; often they are socially timid. Sometimes, like eunuchs in Oriental monarchies, or kings' mistresses elsewhere, they are, for one reason or another, debarred from titular leadership. Their influence is greatest where nominal power is hereditary, and least where it is the reward of personal skill and energy. Such men, however, even in the most modern forms of government, inevitably have considerable power in those departments which average men consider mysterious. Of these the most important, in our time, are currency and foreign policy. In the time of the Kaiser William II, Baron Holstein (permanent Head of the German Foreign Office) had immense power, although he made no public appearances. How great is the power of the permanent officials in the British Foreign Office at the present day, it is impossible for us to know; the necessary documents may become known to our children. The qualities required for power behind the scenes are very different from those required for all other kinds, and as a rule, though not always, they are undesirable qualities. A system which accords much power to the courtier or the wire-puller is, therefore, in general not a system likely to promote the general welfare.

2

Domination by Economic Power and by Authority

MAX WEBER

Domination in the most general sense is one of the most important elements of social action. Of course, not every form of social action reveals a structure of dominancy. But in most of the varieties of social action domination plays a considerable role, even where it is not obvious at first sight. Thus, for example, in linguistic communities the elevation by authoritative fiat of a dialect to the status of an official language of a political entity has very often had a decisive influence on the development of a large community with a common literary language, as, for instance, Germany.[1] On the other hand, political separation has determined the final form of a corresponding linguistic differentiation, as, for instance, in the case of Holland as against Germany.[2] Furthermore, the domination exercised in the schools stereotypes the form and the predominance of the official school language most enduringly and decisively. Without exception every sphere of social action is profoundly influenced by structures of dominancy. In a great number of cases the emergence of rational association from amorphous social action has been due to domination and the way in which it has been exercised. Even where this is not the case, the structure of dominancy and its unfolding is decisive in determining the form of social action and its orientation toward a 'goal'. Indeed, domination has played the decisive role particularly in the economically most important social structures of the past and present, viz., the manor on the one hand, and the large-scale capitalistic enterprise on the other.

Domination constitutes a special case of power, as we shall see presently. As in the case of other forms of power, those who exercise domination do not apply it exclusively, or even usually, to

Reprinted with permission from Max Weber, *Economy and Society*, edited by G. Roth and C. Wittich, Berkeley and Los Angeles: University of California Press, 1978, chapter X, pp. 941–8.

the pursuit of purely economic ends, such as, for example, a plentiful supply of economic goods. It is true, however, that the control over economic goods, i.e., economic power, is a frequent, often purposively willed, consequence of domination as well as one of its most important instruments. Not every position of economic power, however, represents domination in our sense of the word. Nor does domination utilize in every case economic power for its foundation and maintenance. But in the vast majority of cases, and indeed in the most important ones, this is just what happens in one way or another and often to such an extent that the mode of applying economic means for the purpose of maintaining domination, in turn, exercises a determining influence on the structure of domination. Furthermore, the great majority of all economic organizations, among them the most important and the most modern ones, reveal a structure of dominancy. The crucial characteristics of any form of domination may, it is true, not be correlated in any clearcut fashion with any particular form of economic organization. Yet, the structure of dominancy is in many cases both a factor of great economic importance and, at least to some extent, a result of economic conditions.

Our first aim here is that of stating merely general propositions regarding the relationship between forms of economic organization and of domination. Because of this very general character, these propositions will inevitably be abstract and sometimes also somewhat indefinite. For our purpose we need, first of all, a more exact definition of what we mean by 'domination' and its relationship to the general term 'power'. Domination in the quite general sense of power, i.e., of the possibility of imposing one's own will upon the behavior of other persons, can emerge in the most diverse forms. If, as has occasionally been done, one looks upon the claims which the law accords to one person against one or more others as a power to issue commands to debtors or to those to whom no such claim is accorded, one may thereby conceive of the whole system of modern private law as the decentralization of domination in the hands of those to whom the legal rights are accorded. From this angle, the worker would have the power to command, i.e., 'domination', over the entrepreneur to the extent of his wage claim, and the civil servant over the king to the extent of his salary claim. Such a terminology would be rather forced and, in any case, it would not be of more than provisional value since a distinction in kind must be made between 'commands' directed by the judicial authority to an adjudged debtor and 'commands' directed by the claimant himself to a debtor prior to judgment. However, a position ordinarily designated as 'dominating' can emerge from the social relations in a drawing room as well as in the market, from the rostrum of a lecture-hall as well as from the command post of a regiment, from an erotic or charitable relationship as well as from scholarly discussion or athletics. Such a broad definition would, however, render the term 'domination' scientifically useless. A comprehensive classification of all forms, conditions, and concrete contents of 'domination' in that widest sense is impossible here. We will only call to mind that, in addition to numerous other possible types, there are two diametrically contrasting types of domination, viz., domination by virtue of a constellation of interests (in particular: by virtue of a position of monopoly), and domination by virtue of authority, i.e., power to command and duty to obey.

The purest type of the former is monopolistic domination in the market; of the latter, patriarchal, magisterial or princely power. In its purest form, the first is based upon influence derived exclusively from the possession of goods or marketable skills guaranteed in some way and acting upon the conduct of those dominated, who remain, however, formally free and are motivated simply by the pursuit of their own interests. The latter kind of domination rests upon alleged absolute duty to obey, regardless of personal motives or interests. The borderline between these two types of domination is fluid. Any large central bank or credit institution, for instance, exercises a 'dominating' influence on the capital market by virtue of its monopolistic position. It can impose upon its potential debtors conditions for the granting of credit, thus influencing to a marked degree their economic behavior for the sake of the liquidity of its own resources. The potential debtors, if they really need the credit, must in their own interest submit to these conditions and must even guarantee this submission by supplying collateral security. The credit banks do not, however, pretend that they exercise 'authority', i.e., that they claim 'submission' on the part of the dominated without regard to the latter's own interests; they simply pursue their own interests and realize them best when the dominated persons, acting with formal freedom, rationally pursue their own interests as they are forced upon them by objective circumstances.

Even the owner of an incomplete monopoly finds himself in that same position if, despite existing competition, he is able by and large to 'prescribe' prices to both exchange partners and competitors; in other words, if by his own conduct he can impose upon them a way of conduct according to his own interest, without, however, imposing on them the slightest 'obligation' to submit to this domination. Any type of domination by virtue of constellation of interests may, however, be transformed gradually into domination by authority. This applies particularly to domination originally founded on a position of monopoly. A bank, for instance, in order to control more effectively a debtor corporation, may demand as a condition for credit that some member of its board be made a member of the board of the debtor corporation. That board, in turn, can give decisive orders to the management by virtue of the latter's obligation to obey.

Or a central bank of issue causes the credit institutions to agree on uniform terms of credit and in this way tries, by virtue of its position of power, to secure to itself a continuous control and supervision of the relationships between the credit institutions and their customers. It may then utilize its control for ends of currency management or for the purpose of influencing the business cycle or for political ends such as, for instance, the preparation of financial readiness for war. The latter kind of use will be made in particular where the central bank itself is exposed to influence from the political power. Theoretically, it is conceivable that such controls can actually be established, that the ends for and the ways of its exercise become articulated in reglementations, that special agencies are created for its exercise and special appellate agencies for the resolution of questions of doubt, and that, finally, the controls are constantly made more strict. In such a case this kind of domination might become quite like the authoritative domination of a bureaucratic state agency over its subordinates, and the subordination would assume the character of a relationship of obedience to authority.

The same observation can be made with respect to the domination by the breweries over the tavern owners whom they supply with their equipment, or the domination to which book dealers would have to submit if there should some day be a German publishers' cartel with power to issue and withhold retailers' licenses, or the domination of the gasoline dealers by the Standard Oil Company, or the domination exercised through their common sales office by the German coal producers over the coal dealers. All these retailers may well be reduced to employed sales agents, little different from linemen working outside the employer's plant or other private employees but subject to the authority of a department chief. The transitions are gradual from the ancient debtor's factual dependency on his creditor to formal servitude for debt; or, in the Middle Ages and in modern times, from the craftsman's dependence on the market-wise exporter over the various forms of dependency of the home industry to the completely authoritarian labor regulation of the sweatshop worker. And from there other gradations lead to the position of the secretary, the engineer, or the worker in the office or plant, who is subject to a discipline no longer different in its nature from that of the civil service or the army, although it has been created by contract concluded in the labor market by formally 'equal' parties through the 'voluntary' accept-ance of the terms offered by the employer. More important than the difference between private and public employment is certainly that between the military service and the other situations. The latter are concluded and terminated voluntarily, while the former is imposed by compulsion, at least in those countries where, as in ours, the ancient system of mercenary service has been replaced by the draft. Yet, even the relationship of political allegiance can be entered into and, to some extent, be dissolved voluntarily; the same holds true of the feudal and, under certain circumstances, even of the patri-monial dependency relationships of the past. Thus even in these cases the transitions are but gradual to those relationships of authority, for instance slavery, which are completely involuntary and, for the subject, normally nonterminable. Obviously, a certain minimum interest of the subordinate in his own obeying will norm-ally constitute one of the indispensable motives of obedience even in the completely authoritarian duty-relationship. Throughout, transitions are thus vague and changing. And yet, if we wish at all to obtain fruitful distinctions within the continuous stream of actual phenomena, we must not overlook the clear-cut antithesis between factual power which arises completely out of possession and by way of interest compromises in the market, and, on the other hand, the authoritarian power of a patriarch or monarch with its appeal to the duty of obedience simply as such. The varieties of power are in no way exhausted by the examples just given. Even mere possession can be a basis of power in forms other than that of the market. As we pointed out before, even in socially undifferen-tiated situations wealth, accompanied by a corresponding way of life, creates prestige, corresponding to the position in present society of one who 'keeps an open house' or the lady who has her 'salon'. Under certain circumstances, every one of these relation-ships may assume authoritarian traits. Domination in the broader sense can be produced not only by the exchange relationships of the market but also by those of 'society'; such phenomena may range all the way from the 'drawing room lion' to the patented *arbiter elegantiarum*[3] of imperial Rome or the courts of love of the ladies of Provence.[4] Indeed, such situations of domination can be found also outside the sphere of private markets and relationships. Even without any formal power of command an 'empire state' or, more correctly, those individuals who are the decisive ones within it either through authority or through the market, can exercise a far-reaching and occasionally even a despotic hegemony. A typical illustration is afforded by Prussia's position within the German Customs Union or, later, in the German Reich. To some, although much lesser extent, New York's position within the United States affords another illustration. In the German Customs Union the Prussian officials were dominant, because their state's territory constituted the largest and thus the decisive market; in the German Reich they are paramount because they dispose of the largest net of railroads, the greatest number of university positions, etc., and can thus cripple the corresponding administrative departments of the other, formally equal, states. New York can exercise political power because it is the seat of the great financial powers. All such forms of power are based upon constellations of interests. They thus resemble those which occur in the market, and in the course of development they can easily be transformed into formally regulated relationships of authority or, more correctly, into associations with heterocephalous power of command and coercive apparatus. Indeed, because of the very absence of rules, domination which originates in the market or other interest constellations may be felt to be much more oppressive than an authority in which the duties of obedience are set out clearly and expressly. That aspect must not affect, however, the terminology of the sociologist.

In the following discussion [of Weber's text, not reprinted here] we shall use the term domination exclusively in that narrower sense which excludes from its scope those situations in which power has its source in a formally free interplay of interested parties such as occurs especially in the market. In other words, in our terminology *domination* shall be identical with *authoritarian power of command*.

To be more specific, *domination* will thus mean the situation in which the manifested will (*command*) of the *ruler* or rulers is meant to influence the conduct of one or more others (*the ruled*) and actually does influence it in such a way that their conduct to a socially relevant degree occurs as if the ruled had made the content of the command the maxim of their conduct for its very own sake. Looked upon from the other end, this situation will be called *obedience*.

Further Notes

1 The definition sounds awkward, especially due to the use of the 'as if' formula. This cannot be avoided, however. The merely external fact of the order being obeyed is not sufficient to signify domination in our sense; we cannot overlook the meaning of the fact that the command is accepted as a 'valid' norm. On the other hand, however, the causal chain extending from the command to the actual fact of compliance can be quite varied. Psychologically, the command may have achieved its effect upon the ruled either through empathy or through inspiration or through persuasion by rational argument or through some combination of these three principal types of influence of one person over another.[5] In a concrete case the performance of the command may have been motivated by the ruled's own conviction of its propriety, or by his sense of duty, or by fear, or by 'dull' custom, or by a desire to obtain some benefit for himself. Sociologically, those differences are not necessarily relevant. On the other hand, the sociological character of domination will differ according to the basic differences in the major modes of legitimation.
2 Many transitions exist, as we have seen, between that narrower concept of domination as we have defined it now and those situations of setting the tone in the market, the drawing room, in a discussion, etc., which we have discussed earlier. We shall briefly revert to some of these latter cases so as to elucidate more clearly the former.

It is obvious that relationships of domination may exist reciprocally. In modern bureaucracy, among officials of different departments, each is subject to the others' powers of command insofar as the latter have jurisdiction. There are no conceptual difficulties involved, but where a customer places with a shoemaker an order for a pair of shoes, can it then be said that either one has control over the other? The answer will depend upon the circumstances of each individual case, but almost always will it be found that in some limited respect the will of the one has influenced that of the other even against that other's reluctance and that, consequently, to that extent one has dominated over the other. No precise concept of domination could be built up, however, upon the basis of such considerations; and this statement holds true for all relationships of exchange, including those of intangibles. Or what shall we say of the village craftsman who, as is often the case in Asia, is employed at fixed terms by the village? Is he, within his vocational jurisdiction, a ruler, or is he the ruled, and, if so, by whom? One will be inclined rather not to apply the concept of domination to such relationships, except with respect to the powers which he, the craftsman, exercises over his assistants or which are exercised over him by those persons who are to control him by virtue of their official position. As soon as we do this, we narrow the concept of domination to that technical one which we have defined above. Yet, the position of a village chief, that is, a person of official authority, may be exactly like that of the village craftsman. The distinction between private business and public office, as we know it, is the result of development and it is not at all so firmly rooted elsewhere as it is with us in Germany. In the popular American view, a judge's job is a business just as a banker's. He, the judge, simply is a man who has been granted the monopoly to give a person a decision with the help of which the latter may enforce some performance against another or, as the case may be, may shield himself against the claims of others. By virtue of this monopoly the judge enjoys directly or indirectly a number of benefits, legitimate or illegitimate, and for their enjoyment he pays a portion of his fees to the party boss to whom he owes his job.

To all of these, the village chief, the judge, the banker, the craftsman, we shall ascribe domination, wherever they claim, and to a socially relevant degree find obedience to, commands given and received as such. No usable concept of domination can be defined in any way other than by reference to power of command; but we must never forget that here, as everywhere else in life, everything is 'in transition'. It should be self-evident that the sociologist is guided exclusively by the factual existence of such a power of command, in contrast to the lawyer's interest in the theoretical content of a legal norm. As far as sociology is concerned, power of command does not exist unless the authority which is claimed by somebody is actually heeded to a socially relevant degree. Yet, the sociologist will normally start from the observation that 'factual' powers of command usually claim to exist 'by virtue of law'. It is exactly for this reason that the sociologist cannot help operating with the conceptual apparatus of the law.

NOTES

1 Among numerous German dialects and ways in which the language was used in poetry, literature, and polite parlance, acceptance as the standard was achieved by that form which was used in the late fourteenth and fifteenth centuries by the imperial chancery, first in

Prague and then in Vienna, especially when a style close to it was used by Luther in his translation of the Bible.

2 The low-German dialect spoken in the present Netherlands achieved, in the form in which it is used in the Province of South Holland, the status of a separate language when the United Provinces separated from Germany and the Dutch dialect became the language of official-dom and of the Bible translation (Statenbijbel, 1626–35). Significantly no such status as a separate language was achieved by any one of the Swiss German dialects; as there was no central chancery in the loose Swiss Confederation, High German remained the official language in spite of the political separation from Germany, which took place a century earlier than that of the Netherlands.

3 *Arbiter elagantiarum* – According to Tacitus (Annals XVI, 18), Gaius Petronius, who is probably identical with the satirist Petronius Arbiter, was called by Nero the 'arbiter of elegance' to whose judgement he bowed in matters of taste. Petronius and his title have been popularized through Henry Sienkiewicz' novel *Quo Vadis*.

4 On courts of love, see part two, chapter I, n. 10 of Max Weber, *Economy and Society*, translated by G. Roth and C. Wittich (University of California Press, Berkeley and Los Angeles, 1978).

5 On empathy and inspiration as factors influencing the attitude of other persons, see part two, chapter I:2:B of Weber, *Economy and Society*.

3
Power as the Control of Behavior

ROBERT DAHL

In approaching the study of politics through the analysis of power, one assumes, at a minimum, that relations of power are among the significant aspects of a political system. This assumption, and therefore the analysis of power, can be applied to any kind of political system, international, national, or local, to associations and groups of various kinds, such as the family, the hospital, and the business firm, and to historical developments.

At one extreme, an analysis of power may simply postulate that power relations are one feature of politics among a number of others – but nonetheless a sufficiently important feature to need emphasis and description. At the other extreme, an analyst may hold that power distinguishes 'politics' from other human activity; to analysts of this view 'political science, as an empirical discipline, is the study of the shaping and sharing of power'.[1]

In either case, the analyst takes it for granted that differences between political systems, or profound changes in the same society, can often be interpreted as differences in the way power is distributed among individuals, groups, or other units. Power may be relatively concentrated or diffused, and the share of power held by different individuals, strata, classes, professional groups, ethnic, racial, or religious groups, etc., may be relatively great or small. The analysis of power is often concerned, therefore, with the identification of elites and leadership, the discovery of the ways in which power is allocated to different strata, relations among leaders and between leaders and non-leaders, and so forth.

Although the approach to politics through the study of power relations is sometimes thought to postulate that everyone seeks power as the highest value, analysts of power generally reject this assumption as psychologically untenable; the analysis of power does not logically imply any particular psychological assumptions. Sometimes critics also regard the analysis of power as implying that the pursuit of power is morally good or at any rate that it should not be condemned. But an analysis of power may be neutral as to values; or the analyst may be concerned with power, not to glorify it, but in order to modify the place it holds in human relations and to increase the opportunities for dignity, respect, freedom, or other values.[2]

Indeed, it would be difficult to explain the extent to which political theorists for the past 25 centuries have been concerned with relations of power and authority were it not for the moral and practical significance of power to any person interested in political life, whether as observer or activist. Some understanding of power is usually thought to be indispensable for moral or ethical appraisals of political systems. From a very early time – certainly since Socrates, and probably before – men have been inclined to judge the relative desirability of different types of political systems by, among other characteristics, the relations of power and authority in these systems. In addition, intelligent *action* to bring about a result of some kind in a political system, such as a change in a law or a policy, a revolution, or a settlement of an international dispute requires knowledge of how to produce or 'cause' these results. In political action, as in other spheres of life, we try to produce the results we want by acting appropriately on the relevant causes. As we shall see, power relations can be viewed as causal relations of a particular kind.

It therefore seems most unlikely that the analysis of power will disappear as an approach to the study of politics. However, the fact that this approach is important and relevant does not shield it from some serious difficulties. These have become particularly manifest as the approach has been more earnestly and systematically employed.

ORIGINS

The attempt to study and explain politics by analyzing relations of power is, in a loose sense, ancient. To Aristotle, differences in the location of power, authority, or rule among the citizens of a political society served as one criterion for differentiating among actual constitutions, and it entered into his distinction between good constitutions and bad ones. With few exceptions (most notably Thomas Hobbes) political theorists did not press their investigations very far into certain aspects of power that have seemed important to social scientists in the twentieth century. For example, most political theorists took it for granted, as did Aristotle, that key terms like *power, influence, authority*, and *rule* (let us call them 'power terms') needed no great elaboration, presumably because the meaning of these words was clear to men of common sense. Even Machiavelli, who marks a decisive turning point from classical–normative to modern–empirical theory, did not consider political terms in general as particularly technical. Moreover, he strongly preferred the concrete to the abstract. In his treatment of power relations Machiavelli frequently described a specific event as an example of a general principle; but often the general principle was only implied or barely alluded to, and he used a variety of undefined terms such as *imperio, forza, potente*, and *autorità*.

From Aristotle to Hobbes political theorists were mainly concerned with power relations within a given community. But external relations even more than internal ones force attention to questions of relative power. The rise of the modern nation-state therefore compelled political theorists to recognize the saliency of power in politics, and particularly, of course, in international politics.[3]

Thus political 'realists' found it useful to define, distinguish, and interpret the state in terms of its power. Max Weber both reflected this tradition of 'realism' and opened the way for new developments in the analysis of power. '"Power" (*Macht*) is the probability that one actor within a social relationship will be in a position to carry out his own will despite resistance, regardless of the basis on which this probability rests.'[4] This definition permitted Weber to conclude that 'the concept of power is highly comprehensive from the point of view of sociology. All conceivable . . . combinations of circumstances may put him [the actor] in a position to impose his will in a given situation.' It follows that the state is not distinguishable from other associations merely because it employs a special and peculiarly important kind of power–force. In a famous and highly influential definition, Weber characterized the state as follows: 'A compulsory political association with continuous organization (*politischer Anstaltsbetrieb*) will be called a "state" if and in so far as its administrative staff successfully upholds a claim to the *monopoly* of the *legitimate* use of physical force in the enforcement of its order.'

In his well-known typologies and his analyses of political systems, however, Weber was less concerned with power in general than with a special kind that he held to be unusually important – legitimate power, or authority.

Later theorists, practically all of whom were directly or indirectly influenced by Weber, expanded their objectives to include a fuller range of power relations. In the United States attempts to suggest or develop systematic and comprehensive theories of politics centring about power relations appeared in books by Catlin,[5] an important essay by Goldhamer and Shils,[6] and numerous works of the Chicago school – principally Merriam,[7] Lasswell,[8] and, in international politics, Morgenthau.[9] In the decade after World War II the ideas of the Chicago school were rapidly diffused throughout American political science.

ELEMENTS IN THE ANALYSIS OF POWER

Power terms evidently cover a very broad category of human relations. Considerable effort and ingenuity have gone into schemes for classifying these relations into various types, labelled power, influence, authority, persuasion, dissuasion, inducement, coercion, compulsion, force, and so on, all of which we shall subsume under the collective label power terms. The great variety and heterogeneity of these relations may, in fact, make it impossible – or at any rate not very fruitful – to develop general theories of power intended to cover them all.

At the most general level, power terms in modern social science refer to *subsets of relations among social units such that the behaviors of one or more units* (the responsive units, R) *depend in some circumstances on the behavior of other units* (the controlling units, C). (In the following discussion, R will always symbolize the responsive or dependent unit, C the controlling unit. These symbols will be used throughout and will be substituted even in direct quotations where the authors themselves have used different letters.) By this broad definition, then, power terms in the social sciences exclude relations with inanimate or even non-human objects; the control of a dog by his master or the power of a scientist over 'nature' provided by a nuclear reactor would fall, by definition, in a different realm of discourse. On the other hand, the definition could include the power of one nation to affect the actions of another by threatening to use a nuclear reactor as a bomb or by offering to transfer it by gift or sale.

If power-terms include *all* relations of the kind just defined, then they spread very widely over the whole domain of human relations. In practice, analysts of power usually confine their attention to smaller subsets. One such subset consists, for example, of relations in which 'severe sanctions . . . are expected to be used or are in fact applied to sustain a policy against opposition' – a subset that Lasswell and Kaplan call power.[10] However, there is no agreement on the common characteristics of the various subsets covered by power terms, nor are different labels applied with the same meaning by different analysts.

Despite disagreement on how the general concept is to be defined and limited, the variety of smaller subsets that different writers find interesting or important, and the total lack of a standardized classification scheme and nomenclature, there is nonetheless some underlying unity in the various approaches to the analysis of power. In describing and explaining patterns of power, different writers employ rather similar elements.[11] What follows is an attempt to clarify these common elements by ignoring many differences in terminology, treatment, and emphasis.

Some Descriptive Characteristics

For purposes of exposition it is convenient to think of the analysis of power in terms of the familiar distinction between dependent and independent variables. The attempt to understand a political system may then be conceived of as an effort to *describe* certain characteristics of the system: the dependent variables; and to *explain* why the system takes on these particular characteristics, by showing the effects on these characteristics of certain other factors: the independent variables. Some of the characteristics of a political system that analysts seek to explain are the *magnitude* of the power of the C's with respect to the R's, how this power is *distributed* in the system, and the *scope*, and *domain*, of control that different individuals or actors have, exercise, or are subject to.

Magnitude

Political systems are often characterized explicitly or implicitly by the differences in the 'amounts' of power (over the actions of the government or state) exercised by different individuals, groups, or strata. The magnitude of C's power with respect to R is thought of as measurable, in some sense, by at least an ordinal scale; frequently, indeed, a literal reading would imply that power is subject to measurement by an interval scale. How to compare and measure different magnitudes of power poses a major unsolved problem; we shall return to it briefly later on. Meanwhile, we shall accept the assumption of practically every political theorist for several thousand years, that it is possible to speak meaningfully of different amounts of power. Thus a typical question in the analysis of a political system would be: Is control over government highly concentrated or relatively diffused?

Distribution

An ancient and conventional way of distinguishing among political systems is according to the way control over the government or the state is distributed to individuals or groups in the systems. Aristotle, for example, stated: 'The proper application of the term "democracy" is to a constitution in which the free-born and poor control the government – being at the same time a majority; and similarly the term "oligarchy" is properly applied to a constitution in which the rich and better-born control the government – being at the same time a minority'.[12]

Control over government may be conceived as analogous to income, wealth, or property; and in the same way that income or wealth may be distributed in different patterns, so too the distribution of power over government may vary from one society or historical period to another. One task of analysis, then, is to classify and describe the most common distributions and to account for the different patterns. Typical questions would be: What are the characteristics of the C's and of the R's? How do the C's and R's compare in numbers? Do C's and R's typically come from different classes, strata, regions, or other groups? What historical changes have occurred in the characteristics of C and R?

Scope

What if C's are sometimes not C's, or C's sometimes R's, or R's sometimes C's? The possibility cannot be ruled out that individuals or groups who are relatively powerful with respect to one kind of activity may be relatively weak with respect to other activities. Power need not be general; it may be specialized. In fact, in the absence of a single world ruler, some specialization is inevitable; in any case, it is so commonplace that analysts of power have frequently insisted that a statement about the power of an individual, group, state, or other actor is practically meaningless unless it specifies the power of actor C with respect to some class of R's activities. Such a class of activities is sometimes called the range[12] or the scope of C's power.[13] There is no generally accepted way of defining and classifying different scopes. However, a typical question about a political system would be: Is power generalized over many scopes, or is it specialized? If it is specialized, what are the characteristics of the C's, the elites, in the different scopes? Is power specialized by individuals in the sense that C_a and C_b exercise power over different scopes, or is it also specialized by classes, social strata, skills, professions, or other categories?

Domain

C's power will be limited to certain individuals: the R's over whom C has or exercises control constitute what is sometimes called the 'domain', or 'extension', of C's power.[14] Typical questions thus might be: Who are the R's over whom C has control? What are their characteristics? How numerous are they? How do they differ in numbers or characteristics from the R's not under C's control?

Given the absence of any standard unit of measure for amounts, distributions, scopes, domains, and other aspects of power, and the variety of ways of describing these characteristics, it is not at all surprising that there is an abundance of schemes for classifying political systems according to some characteristic of power. Most such schemes use, implicitly or explicitly, the idea of a *distribution of power over the behavior of government*. The oldest, most famous, and most enduring of these is the distinction made by the Greeks between rule by one, the few, and the many.[15] Some variant of this scheme frequently reappears in modern analyses of power.[16] Often, as with Aristotle himself, the distribution of power is combined with one or more other dimensions.[17] Rough dichotomous schemes are common. One based on 'the degree of autonomy and interdependence of the several power holders' distinguishes two polar types, called autocracy and constitutionalism.[18] American community studies have in recent years called attention to differences between 'pluralistic' systems and unified or highly stratified 'power structures'. In one study that compares four communities the authors developed a more complex typology of power structures by combining a dimension of 'distribution of political power among citizens' with the degree of convergence or divergence in the ideology of leaders; the four types of power structures produced by dichotomizing these two dimensions are in turn distinguished from regimes.[19]

Some Explanatory Characteristics

Given the different types of political systems, how are the differences among them to be explained? If, for example, control over government is sometimes distributed to the many, often to the few, and occasionally to one dominant leader, how can we account for the differences? Obviously these are ancient, enduring, and highly complex problems; and there is slight agreement on the answers. However, some factors that are often emphasized in modern analysis can be distinguished.

Resources

Differences in patterns or structures of power may be attributed primarily, mainly, or partly to the way in which 'resources', or 'base values', are distributed among the individuals, strata, classes and groups in different communities, countries, societies and historical periods. This is an ancient, distinguished, widespread and persuasive mode of explanation, used by Aristotle in Greece in the fourth century BC, by James Harrington in seventeenth-century England, by the fathers of the American constitution in the late eighteenth century, by Marx and Engels in the nineteenth century, and by a great many social scientists in the twentieth century. A central hypothesis in most of these theories is that the greater one's resources, the greater one's power. Although explanations of this kind do not always go beyond tautology (by defining power in terms of resources), logical circularity is certainly not inherent in this mode of explanation. However, there is no accepted way of classifying resources or bases. Harold Lasswell has constructed a comprehensive scheme of eight base values which, although not necessarily exhaustive, are certainly inclusive; these are power (which can serve as a base for more power), respect, rectitude or moral standing, affection, well-being, wealth, skill, and enlightenment.[20] Other writers choose more familiar categories to classify resources: for example, in trying to account for the patterns of influence in one community, the author described the patterns of social standing; the distribution of cash, credit and wealth; access to legality, popularity and control over jobs; and control over sources of information.[21]

Skill

Two individuals with access to approximately the same resources may not exercise the same degree of power (over, let us say, government decisions). Indeed, it is a common observation that individuals of approximately equal wealth or social status may differ greatly in power. To be sure, this might be accounted for by differences in access to other resources, such as the greater legality, bureaucratic knowledge, and public affection that fall to any individual who is chosen, say, to be prime minister of Britain or president of the United States. Another factor, however, one given particular prominence by Machiavelli, is political skill. Formally, skill could be treated as another resource. Nonetheless, it is generally thought to be of critical importance in explaining differences in the power of different leaders – different presidents, for example, as in Neustadt's comparison of presidents Roosevelt, Truman, and Eisenhower.[22] However, despite many attempts at analysis, from Machiavelli to the present day, political skill has remained among the more elusive aspects in the analysis of power.

Motivations

Two individuals with access to the same resources may exercise different degrees of power (with respect to some scope) because of different motivations: the one may use his resources to increase his power; the other may not. Moreover, since power is a relationship between C's and R's, the motivations not only of the C's but also of the R's are important. One person may worship authority, while another may defy it. A number of writers have explored various aspects of motivations involved in power relations.[23]

Costs

Motivations can be related to resources by way of the economists' language of cost – a factor introduced into the analysis of power by a mathematical economist.[24] In order to control R, C may have to use some of his resources. Thus C's supply of resources is likely to have a bearing on how far he is willing to go in trying to control R. And variations in C's resources are likely to produce variations in C's power. C's *opportunity costs* in controlling R – that is, what C must forgo or give up in other opportunities as a result of using some of his resources to control R – are less (other things being equal) if he is rich in resources than if he is poor in resources. In concrete terms, to a rich man the sacrifice involved in a campaign contribution of $100 is negligible; to a poor man the sacrifice entailed in a contribution of $100 is heavy. C's willingness to use his resources to control R will also depend on the value to C of R's response; the value of R's response is, in turn, dependent in part on C's motivations. The relationship may also be examined from R's point of view. R's opportunity costs consist of what he is then unable to do if he complies with C. In R's case, as in C's, his supply of resources and his motivations help determine his opportunity costs. Thus a power relation can be interpreted as a sort of transaction between C and R.

PROBLEMS OF RESEARCH

Like all other approaches to an understanding of complex social phenomena, the analysis of power is beset with problems. At a very general level, attempts to analyze power share with many – perhaps most – other strategies of inquiry in the social sciences the familiar dilemma of rigor versus relevance, and the dilemma has led to familiar results. Attempts to meet high standards of logical rigor or empirical verification have produced some intriguing experiments and a good deal of effort to clarify concepts and logical relationships but not rounded and well-verified explanations of complex political systems in the real world. Conversely, attempts to arrive at a better understanding of the more concrete phenomena of political life and institutions often sacrifice a good deal in rigor of logic and verification in order to provide more useful and reliable guides to the real world.

There are, however, a number of more specific problems in the analysis of power, many of which have only been identified in the last few decades. Relevant work is quite recent and seeks (1) to clarify the central concepts, partly by expanding on the analogy between power relations and causal relations, (2) to specify particular subsets that are most interesting for social analysis, (3) to develop methods of measurement, and (4) to undertake empirical investigations of concrete political phenomena.

Power and Cause

The closest equivalent to the power relation is the causal relation. For the assertion 'C has power over R', one can substitute the assertion, 'C's behavior causes R's behavior'. If one can define the causal relation, one can define influence, power, or authority, and vice-versa.[25]

Since the language of cause is no longer common in the formal theoretical language of the natural sciences, it might be argued that social scientists should also dispense with that language and that insofar as power is merely a term for a causal relation involving human beings, power-terms should simultaneously be dispensed with. But it seems rather unlikely that social scientists will, in fact, reject causal language. For the language of cause, like the language of power, is used to interpret situations in which there is the possibility that some event will intervene to change the order of other events. In medical research it is natural and meaningful to ask, Does cigarette smoking cause lung cancer and heart disease? In social situations the notion of cause is equally or even more appropriate. What makes causal analysis important to us is our desire to act on causes in the real world in order to bring about effects – reducing death rates from lung cancer, passing a civil-rights bill through Congress, or preventing the outbreak of war.

To interpret the terms *power, influence, authority*, etc., as instances of causal relations means, however, that the attempt to detect true rather than spurious power relations must run into the same difficulties that have beset efforts to distinguish true from spurious causal relations. Some analysts have confronted the problem; others have noted it only to put it aside; most have ignored it entirely, perhaps on the assumption that if social scientists tried to solve the unsolved problems of philosophy they would never get around to the problems of the social sciences. Yet if power is analogous to cause – or if power relations are logically a subset of causal relations – then recent analyses of causality must have relevance to the analysis of power.

In the first place, properties used to distinguish causation also serve to define power relations: covariation, temporal sequence, and asymmetry, for example. The appropriateness of these criteria has in fact been debated, not always conclusively, by various students of power.[26]

Thus, the problem whether *A* can be said to cause *B* if *A* is a necessary condition for *B*, or a sufficient condition, or *both* necessary *and* sufficient, has also plagued the definition of power-terms. Some writers have explicitly stated or at least implied that relations of power mean that some action by *C* is a necessary condition for *R*'s response.[27] Oppenheim has argued, however, that such definitions permit statements that run flatly counter to common sense; he holds that it would be more appropriate to require only that *C*'s action be sufficient to produce *R*'s response.[28] Riker has suggested in turn that 'the customary definition of power be revised . . . to reflect the necessary-and-sufficient condition theory of causality'.[29] However, Blalock in his *Causal Inferences in Non-experimental*

Research[30] has shown that defining cause in terms of necessary and sufficient conditions leads to great practical difficulties in research. 'In real-life situations we seldom encounter instances where *B* is present if and only if *A* is also present'; moreover, specifying necessary and sufficient conditions requires the researcher 'to think always in terms of attributes and dichotomies', whereas 'there are most certainly a number of variables which are best conceived as continuously distributed, even though we may find it difficult to measure them operationally in terms of a specified unit of some kind.' 'The use of "necessary and sufficient" terminology . . . may work well for the logician but not [for] the social scientist.' Blalock's criticism, and indeed his whole effort to explore problems of causal inference in non-experimental research, are highly relevant to the analysis of power.

Aside from these somewhat rarefied philosophical and definitional questions, which many social scientists are prepared to abandon to metaphysicians or philosophers of science, the analogy between power and cause argues that the problem of distinguishing cause from correlation, or true from spurious causation, is bound to carry over into the analysis of power. And indeed it does. The difficulty of distinguishing true from spurious power relations has proved to be quite formidable.

The most rigorous method of distinguishing true from spurious causation is, of course, experimentation, and this would be the most rigorous method for distinguishing true from spurious power relations, provided the proper experimental conditions were present. Unfortunately, however, as in many areas of the social sciences, so too in the analysis of power, experimental methods have so far been of limited value, and for similar reasons. In non-experimental situations the optimal requirements for identifying causal relations seem to be the existence of satisfactory interval measures, a large supply of good data employing these measures, and an exhaustive analysis of alternative ways of accounting for the observations.[31] Unfortunately, in the analysis of power, existing methods of measurement are rather inadequate, the data are often inescapably crude and limited, a variety of simple alternative explanations seem to fit the data about equally well, and in any case the complexity of the relations requires extraordinarily complex models.

The shortage of relevant models of power may disappear in time. In fact, the causal analogue suggests that the development of a great array of carefully described alternative models to compare with observations is probably a prerequisite for further development in the analysis of power. Again, the analogy between power and cause readily reveals why this would seem to be the case. In trying to determine the cause of a phenomenon it is of course impossible to know whether all the relevant factors in the real world are actually controlled during an investigation. Consequently, it is never possible to demonstrate causality.

> It is possible to make causal *inferences* concerning the adequacy of causal models, at least in the sense that we can proceed by eliminating inadequate models that make predictions that are not consistent with the data. . . . [Such] causal models involve (1) a finite set of explicitly defined variables, (2) certain asumptions about how these variables are interrelated causally, and (3) assumptions to the effect that outside variables, while operating, do not have confounding influences that disturb the causal patterning among the variables explicitly being considered.[32]

If power relations are a subset of causal relations, these requirements would also be applicable in the analysis of power.

In analyzing power, why have analysts so rarely attempted to describe, in rigorous language at any rate, the alternative causal models relevant to their inquiry? There seem to be several reasons. First, students of power have not always been wholly aware that distinguishing true from spurious power relations requires intellectual strategies at a rather high level of sophistication. Second, the crude quality of the observations usually available in studying power may discourage efforts to construct elegant theoretical models. Third, until recent times the whole approach to power analysis was somewhat speculative: there were a good many impressionistic works but few systematic empirical studies of power relations. Of the empirical studies now available most are investigations of power relations in American communities undertaken since 1950. These community studies have provoked a good deal of dispute over what are, in effect, alternative models of causation. So far, however, investigators have usually not described clearly the array of alternative models that might be proposed to explain their data, nor have they clearly specified the criteria they use for rejecting all the alternatives except the one they accept as their preferred explanation.

Theories about power relations in various political systems are of course scattered through the writings of a number of analysts.[33] But a straightforward presentation of an empirical theory of power relations in political systems is a rarity. A notable exception is offered by March's formulation of six models of social choice that involve, in some sense, relationships of power.

The analogy between cause and power calls attention to one further point: any attempt to develop an empirical theory of power will run headlong into the fact that a causal chain has many links; that the links one specifies depend on what one wishes to explain; and that what one wishes to explain depends, in part, on the theory with which one begins. In causal analysis, it is usually

> possible to insert a very large number of additional variables between any two supposedly directly related factors. We must stop somewhere and consider the theoretical system closed. Practically, we may choose to stop at the point 'where the additional variables are either difficult or expensive to measure, or where they have not been associated with any operations at all. . . . A relationship that is direct in one theoretical system may be indirect in another, or it may even be taken as spurious.[34]

Some of the links that a power analyst may take as 'effects' to be explained by searching for causes are the outcomes of specific decisions; the current values, attitudes, and expectations of decision makers; their earlier or more fundamental attitudes and values; the attitudes and values of other participants – or non-participants – whose participation is in some way significant; the processes of selection, self-selection, recruitment, or entry by which decision makers arrive at their locations in the political system; the rules of decision making, the structures, the constitutions. No doubt a 'complete' explanation of power relations in a political system would try to account for all of these effects, and others. Yet this is an enormously ambitious task. Meanwhile, it is important to specify which effects are at the focus of an explanatory theory and which are not. A good deal of confusion, and no little controversy, are produced when different analysts focus on different links in the chain of power and causation without specifying clearly what effects they wish to explain; and a good deal of criticism of dubious relevance is produced by critics who hold that an investigator has focused on the 'wrong' links or did not provide a 'complete' explanation.

Classifying Types of Power

Even though the analysis of power has not produced many rigorous causal models, it has spawned a profusion of schemes for classifying types of power relations.[35]

Among the characteristics most often singled out for attention are (1) legitimacy: the extent to which *R* feels normatively obliged to comply with *C*; (2) the nature of the sanctions: whether *C* uses rewards or deprivations, positive or negative sanctions; (3) the magnitude of the sanctions: extending from severe coercion to no sanctions at all; (4) the means or channels employed: whether *C* controls *R* only by means of information that changes *R*'s intentions or by actually changing *R*'s situation or his environment of rewards and deprivations. These and other characteristics can be combined to yield many different types of power relations.

As we have already indicated, no single classification system prevails, and the names for the various categories are so completely unstandardized that what is labeled power in one scheme may be called coercion or influence in another. Detached from empirical theories, these schemes are of doubtful value. In the abstract it is impossible to say why one classification system should be preferred over another.

Nonetheless, there are some subsets of power relations – types of power, as they are often called – that call attention to interesting problems of analysis and research. One of these is the distinction between *having* and *exercising* power or influence.[36] This distinction is also involved in the way anticipated reactions function as a basis for influence and power.[37]

To illustrate the problem by example, let us suppose that even in the absence of any previous communication from the president to Senator *R*, or indeed any previous action of any kind by the president, Senator *R* regularly votes *now* in a way he thinks will insure the president's favor *later*. The senator calculates that if he loses the next election, he may, as a result of the president's favorable attitude, be in line to receive a presidential appointment to a federal court. Thus, while Senator *R*'s voting behavior is oriented toward future rewards, expected or hoped for, his votes are not the result of any specific action by the president.

If one holds that *C* cannot be a cause of *R* if *C* follows *R* in time, then no act of the incumbent president *need* be a cause of Senator *R*'s favorable vote. Obviously this does not mean that Senator *R*'s actions are 'uncaused'. The immediate determinant of his vote is his expectations. If we ask what 'caused' his expectations, there are many possible answers. For example, he might have concluded that in American society if favors are extended to *C*, this makes it more likely that *C* will be indulgent later on. Or he may have acquired from political lore the understanding that the general rule applies specifically to relations of senators and presidents. Thus, the causal chain recedes into the senator's previous learning – but not necessarily to any specific *past* act of the incumbent president or any other president.

This kind of phenomenon is commonplace, important, and obviously relevant to the analysis of power. Yet some studies, critics have said, concentrate on the exercise of power and fail to account for individuals or groups in the community who, though they do not exercise power, nonetheless have power, in the sense that many people try assiduously to anticipate their reactions.[38] This failure may be a result of certain paradoxical aspects of having power that can make it an exceedingly difficult phenomenon to study.

For in the limiting case of anticipated reactions, it appears, paradoxically, that it is not the president who controls the senator, but the senator who controls the president – i.e., it is the senator who, by his loyal behavior, induces the president to appoint him to a federal court. Thus, it is not C who controls or even attempts to control R, but R who attempts to control C – and to the extent that R anticipates C's reactions correctly, R does in fact control C. It is, then, not the king who controls the courtier but the courtier who controls the king.

Now if we examine this paradox closely we quickly discover that it arises simply because we have tried to describe the relationship between king and courtier, president and senator, C and R by distinguishing only one aspect, namely, the exercise of power. The courtier does indeed exercise power over the king by successfully anticipating the reactions of the monarch and thereby gaining a duchy. But it was not this that we set out to explain. For it is the king who has, holds, or possesses the capacity to confer that dukedom, and even though he does not *exercise* his power, he gains the willing compliance of the courtier.

What is it, then, that distinguishes having power from exercising power? The distinction could hinge upon the presence or absence of a manifest intention. We could define the *exercise* of power in such a way as to require C to manifest an intention to act in some way in the future, his action to be contingent on R's behavior. By contrast, C might be said to *have* power when, though he does not manifest an intention, R imputes an intention to him and shapes his behaviour to meet the imputed intention. If one were to accept this distinction, then in studying the *exercise* of power, one would have to examine not only R's perceptions and responses but also C's intentions and actions. In studying relationships in which C is thought to *have* power, even though he does not exercise it, one would in principle need only to study R's perceptions, the intentions R imputes to C, and the bearing of these on R's behavior. Carried to the extreme, then, this kind of analysis could lead to the discovery of as many different power structures in a political system as there are individuals who impute different intentions to other individuals, groups, or strata in the system.

The distinction between having and exercising power could also turn on the directness involved in the relation between C and R and on the specificity of the actions. In the most direct relationship R's response would be tripped off by a signal directly from C. In this case, C is exercising power. But some relationships are highly indirect; for example, C may modify R's environment in a more or less lasting way, so that R continues to respond as C had intended, even though C makes no effort to control R. In these cases, one might say that although C does not exercise control over R, he does *have* control over R. There are a variety of these indirect, or 'roundabout', controls.[39]

Measuring Power

Even more than with power terms themselves, notions of 'more' or 'less' power were in classical theory left to the realm of common sense and intuition. Efforts to develop systematic measures of power date almost wholly from the 1950s. Of those, some are stated partly in mathematical formulas, some entirely in non-mathematical language. Since the essential features can be suggested without mathematics, we shall describe these measures in ordinary language.[40]

In a rough way, the various criteria for measuring power can be classified into three types: game-theoretical, Newtonian, and economic.

Game-theoretical Criteria

Shapley, a mathematician, and Shubik, an econometrician, have jointly formulated a 'method for evaluating the distribution of power in a committee system'.[41] This is intended to measure the power accruing to a voter where the outcome or decision is determined exclusively by voting. In these cases the rules prescribe what proportion of votes constitutes a winning proportion (e.g., a simple majority of all committee members). Thus each member has a

Robert Dahl

certain abstract probability of casting the last vote that would be needed to complete a winning coalition, in other words to occupy a pivotal position with respect to the outcome. By adding his vote at this crucial juncture, a voter may be conceived of as having made a particularly decisive contribution to the outcome; thus, gaining his vote might have considerable value to the other members of a coalition that would lose without his vote. Shapley and Shubik proposed measuring the power of a voter by the probability that he would be the pivotal voter in a winning coalition. Because their measure is entirely limited to voting situations and excludes all outcomes other than the act of voting itself, the utility of the measure is limited to cases where most of the other familiar elements of political life – various forms of persuasion, inducement, and coercion – are lacking.

Newtonian Criteria

On the analogy of the measurement of force in classical mechanics, a number of analysts propose to measure power by the amount of change in R attributable to C. The greater the change in R, the greater the power of C; thus C_a is said to exert more power than C_b if C_a induces more change in R_a than C_b induces in R_a (or in some other R). Measures of this kind have been more frequently proposed than any other.[42]

'Change in R' is not, however, a single dimension, since many different changes in R may be relevant. Some of the important dimensions of the 'change in R' brought about by C that have been suggested for measuring the amount of C's power are (1) the probability that R will comply; (2) the number of persons in R; (3) the number of distinct items, subjects, or values in R; (4) the amount of change in R's position, attitudes, or psychological state; (5) the speed with which R changes; (6) the reduction in the size of the set of outcomes or behaviors available to R; and (7) the degree of R's threatened or expected deprivation.

Economic Criteria

Where the game-theoretical measure focuses on the pivotal position of C, and Newtonian measures on changes in R, a third proposal would include 'costs' to both C and R in measuring C's power. Harsanyi has argued that a complete measure of power should include (1) the opportunity costs to C of attempting to influence R, which Harsanyi calls the *costs* of C's power, and (2) the opportunity costs to R of refusing to comply with C, which Harsanyi calls the *strength* of C's power over R.[43] The measure Harsanyi proposes is not inherently limited to the kinds of cost most familiar to economists but could be extended – at least in principle – to include psychological costs of all kinds.

Designing Operational Definitions

Empirical studies discussed by Cartwright,[44] March,[45] and others, and particularly community studies, have called attention to the neglected problem of designing acceptable operational definitions.

The concepts and measures discussed in this article have not been clothed in operational language. It is not yet clear how many of them can be. Yet the researcher who seeks to observe, report, compare, and analyze power in the real world, in order to test a particular hypothesis or a broader theory, quickly discovers urgent need for operationally defined terms. Research so far has called attention to three kinds of problems. First, the gap between concept and operational definition is generally very great, so great, indeed, that it is not always possible to see what relation there is between the operations and the abstract definition. Thus a critic is likely to conclude that the studies are, no doubt, reporting something in the real world, but he might question whether they are reporting the phenomena we mean when we speak of power. Second, different operational measures do not seem to correlate with one another,[46] which suggests that they may tap different aspects of power relations. Third, almost every measure proposed has engendered controversy over its validity.

None of these results should be altogether surprising or even discouraging. For despite the fact that the attempt to understand political systems by analyzing power relations is ancient, the systematic empirical study of power relations is remarkably new.

NOTES

1 Harold D. Lasswell and Abraham Kaplan, *Power and Society: A Framework for Political Enquiry*, Yale Law School Studies, vol. 2 (Yale University Press, New Haven, 1950; paperback edn 1963), p. xiv.

2 Lasswell and Kaplan, *Power and Society*; Bertrand de Jouvenel, *Power: The Natural History of its Growth* (Batchworth, London, 1952; first published in French). See also Felix E. Oppenheim, *Dimensions of Freedom: An Analysis* (St. Martins, New York; Macmillan, London, 1961), chapters 8 and 9.

3 Friedrich Meinecke, *Machiavellism: The Doctrine of Raison d'État and its Place in Modern History* (Yale University Press, New Haven, 1957, first published as *Die Idee der Staatsräson in der neueren Geschichte,* 1924).

4 Max Weber, *The Theory of Social and Economic Organization,* ed. Talcott Parsons (The Free Press, Glencoe, Ill., 1957; first published as part 1 of *Wirtschaft und Gesellschaft,* 1922), p. 152. Further quotations from pp. 153, 154.

5 George E. G. Catlin, *The Science and Method of Politics* (Knopf, New York; Routledge, London, 1927) and *A Study of the Principles of Politics, Being an Essay Towards Political Rationalization* (Macmillan, New York, 1930).

6 Herbert Goldhamer and Edward Shils, 'Types of power and status', *American Journal of Sociology,* 45 (1939), pp. 171–82.

7 Charles E. Merriam, *Political Power: Its Composition and Incidence* (McGraw-Hill, New York, 1934; paperback edn 1964 by Collier).

8 Harold D. Lasswell, *Politics: Who Gets What When, How?* (McGraw-Hill, New York, 1936).

9 Hans J. Morgenthau, *Politics Among Nations: The Struggle for Power and Peace,* 4th edn (Knopf, New York, 1967).

10 Lasswell and Kaplan, *Power and Society,* pp. 74–5.

11 Compare Dorwin Cartwright, 'Influence, leadership, control' in James G. March (ed.), *Handbook of Organizations* (Rand McNally, Chicago, 1965), pp. 1–47.

12 Aristotle, *The Politics of Aristotle,* translated and edited by Ernest Barker (Oxford University Press, New York, 1962), p. 164.

13 Lasswell and Kaplan, *Power and Society,* p. 73.

14 Lasswell and Kaplan, *Power and Society,* p. 73; John C. Harsanyi, 'Measurement of social power, opportunity costs, and the theory of two-person bargaining games', *Behavioral Science,* 7 (1962), pp. 67–80, esp. p. 67.

15 Aristotle, *The Politics of Aristotle,* pp. 110 ff.

16 Lasswell and Kaplan, *Power and Society,* p. 218.

17 Robert A. Dahl, *Modern Political Analysis* (Prentice-Hall, Englewood Cliffs, N.J., 1963), p. 38.

18 Karl Loewenstein, *Political Power and the Governmental Process* (University of Chicago Press, Chicago, 1957), p. 29.

19 Robert E. Agger, Daniel Goldrich and Bert Swanson, *The Rulers and the Ruled: Political Power and Impotence in American Communities* (Wiley, New York, 1964), pp. 73 ff.

20 Lasswell and Kaplan, *Power and Society,* p. 87.

21 Robert A. Dahl, *Who Governs? Democracy and Power in an American City* (Yale University Press, New Haven, 1961, 1963), pp. 229 ff.

22 Richard E. Neustadt, *Presidential Power: The Politics of Leadership* (Wiley, New York, 1960, paperback edn 1962), pp. 152 ff.

23 E.g. Harold D. Lasswell, *Psychopathology and Politics,* new edn, with afterthoughts by the author (Viking, New York, 1960); Arnold A.

Rogow and Harold D. Lasswell, *Power, Corruption and Rectitude* (Prentice-Hall, Englewood Cliffs, N.J., 1963); Dorwin Cartwright (ed.), *Studies in Social Power*, Research Center for Group Dynamics, publication no. 6 (University of Michigan, Institute for Social Research, Ann Arbor, 1959).

24 Harsanyi, 'Measurement of social power, opportunity costs, etc.'; John C. Harsanyi, 'Measurement of social power in *n*-person reciprocal power situations', *Behavioral Science*, 7 (1962), pp. 81–91.

25 Herbert A. Simon, *Models of Man: Social and Rational; Mathematical Essays on Rational Human Behavior in a Social Setting* (Wiley, New York, 1947–56, 1957), p. 5.

26 Simon, *Models of Man*, pp. 5, 11, 12, 66; Robert A. Dahl, 'The concept of power', *Behavioral Science*, 2 (1957), pp. 201–15, esp. p. 204; Cartwright, *Studies in Social Power*, p. 197; Oppenheim, *Dimensions of Freedom*, p. 104.

27 Herbert A. Simon, 'Notes on the observation and measurement of political power', *Journal of Politics*, 15 (1953), pp. 500–16, esp. p. 504; James G. March, 'An introduction to the theory and measurement of influence', *American Political Science Review*, 49 (1955), pp. 431–51, esp. p. 435; Dahl, 'The concept of power', p. 203.

28 Oppenheim, *Dimensions of Freedom*, p. 41.

29 William H. Riker, 'Some ambiguities in the notion of power', *American Political Science Review*, 58 (1964), pp. 341–9, esp. p. 348.

30 Hubert M. Blalock Jr, *Causal Inferences in Nonexperimental Research* (University of North Carolina Press, Chapel Hill, 1964), quotations from pp. 30, 32, 34.

31 Blalock, *Causal Inferences*.

32 Ibid., p. 62.

33 E.g. Vilfredo Pareto, *The Mind and Society: A Treatise on General Sociology*, 4 vols (Dover, New York, 1963; first published as *Trattato di sociologia generale*. Volume 1: *Non-logical Conduct*. Volume 2: *Theory of Residues*. Volume 3: *Theory of Derivations*. Volume 4: *The General Form of Society*), vol. 4; C. Wright Mills, *The Power Elite* (Oxford University Press, New York, 1956) *passim*; Lasswell and Kaplan, *Power and Society*, chapters 9 and 10. See also Dahl, *Who Governs?*; Gaetano Mosca, *The Ruling Class* (McGraw-Hill, New York 1939, first published as *Elementi di scienza politica*, 1896); Peter H. Rossi, 'Power and community structure', *Midwest Journal of Political Science*, 4 (1960), pp. 390–401; Nelson W. Polsby, *Community Power and Political Theory*, Yale Studies in Political Science, vol. 7 (Yale University Press, New Haven, 1963); Talcott Parsons, 'On the concept of influence', *Public Opinion Quarterly*, 27 (1963), pp. 37–62 (a comment by J. S. Coleman appears on pp. 63–83; a communication by R. A. Bauer on pp. 83–6; and a rejoinder by Talcott Parsons on pp. 87–92); Talcott Parsons, 'On the concept of political power', American Philosophical Society, *Proceedings*, 107 (1963), pp. 232–62.

34 Blalock, *Causal Inferences*, p. 18.

35 Oppenheim, *Dimensions of Freedom*; Cartwright, 'Influence, leadership, control'; Parsons, 'On the concept of influence'; Parsons, 'On the concept of political power'; John R. P. French and Bertram Raven, 'The bases of social power', in Dorwin Cartwright (ed.) *Studies in Social Power*, Research Center for Group Dynamics, publication no. 6 (University of Michigan, Institute for Social Research, Ann Arbor, 1959), pp. 150–67.

36 Lasswell and Kaplan, *Power and Society*, p. 71; Oppenheim, *Dimensions of Freedom*, chapters 2 and 3.

37 Carl J. Friedrich, *Man and His Government: An Empirical Theory of Politics* (McGraw-Hill, New York, 1963), chapter 11.

38 Peter Bachrach and Morton Baratz, 'Two faces of power', *American Political Science Review*, 56 (1962), pp. 947–52.

39 Robert A. Dahl and Charles E. Lindblom, *Politics, Economics, and Welfare: Planning and Politico-economic Systems Resolved into Basic Social Processes* (Harper, New York, 1953; paperback edn 1963), pp. 110 ff.

40 The reader should consult the sources cited for the precise formulations. Most of the best-known measures are presented and discussed in Riker, 'Some ambiguities'.

41 L. S. Shapley and Martin Shubik, 'A method for evaluating the distribution of power in a committee system', *American Political Science Review*, 48 (1954), pp. 787–92.

42 See Oppenheim, *Dimensions of Freedom*, chapter 8; Dahl, *Modern Political Analysis*, chapter 5; Cartwright, *Studies in Social Power*; Simon, *Models of Man*; Dahl, 'The concept of power'; James G. March, 'Measurement concepts in the theory of influence', *Journal of Politics*, 19 (1957), pp. 202–26.

43 Harsanyi, 'Measurement of social power, opportunity costs, etc.', pp. 68 ff.

44 Cartwright, 'Influence, leadership, control'.

45 James G. March (ed.) *Handbook of Organizations* (Rand McNally, Chicago, 1965).

46 James G. March, 'Influence measurement in experimental and semi-experimental groups', *Sociometry*, 19 (1956), pp. 260–71.

4

Communicative Power

HANNAH ARENDT

It is against the background of these experiences that I propose to raise the question of violence in the political realm. This is not easy; what Sorel remarked over 60 years ago, 'The problems of violence still remain very obscure',[1] is as true today as it was then. I mentioned the general reluctance to deal with violence as a phenomenon in its own right, and I must now qualify this statement. If we turn to discussions of the phenomenon of power, we soon find that there exists a consensus among political theorists from Left to Right to the effect that violence is nothing more than the most flagrant manifestation of power. 'All politics is a struggle for power; the ultimate kind of power is violence', said C. Wright Mills, echoing, as it were, Max Weber's definition of the state as 'the rule of men over men based on the means of legitimate, that is allegedly legitimate, violence'.[2] The consensus is very strange; for to equate political power with 'the organization of violence' makes sense only if one follows Marx's estimate of the state as an instrument of oppression in the hands of the ruling class. Let us therefore turn to authors who do not believe that the body politic and its laws and institutions are merely coercive superstructures, secondary manifestations of some underlying forces. Let us turn, for instance, to Bertrand de Jouvenel, whose book *Power* is perhaps the most prestigious and, anyway, the most interesting recent treatise on the subject. 'To him', he writes, 'who contemplates the unfolding of the ages war presents itself as an activity of States *which pertains to their essence*.'[3] This may prompt us to ask whether the end of warfare, then, would mean the end of states. Would the disappearance of violence in relationships between states spell the end of power?

The answer, it seems, will depend on what we understand by

From Hannah Arendt, *On Violence*, Florida: Harcourt Brace, 1969; London: Allen Lane, 1970 copyright © 1969, 1970 by Hannah Arendt. Reprinted by permission of Harcourt Brace Jovanovich, Inc. and Penguin Books Ltd.

power. And power, it turns out, is an instrument of rule, while rule, we are told, owes its existence to 'the instinct of domination'.[4] We are immediately reminded of what Sartre said about violence when we read in Jouvenel that 'a man feels himself more of a man when he is imposing himself and making others the instruments of his will', which gives him 'incomparable pleasure'.[5] 'Power', said Voltaire, 'consists in making others act as I choose'; it is present wherever I have the chance 'to assert my own will against the resistance' of others, said Max Weber, reminding us of Clausewitz's definition of war as 'an act of violence to compel the opponent to do as we wish'. The word, we are told by Strausz-Hupé, signifies 'the power of man over man'.[6] To go back to Jouvenel: 'To command and to be obeyed: without that, there is no Power – with it no other attribute is needed for it to be. . . . The thing without which it cannot be: that essence is command.'[7] If the essence of power is the effectiveness of command, then there is no greater power than that which grows out of the barrel of a gun, and it would be difficult to say in 'which way the order given by a policeman is different from that given by a gunman'. (I am quoting from the important book *The Notion of the State*, by Alexander Passerin d'Entrèves, the only author I know who is aware of the importance of distinguishing between violence and power. 'We have to decide whether and in what sense "power" can be distinguished from "force", to ascertain how the fact of using force according to law changes the quality of force itself and presents us with an entirely different picture of human relations', since 'force, by the very fact of being qualified, ceases to be force'. But even this distinction, by far the most sophisticated and thoughtful one in the literature, does not go to the root of the matter. Power in Passerin d'Entrèves's understanding is 'qualified' or 'institutionalized force'. In other words, while the authors quoted above define violence as the most flagrant manifestation of power, Passerin d'Entrèves defines power as a kind of mitigated violence. In the final analysis, it comes to the same.)[8] Should everybody from Right to Left, from Bertrand de Jouvenel to Mao Tse-tung agree on so basic a point in political philosophy as the nature of power?

In terms of our traditions of political thought, these definitions have much to recommend them. Not only do they derive from the old notion of absolute power that accompanied the rise of the sovereign European nation-state, whose earliest and still greatest spokesmen were Jean Bodin, in sixteenth-century France, and Thomas Hobbes, in seventeenth-century England; they also coincide with the terms used since Greek antiquity to define the forms of government as the rule of man over man – of one or the few in monarchy and oligarchy, of the best or the many in aristocracy and democracy. Today we ought to add the latest and perhaps most formidable form of such dominion: bureaucracy or the rule of an intricate system of bureaus in which no men, neither one nor the best, neither the few nor the many, can be held responsible, and which could be properly called rule by Nobody. (If, in accord with traditional political thought, we identify tyranny as government that is not held to give account of itself, rule by Nobody is clearly the most tyrannical of all, since there is no one left who could even be asked to answer for what is being done. It is this state of affairs, making it impossible to localize responsibility and to identify the enemy, that is among the most potent causes of the current world-wide rebellious unrest, its chaotic nature, and its dangerous tendency to get out of control and to run amuck.)

Moreover, this ancient vocabulary was strangely confirmed and fortified by the addition of the Hebrew-Christian tradition and its 'imperative conception of law'. This concept was not invented by the 'political realists' but was, rather, the result of a much earlier, almost automatic generalization of God's 'Commandments', according to which 'the simple relation of command and obedience' indeed sufficed to identify the essence of law.[9] Finally, more modern scientific and philosophical convictions concerning man's nature have further strengthened these legal and political traditions. The many recent discoveries of an inborn instinct of domination and an innate aggressiveness in the human animal were preceded by very similar philosophic statements. According to John Stuart Mill, 'the first lesson of civilization [is] that of obedience', and he speaks of 'the two states of the inclinations . . . one the desire to exercise power over others; the other . . . disinclination to have power exercised over themselves'.[10] If we would trust our own experiences in these matters, we should know that the instinct of submission, an ardent desire to obey and be ruled by some strong man, is at least as prominent in human psychology as the will to power, and, politically, perhaps more relevant. The old adage 'How fit he is to sway/ That can so well obey', some version of which seems to have been known to all centuries and all nations,[11] may point to a psychological truth: namely, that the will to power and the will to submission are interconnected. 'Ready submission to tyranny', to use Mill once more, is by no means always caused by 'extreme passiveness'. Conversely, a strong disinclination to obey is often accompanied by an equally strong disinclination to dominate and command. Historically speaking, the ancient institution of slave economy would be inexplicable on the grounds of Mill's psychology. Its express purpose was to liberate citizens from the burden of household affairs and to permit them to enter the public life of the community, where all were equals; if it were true that nothing is sweeter than to give commands and to rule others, the master would never have left his household.

However, there exists another tradition and another vocabulary no less old and time-honored. When the Athenian city-state called its constitution an isonomy, or the Romans spoke of the *civitas* as their form of government, they had in mind a concept of power and law whose essence did not rely on the command–obedience relationship and which did not identify power and rule or law and command. It was to these examples that the men of the eighteenth-century revolutions turned when they ransacked the archives of antiquity and constituted a form of government, a republic, where the rule of law, resting on the power of the people, would put an end to the rule of man over man, which they thought was a 'government fit for slaves'. They too, unhappily, still talked about obedience – obedience to laws instead of men; but what they actually meant was support of the laws to which the citizenry had given its consent.[12] Such support is never unquestioning, and as far as reliability is concerned it cannot match the indeed 'unquestioning obedience' that an act of violence can exact – the obedience every criminal can count on when he snatches my pocketbook with the help of a knife or robs a bank with the help of a gun. It is the people's support that lends power to the institutions of a country, and this support is but the continuation of the consent that brought the laws into existence to begin with. Under conditions of representative government the people are supposed to rule those who govern them. All political institutions are manifestations and materializations of power; they petrify and decay as soon as the living power of the people ceases to uphold them. This is what Madison meant when he said 'all governments rest on opinion', a word no less true for the various forms of monarchy than for democracies. ('To suppose that majority rule functions only in democracy is a fantastic illusion', as Jouvenel points out: 'The king, who is but one solitary individual, stands far more in need of the general support of Society than any other form of government.'[13] Even the tyrant, the One who rules against all, needs helpers in the business of violence, though their number may be rather restricted.) However, the strength of opinion, that is, the power of the government, depends on numbers; it is 'in proportion to the number with which it is associated',[14] and tyranny, as Montesquieu discovered, is therefore the most violent and least powerful of forms of government. Indeed one of the most obvious distinctions between power and violence is that power always stands in need of numbers, whereas violence up to a point can manage without them because it relies on implements. A legally unrestricted majority rule, that is, a democracy without a constitution, can be very formidable in the suppression of the rights of minorities and very effective in the suffocation of dissent without any use of violence. But that does not mean that violence and power are the same.

The extreme form of power is All against One, the extreme form of violence is One against All. And this latter is never possible without instruments. To claim, as is often done, that a tiny unarmed minority has successfully, by means of violence – shouting, kicking up a row, et cetera – disrupted large lecture classes whose overwhelming majority had voted for normal instruction procedures is therefore very misleading. (In a recent case at some German university there was even one lonely 'dissenter' among several hundred students who could claim such a strange victory.) What actually happens in such cases is something much more serious: the majority clearly refuses to use its power and overpower the disrupters; the academic processes break down because no one is willing to raise more than a voting finger for the *status quo*. What the universities are up against is the 'immense negative unity' of which Stephen Spender speaks in another context. All of which proves only that a minority can have a much greater potential power than one would expect by counting noses in public-opinion polls. The merely onlooking majority, amused by the spectacle of a shouting match between student and professor, is in fact already the latent ally of the minority. (One need only imagine what would have happened had one or a few unarmed Jews in pre-Hitler Germany tried to disrupt the lecture of an anti-Semitic professor in order to understand the absurdity of the talk about the small 'minorities of militants'.)

It is, I think, a rather sad reflection on the present state of political science that our terminology does not distinguish among such key words as 'power', 'strength', 'force', 'authority', and, finally, 'violence' – all of which refer to distinct, different phenomena and would hardly exist unless they did. (In the words of d'Entrèves, 'might, power, authority: these are all words to whose exact implications no great weight is attached in current speech; even the greatest thinkers sometimes use them at random. Yet it is fair to presume that they refer to different properties, and their meaning should therefore be carefully assessed and examined. . . .

The correct use of these words is a question not only of logical grammar, but of historical perspective.')[15] To use them as synonyms not only indicates a certain deafness to linguistic meanings, which would be serious enough, but it has also resulted in a kind of blindness to the realities they correspond to. In such a situation it is always tempting to introduce new definitions, but – though I shall briefly yield to temptation – what is involved is not simply a matter of careless speech. Behind the apparent confusion is a firm conviction in whose light all distinctions would be, at best, of minor importance: the conviction that the most crucial political issue is, and always has been, the question of Who rules Whom? Power, strength, force, authority, violence – these are but words to indicate the means by which man rules over man; they are held to be synonyms because they have the same function. It is only after one ceases to reduce public affairs to the business of dominion that the original data in the realm of human affairs will appear, or, rather, reappear, in their authentic diversity.

These data, in our context, may be enumerated as follows:

Power corresponds to the human ability not just to act but to act in concert. Power is never the property of an individual; it belongs to a group and remains in existence only so long as the group keeps together. When we say of somebody that he is 'in power' we actually refer to his being empowered by a certain number of people to act in their name. The moment the group, from which the power originated to begin with (*potestas in populo*, without a people or group there is no power), disappears, 'his power' also vanishes. In current usage, when we speak of a 'powerful man' or a 'powerful personality', we already use the word 'power' metaphorically; what we refer to without metaphor is 'strength'.

Strength unequivocally designates something in the singular, an individual entity; it is the property inherent in an object or person and belongs to its character, which may prove itself in relation to other things or persons, but is essentially independent of them. The strength of even the strongest individual can always be overpowered by the many, who often will combine for no other purpose than to ruin strength precisely because of its peculiar independence. The almost instinctive hostility of the many toward the one has always, from Plato to Nietzsche, been ascribed to resentment, to the envy of the weak for the strong, but this psychological interpretation misses the point. It is in the nature of a group and its power to turn against independence, the property of individual strength.

Force, which we often use in daily speech as a synonym for violence, especially if violence serves as a means of coercion, should be reserved, in terminological language, for the 'forces of nature' or the 'force of circumstances' (*la force des choses*), that is, to indicate the energy released by physical or social movements.

Authority, relating to the most elusive of these phenomena and therefore, as a term, most frequently abused,[16] can be vested in persons – there is such a thing as personal authority, as, for instance, in the relation between parent and child, between teacher and pupil – or it can be vested in offices, as, for instance, in the Roman senate (*auctoritas in senatu*) or in the hierarchical offices of the Church (a priest can grant valid absolution even though he is drunk). Its hallmark is unquestioning recognition by those who are asked to obey; neither coercion nor persuasion is needed. (A father can lose his authority either by beating his child or by starting to argue with him, that is, either by behaving to him like a tyrant or by treating him as an equal.) To remain in authority requires respect for the person or the office. The greatest enemy of authority, therefore, is contempt, and the surest way to undermine it is laughter.[17]

Violence, finally, as I have said, is distinguished by its instrumental character. Phenomenologically, it is close to strength, since the implements of violence, like all other tools, are designed and used for the purpose of multiplying natural strength until, in the last stage of their development, they can substitute for it.

It is perhaps not superfluous to add that these distinctions, though by no means arbitrary, hardly ever correspond to watertight compartments in the real world, from which nevertheless they are drawn. Thus institutionalized power in organized communities often appears in the guise of authority, demanding instant, unquestioning recognition; no society could function without it. (A small, and still isolated, incident in New York shows what can happen if authentic authority in social relations has broken down to the point where it cannot work any longer even in its derivative, purely functional form. A minor mishap in the subway system – the doors on a train failed to operate – turned into a serious shutdown on the line lasting four hours and involving more than 50,000 passengers, because when the transit authorities asked the passengers to leave the defective train, they simply refused.)[18] Moreover, nothing, as we shall see, is more common than the combination of violence and power, nothing less frequent than to find them in their pure and therefore extreme form. From this, it does not follow that authority, power, and violence are all the same.

Still it must be admitted that it is particularly tempting to think of power in terms of command and obedience, and hence to equate power with violence, in a discussion of what actually is only one of power's special cases – namely, the power of government. Since in foreign relations as well as domestic affairs violence appears as a last resort to keep the power structure intact against individual challengers – the foreign enemy, the native criminal – it looks indeed as though violence were the prerequisite of power and power nothing but a façade, the velvet glove which either conceals the iron hand or will turn out to belong to a paper tiger. On closer inspection, though, this notion loses much of its plausibility. For our purpose, the gap between theory and reality is perhaps best illustrated by the phenomenon of revolution.

Since the beginning of the century theoreticians of revolution have told us that the chances of revolution have significantly decreased in proportion to the increased destructive capacities of weapons at the unique disposition of governments.[19] The history of the last 70 years, with its extraordinary record of successful and unsuccessful revolutions, tells a different story. Were people mad who even tried against such overwhelming odds? And, leaving out instances of full success, how can even a temporary success be explained? The fact is that the gap between state-owned means of violence and what people can muster by themselves – from beer bottles to Molotov cocktails and guns – has always been so enormous that technical improvements make hardly any difference. Textbook instructions on 'how to make a revolution' in a step-by-step progression from dissent to conspiracy, from resistance to armed uprising, are all based on the mistaken notion that revolutions are 'made'. In a contest of violence against violence the superiority of the government has always been absolute; but this superiority lasts only as long as the power structure of the government is intact – that is, as long as commands are obeyed and the army or police forces are prepared to use their weapons. When this is no longer the case, the situation changes abruptly. Not only is the rebellion not put down, but the arms themselves change hands – sometimes, as in the Hungarian revolution, within a few hours. (We should know about such things after all these years of futile fighting in Vietnam, where for a long time, before getting massive Russian aid, the National Liberation Front fought us with weapons that were made in the United States.) Only after this has happened, when the disintegration of the government in power has permitted the rebels to arm themselves, can one speak of an 'armed uprising', which often does not take place at all or occurs when it is no longer necessary. Where commands are no longer obeyed, the means of violence are of no use; and the question of this obedience is not decided by the command–obedience relation but by opinion, and, of course, by the number of those who share it. Everything depends on the power behind the violence. The sudden dramatic breakdown of power that ushers in revolutions reveals in a flash how civil obedience – to laws, to rulers, to institutions – is but the outward manifestation of support and consent.

Where power has disintegrated, revolutions are possible but not necessary. We know of many instances when utterly impotent regimes were permitted to continue in existence for long periods of time – either because there was no one to test their strength and reveal their weakness or because they were lucky enough not to be engaged in war and suffer defeat. Disintegration often becomes manifest only in direct confrontation; and even then, when power is already in the street, some group of men prepared for such an eventuality is needed to pick it up and assume responsibility. We have recently witnessed how it did not take more than the relatively harmless, essentially nonviolent French students' rebellion to reveal the vulnerability of the whole political system, which rapidly disintegrated before the astonished eyes of the young rebels. Unknowingly they had tested it; they intended only to challenge the ossified university system, and down came the system of governmental power, together with that of the huge party bureaucracies – '*une sorte de désintégration de toutes les hiérarchies*'.[20] It was a textbook case of a revolutionary situation[21] that did not develop into a revolution because there was nobody, least of all the students, prepared to seize power and the responsibility that goes with it. Nobody except, of course, de Gaulle. Nothing was more characteristic of the seriousness of the situation than his appeal to the army, his journey to see Massu and the generals in Germany, a walk to Canossa, if there ever was one, in view of what had happened only a few years before. But what he sought and received was support, not obedience, and the means were not commands but concessions.[22] If commands had been enough, he would never have had to leave Paris.

No government exclusively based on the means of violence has ever existed. Even the totalitarian ruler, whose chief instrument of rule is torture, needs a power basis – the secret police and its net of informers. Only the development of robot soldiers, which, as previously mentioned, would eliminate the human factor completely and, conceivably, permit one man with a push button to destroy whomever he pleased, could change this fundamental ascendancy of power over violence. Even the most despotic domination we know of, the rule of master over slaves, who always outnumbered him, did not rest on superior means of coercion as such, but on a superior organization of power – that is, on the organized solidarity of the masters.[23] Single men without others to support them never have enough power to use violence successfully. Hence, in domestic affairs, violence functions as the last resort of power against criminals or rebels – that is, against single individuals who, as it were, refuse to be overpowered by the consensus of the majority. And as for actual warfare, we have seen in Vietnam how an enormous superiority in the means of violence can become helpless if confronted with an ill-equipped but well-organized opponent who is much more powerful. This lesson, to be sure, was there to be learned from the history of guerrilla warfare, which is at least as old as the defeat in Spain of Napoleon's still-unvanquished army.

To switch for a moment to conceptual language: Power is indeed of the essence of all government, but violence is not. Violence is by nature instrumental; like all means, it always stands in need of guidance and justification through the end it pursues. And what needs justification by something else cannot be the essence of anything. The end of war – end taken in its twofold meaning – is peace or victory; but to the question 'And what is the end of peace?' there is no answer. Peace is an absolute, even though in recorded history periods of warfare have nearly always outlasted periods of peace. Power is in the same category; it is, as they say, 'an end in itself'. (This, of course, is not to deny that governments pursue policies and employ their power to achieve prescribed goals. But the power structure itself precedes and outlasts all aims, so that power, far from being the means to an end, is actually the very condition enabling a group of people to think and act in terms of the means–end category.) And since government is essentially organized and institutionalized power, the current question 'What is the end of government?' does not make much sense either. The answer will be either question-begging – to enable men to live together – or dangerously utopian – to promote happiness or to realize a classless society or some other nonpolitical ideal, which if tried out in earnest cannot but end in some kind of tyranny.

Power needs no justification, being inherent in the very existence of political communities; what it does need is legitimacy. The common treatment of these two words as synonyms is no less misleading and confusing than the current equation of obedience and support. Power springs up whenever people get together and act in concert, but it derives its legitimacy from the initial getting together rather than from any action that then may follow. Legitimacy, when challenged, bases itself on an appeal to the past, while justification relates to an end that lies in the future. Violence can be justifiable, but it never will be legitimate. Its justification loses in plausibility the farther its intended end recedes into the future. No one questions the use of violence in self-defense, because the danger is not only clear but also present, and the end justifying the means is immediate.

Power and violence, though they are distinct phenomena, usually appear together. Wherever they are combined, power, we have found, is the primary and predominant factor. The situation, however, is entirely different when we deal with them in their pure states – as, for instance, with foreign invasion and occupation. We saw that the current equation of violence with power rests on government's being understood as domination of man over man by means of violence. If a foreign conqueror is confronted by an impotent government and by a nation unused to the exercise of political power, it is easy for him to achieve such domination. In all other cases the difficulties are great indeed, and the occupying invader will try immediately to establish Quisling governments, that is, to find a native power base to support his dominion. The head-on clash between Russian tanks and the entirely non-violent resistance of the Czechoslovak people is a textbook case of a confrontation between violence and power in their pure states. But while domination in such an instance is difficult to achieve, it is not impossible. Violence, we must remember, does not depend on numbers or opinions, but on implements, and the implements of violence, as I mentioned before, like all other tools, increase and multiply human strength. Those who oppose violence with mere power will soon find that they are confronted not by men but by men's artifacts, whose inhumanity and destructive effectiveness increase in proportion to the distance separating the opponents. Violence can always destroy power; out of the barrel of a gun grows the most effective command, resulting in the most instant and perfect obedience. What never can grow out of it is power.

In a head-on clash between violence and power, the outcome is hardly in doubt. If Gandhi's enormously powerful and successful strategy of non-violent resistance had met with a different enemy – Stalin's Russia, Hitler's Germany, even prewar Japan, instead of England – the outcome would not have been decolonization, but massacre and submission. However, England in India and France in Algeria had good reasons for their restraint. Rule by sheer violence comes into play where power is being lost; it is precisely the shrinking power of the Russian government, internally and externally, that became manifest in its 'solution' of the Czechoslovak

problem – just as it was the shrinking power of European imperialism that became manifest in the alternative between decolonization
and massacre. To substitute violence for power can bring victory,
but the price is very high; for it is not only paid by the vanquished,
it is also paid by the victor in terms of his own power. This is
especially true when the victor happens to enjoy domestically the
blessings of constitutional government. Henry Steele Commager is
entirely right: 'If we subvert world order and destroy world peace
we must inevitably subvert and destroy our own political institutions first'.[24] The much-feared boomerang effect of the 'government of subject races' (Lord Cromer) on the home government
during the imperialist era meant that rule by violence in faraway
lands would end by affecting the government of England, that the
last 'subject race' would be the English themselves. The recent gas
attack on the campus at Berkeley, where not just tear gas but also
another gas, 'outlawed by the Geneva Convention and used by the
Army to flush out guerrillas in Vietnam', was laid down while gas-
masked Guardsmen stopped anybody and everybody 'from fleeing
the gassed area', is an excellent example of this 'backlash' phenomenon. It has often been said that impotence breeds violence, and
psychologically this is quite true, at least of persons possessing
natural strength, moral or physical. Politically speaking, the point is
that loss of power becomes a temptation to substitute violence for
power – in 1968 during the democratic convention in Chicago we
could watch this process on television[25] – and that violence itself
results in impotence. Where violence is no longer backed and
restrained by power, the well-known reversal in reckoning with
means and ends has taken place. The means, the means of destruction, now determine the end – with the consequence that the end
will be the destruction of all power.

Nowhere is the self-defeating factor in the victory of violence
over power more evident than in the use of terror to maintain
domination, about whose weird successes and eventual failures we
know perhaps more than any generation before us. Terror is not the
same as violence; it is, rather, the form of government that comes
into being when violence, having destroyed all power, does not
abdicate but, on the contrary, remains in full control. It has often
been noticed that the effectiveness of terror depends almost entirely
on the degree of social atomization. Every kind of organized opposition must disappear before the full force of terror can be let loose.
This atomization – an outrageously pale, academic word for the
horror it implies – is maintained and intensified through the ubi-
quity of the informer, who can be literally omnipresent because he

no longer is merely a professional agent in the pay of the police but potentially every person one comes into contact with. How such a fully developed police state is established and how it works – or, rather, how nothing works where it holds sway – can now be learned in Aleksandr I. Solzhenitsyn's *The First Circle*, which will probably remain one of the masterpieces of twentieth-century literature and certainly contains the best documentation on Stalin's regime in existence.[26] The decisive difference between totalitarian domination, based on terror, and tyrannies and dictatorships, established by violence, is that the former turns not only against its enemies but against its friends and supporters as well, being afraid of all power, even the power of its friends. The climax of terror is reached when the police state begins to devour its own children, when yesterday's executioner becomes today's victim. And this is also the moment when power disappears entirely. There exist now a great many plausible explanations for the de-Stalinization of Russia – none, I believe, so compelling as the realization by the Stalinist functionaries themselves that a continuation of the regime would lead, not to an insurrection, against which terror is indeed the best safeguard, but to paralysis of the whole country.

To sum up: politically speaking, it is insufficient to say that power and violence are not the same. Power and violence are opposites; where the one rules absolutely, the other is absent. Violence appears where power is in jeopardy, but left to its own course it ends in power's disappearance. This implies that it is not correct to think of the opposite of violence as nonviolence; to speak of non-violent power is actually redundant. Violence can destroy power; it is utterly incapable of creating it. Hegel's and Marx's great trust in the dialectical 'power of negation', by virtue of which opposites do not destroy but smoothly develop into each other because contradictions promote and do not paralyze development, rests on a much older philosophical prejudice: that evil is no more than a privative *modus* of the good, that good can come out of evil; that, in short, evil is but a temporary manifestation of a still-hidden good. Such time-honored opinions have become dangerous. They are shared by many who have never heard of Hegel or Marx, for the simple reason that they inspire hope and dispel fear – a treacherous hope used to dispel legitimate fear. By this, I do not mean to equate violence with evil; I only want to stress that violence cannot be derived from its opposite, which is power, and that in order to understand it for what it is, we shall have to examine its roots and nature.

NOTES

1 Georges Sorel, *Reflections on Violence*, 'Introduction to the First Publication' (New York (1906), 1961), p. 60.

2 *The Power Elite* (New York, 1956), p. 171; Max Weber in the first paragraphs of *Politics as a Vocation* (1921). Weber seems to have been aware of his agreement with the Left. He quotes in the context Trotsky's remark in Brest-Litovsk, 'Every state is based on violence', and adds, 'This is indeed true.'

3 *Power: The Natural History of Its Growth* (London (1945), 1952), p. 122.

4 Ibid., p. 93.

5 Ibid., p. 110.

6 See Karl von Clausewitz, *On War* (1832) (New York, 1943), chapter 1; Robert Strausz-Hupé, *Power and Community* (New York, 1956), p. 4; the quotation from Max Weber: '*Macht bedeutet jede Chance, innerhalb einer sozialen Beziehung den eigenen Willen auch gegen Widerstand durchzusetzen*', is drawn from Strausz-Hupé.

7 I chose my examples at random, since it hardly matters to which author one turns. It is only occasionally that one hears a dissenting voice. Thus R. M. McIver states, 'Coercive power is a criterion of the state, but not its essence. . . . It is true that there is no state, where there is no overwhelming force. . . . But the exercise of force does not make a state' (in *The Modern State* (London, 1926), pp. 222–5). How strong the force of this tradition is can be seen in Rousseau's attempt to escape it. Looking for a government of no-rule, he finds nothing better than '*une forme d'association . . . par laquelle chacun s'unissant à tous n'obéisse pourtant qu'à lui-même*'. The emphasis on obedience, and hence on command, is unchanged.

8 *The Notion of the State, An Introduction to Political Theory* was first published in Italian in 1962. The English version is no mere translation; written by the author himself, it is the definitive edition and appeared in Oxford in 1967. For the quotations, see pp. 64, 70 and 105.

9 Ibid., p. 129.

10 *Considerations on Representative Government* (Liberal Arts Library (1861)), pp. 59 and 65.

11 John M. Wallace, *Destiny His Choice: The Loyalism of Andrew Marvell* (Cambridge, 1968), pp. 88–9. I owe this reference to the kind attention of Gregory DesJardins.

12 See appendix XI, p. 97 of Hannah Arendt, *On Violence* (London, 1970).

13 *Power*, p. 98.

14 *The Federalist*, no. 49.

15 *The Notion of the State*, p. 7. Cf. also p. 171, where, discussing the exact meaning of the words 'nation' and 'nationality', he rightly insists that 'the only competent guides in the jungle of so many different meanings are the linguists and the historians. It is to them that we must

turn for help'. And in distinguishing authority and power, he turns to Cicero's *potestas in populo, auctoritas in senatu.*

16 There is such a thing as authoritarian government, but it certainly has nothing in common with tyranny, dictatorship, or totalitarian rule. For a discussion of the historical background and political significance of the term, see my 'What is authority?' in *Between Past and Future: Exercises in Political Thought* (New York, 1968), and part I of Karl-Heinz Lübke's valuable study, *Auctoritas bei Augustin* (Stuttgart, 1968), with extensive bibliography.

17 Sheldon Wolin and John Schaar, 'Berkeley: the Battle of People's Park', *New York Review of Books*, 19 June 1969, are entirely right: 'The rules are being broken because University authorities, administrators and faculty alike, have lost the respect of many of the students.' They then conclude, 'When authority leaves, power enters.' This too is true, but, I am afraid, not quite in the sense they meant it. What entered first at Berkeley was student power, obviously the strongest power on every campus simply because of the students' superior numbers. It was in order to break this power that authorities resorted to violence, and it is precisely because the university is essentially an institution based on authority, and therefore in need of respect, that it finds it so difficult to deal with power in non-violent terms. The university today calls upon the police for protection exactly as the Catholic church used to do before the separation of state and church forced it to rely on authority alone. It is perhaps more than an oddity that the severest crisis of the church as an institution should coincide with the severest crisis in the history of the university, the only secular institution still based on authority. Both may indeed be ascribed to 'the progressing explosion of the atom "obedience" whose stability was allegedly eternal', as Heinrich Böll remarked of the crisis in the churches. See 'Es wird immer später', in *Antwort an Sacharow* (Zürich, 1969).

18 See the *New York Times*, 4 January 1969, pp. 1 and 29.

19 Thus Franz Borkenau, reflecting on the defeat of the Spanish revolution, states: 'In this tremendous contrast with previous revolutions one fact is reflected. Before these latter years, counter-revolution usually depended upon the support of reactionary powers, which were technically and intellectually inferior to the forces of revolution. This has changed with the advent of fascism. Now, every revolution is likely to meet the attack of the most modern, most efficient, most ruthless machinery yet in existence. It means that the age of revolutions free to evolve according to their own laws is over.' This was written more than thirty years ago (*The Spanish Cockpit* (London, 1937; Ann Arbor, 1963), pp. 288–9) and is now quoted with approval by Chomsky, *American Power and the New Mandarins* (New York, 1969), p. 310). He believes that American and French intervention in the civil war in Vietnam proves Borkenau's prediction accurate, 'with substitution of "liberal imperialism" for "fascism".' I think that this example is rather apt to prove the opposite.

20 Raymond Aron, *La Révolution Introuvable* (1968) p. 41.

21 Stephen Spender, *The Year of the Young Rebels*, (New York, 1969), p. 56, disagrees: 'What was so much more apparent than the revolutionary situation [was] the non-revolutionary one'. It may be 'difficult to think of a revolution taking place when . . . everyone looks particularly good humoured', but this is what usually happens in the beginning of revolutions – during the early great ecstasy of fraternity.

22 See appendix XII, p. 98, of Arendt, *On Violence*.

23 In ancient Greece such an organization of power was the polis, whose chief merit, according to Xenophon, was that it permitted the 'citizens to act as bodyguards to one another against slaves and criminals so that none of the citizens may die a violent death'. (*Hiero*, IV, 3.)

24 'Can we limit presidential power?' in *The New Republic*, 6 April 1968.

25 See appendix XIII, p. 98 of Arendt, *On Violence*.

26 See appendix XIV, p. 99 of Arendt, *On Violence*.

5
Hannah Arendt's Communications Concept of Power

JÜRGEN HABERMAS

Max Weber defined (*Macht*) as the possibility of forcing one's own will on the behavior of others. Hannah Arendt, on the contrary, understands power as the ability to agree upon a common course of action in unconstrained communication. Both represent power as a potency that is actualized in actions, but each takes a different model of action as a basis.

'POWER' IN MAX WEBER, TALCOTT PARSONS, AND HANNAH ARENDT

Max Weber takes the teleological model of action as his point of departure: an individual subject (or a group that can be regarded as an individual) chooses the appropriate means to realize a goal that it has set for itself. Goal-attainment or success consists in bringing about a state in the world that fulfills the goal in question. To the extent that his success depends on the behavior of another subject, the actor must have at his disposal the means to instigate the other to the desired behavior. Weber calls this disposition over means to influence the will of another 'power'. Hannah Arendt reserves for it the term 'force' (*Gewalt*). The purposive-rational actor, who is interested only in the success of his action, must dispose of means with which he can compel a subject capable of choice, whether by the threat of sanctions, by persuasion, or by a clever channeling of choices. As Weber puts it: 'Power means every chance within a social relationship to assert one's will even against opposition'.[1] The only alternative to coercion (*Zwang*) exercised by one side against the other is free agreement among participants. But the teleological model of action provides only for actors who are

'Hannah Arendt's communications concept of power', *Social Research*, 44, 1 (1977), pp. 3–24 is reprinted by permission of the journal and author.

oriented to their own success and not to reaching agreement. It admits of agreement processes only to the extent to which they appear to the participants as means for attaining their respective goals. But an agreement of this sort, which is pursued one-sidedly with the proviso of being instrumental for one's own success, is not meant seriously; it does not fulfill the conditions of a consensus brought about without constraint.

Hannah Arendt starts from another model of action, the comunicative:

> Power corresponds to the human ability not just to act but to act in concert. Power is never the property of an individual; it belongs to a group and remains in existence only so long as the group keeps together. When we say of somebody that he is 'in power' we actually refer to his being empowered by a certain number of people to act in their name.[2]

The fundamental phenomenon of power is not the instrumentalization of *another's* will, but the formation of a *common* will in a communication directed to reaching agreement. This could, of course, be understood in such a way that 'power' and 'force' merely designate two different aspects of the same exercise of political rule. 'Power' would then mean the consent of the governed that is mobilized for collective goals, that is, their readiness to support the political leadership; while 'force' would mean the disposition over resources and means of coercion, in virtue of which a political leadership makes and carries through binding decisions in order to realize collective goals. This idea has in fact inspired the systems-theoretic concept of power.

Talcott Parsons understands by power the general capacity of a social system 'to get things done in the interest of collective goals'.[3] The mobilization of consent produces the power which is transformed into binding decisions through the exploitation of social resources.[4] Parsons can bring the two phenomena which Arendt contrasts as power and force under one unified concept of power because he understands power as the property of a system which behaves toward its own components according to the same schema that characterizes the behavior of the purposive-rational actor toward the external world: 'I have defined power as the capacity of a social system to mobilize resources to attain collective goals'.[5] He repeats at the level of systems theory the same teleological concept of power (as the potential to realize goals) that Weber pursued at the level of action theory. In both cases, what is specific to the power of unifying speech, what separates it from force, is lost. The power of agreement-oriented communication to produce consensus is opposed to this force, because seriously intended agreement is an end in itself and cannot be instrumentalized for other ends.

The agreement of those who take counsel together in order to act in common – 'an opinion upon which many publicly are in agreement'[6] – signifies power insofar as it rests on conviction and thus on that peculiarly forceless force with which insights assert themselves. Let us attempt to clarify this. The strength of a consensus brought about in unconstrained communication is not measured against any success but against the claim to rational validity that is immanent in speech. Of course, a conviction that is formed in the give and take of public discussion can also be manipulated; but even successful manipulation must take rationality claims into account. We allow ourselves to be convinced of the truth of a statement, the rightness of a norm, the veracity of an utterance; the authenticity of our conviction stands and falls with belief, that is, with the consciousness that the recognition of those validity claims is rationally motivated. Convictions can be manipulated, but not the rationality claim from which they subjectively draw their force.

In short, the communicatively produced power of common convictions originates in the fact that those involved are oriented to reaching agreement and not primarily to their respective individual successes. It is based on the fact that they do not use language 'perlocutionarily', merely to instigate other subjects to a desired behavior, but 'illocutionarily', that is, for the noncoercive establishment of intersubjective relations. Hannah Arendt disconnects the concept of power from the teleological model; power is built up in communicative action; it is a collective effect of speech in which reaching agreement is an end in itself for all those involved. If, however, power is no longer thought of as a potential for realizing goals, if it is not actualized in purposive-rational action, then in what is it expressed, and for what can it be used?

Hannah Arendt regards the development of power as an end in itself. Power serves to maintain the praxis from which it springs. It becomes consolidated and embodied in political institutions which secure those very forms of life that are centered in reciprocal speech. Power therefore manifests itself (a) in orders that protect liberty, (b) in resistance against forces that threaten political liberty, and (c) in those revolutionary actions that found new institutions of liberty.

It is the people's support that lends power to the institutions of a country, and this support is but the continuation of the

consent that brought the laws into existence to begin
with. . . . All political institutions are manifestations and
materializations of power; they petrify and decay as soon as
the living power of the people ceases to uphold them. This is
what Madison meant when he said 'all government rests on
opinion', a word no less true for the various forms of
monarchy than for democracies.[7]

It becomes clear at this point that the communications concept of
power also has a normative content. Is such a concept scientifically
useful? Is it at all suited to descriptive purposes? I will try to answer
this question in several steps. I will first show how Hannah Arendt
introduces and grounds her concept. Then I would like to offer a
reminder of how she employs it. Finally, I want to deal with a few
weaknesses in the concept; in my view these derive less from its
normative status than from the fact that Arendt remains bound to
the historical and conceptual constellation of classical Greek philosophy.

THE STRUCTURE OF UNIMPAIRED INTERSUBJECTIVITY

Hannah Arendt's principal philosophical work, *The Human Condition* (1958), serves to systematically renew the Aristotelian concept of praxis. The author does not rely on an exegesis of classical
texts; she drafts an anthropology of communicative action – a
counterpart to Arnold Gehlen's anthropology of purposeful action
(*Der Mensch*, 1940, 1950). Whereas Gehlen examines the behavioral circuit of instrumental action as the most important repro-
ductive mechanism of the species, Arendt analyzes the form of
intersubjectivity generated in the praxis of speech as the basic
feature of cultural life. Communicative action is the medium in
which the intersubjectively shared life-world is formed. It is the
'space of appearance' in which actors enter, encounter one another,
are seen and heard. The spatial dimension of the life-world is
determined by the 'fact of human plurality': every interaction
unifies the multiple perspectives of perception and action of those
present, who as individuals occupy an inconvertible standpoint.
The temporal dimension of the life-world is determined by the 'fact
of human natality': the birth of every individual means the possibility of a new beginning; to act means to be able to seize the initiative
and to do the unanticipated. Furthermore, the life-world is essentially charged with securing individual and group identity in social

space and historical time. In communication, individuals appear actively as unique beings and reveal themselves in their subjectivity. At the same time they must recognize one another as equally responsible beings, that is, as beings capable of intersubjective agreement – the rationality claim immanent in speech grounds a radical equality. Finally, the life-world itself is filled, so to speak, with praxis, with the 'web of human relationships'. This comprises the stories in which actors are involved as doers and sufferers.[8]

One may regard the method with which Hannah Arendt develops her practical philosophy – a method reminiscent of Alfred Schutz's social phenomenology – as inadequate; but the intention is clear: she wants to read off of the formal properties of communicative action (or praxis) the general structures of an unimpaired intersubjectivity. These structures set the conditions of normalcy for human existence, indeed for an existence worthy of human beings. Owing to its innovative potential, the domain of praxis is, however, highly unstable and in need of protection. In societies organized around a state, this is looked after by political institutions. These are fed by the power that springs from unimpaired intersubjectivity; and they must in turn protect the susceptible structures of intersubjectivity against deformations if they are not themselves to deteriorate. From this follows the central hypothesis that Hannah Arendt untiringly repeats: no political leadership can with impunity replace power through force; and it can gain power only from a non-deformed public realm. The public-political realm has also been conceived by others as a generator, if not of power then of the legitimation of power; but Hannah Arendt insists that a public-political realm can produce legitimate power only so long as structures of non-distorted communication find their expression in it.

> What first undermines and then kills political communities is loss of power and final impotence; and power cannot be stored up and kept in reserve for emergencies, like the instruments of violence, but exists only in actualization. Where power is not actualized, it passes away, and history is full of examples that the greatest material riches cannot compensate for this loss. Power is actualized only where word and deed have not parted company, where words are not empty and deeds not brutal, where words are not used to violate and destroy but to establish relations and create new realities. Power is what keeps the public realm, the potential space of appearance between acting and speaking men, in existence.[9]

SOME APPLICATIONS OF THE COMMUNICATIONS
CONCEPT OF POWER

Hannah Arendt does not test her hypothesis against examples of the decline of great empires. Her historical investigations resolve instead around two extreme cases: the destruction of political liberty under totalitarian rule (a), and the revolutionary establishment of political liberty (b).[10] Both investigations apply the concept of power, and in such a way that the deformations in Western mass democracies are illuminated from opposite sides.

(a) Every political order that isolates its citizens from one another through mistrust, and cuts off the public exchange of opinions, degenerates to a rule based on violence. It destroys the communicative structures in which alone power can originate. Fear heightened to terror forces each to shut himself off from every other; at the same time it destroys the distances between individuals. It takes from them the power of initiative and robs their interaction of its power to spontaneously unify what is separated: 'pressed together with everyone, each is totally isolated from all'.[11] The totalitarian rule which Hannah Arendt examines in the cases of Nazism and Stalinism is not only a modern version of classical tyrannies; if it were, it would merely silence the communicative movement of the public realm. Its specific achievement, however, is precisely the mobilization of depoliticized masses:

> On the one hand, the police state destroys all relations between men that still remain after the discontinuance of the public-political sphere; on the other hand, it demands that those who have been fully isolated and forsaken by one another be able to be brought into political actions (although naturally not to genuine political action). . . . Totalitarian rule does not only rob men of their capacity to act; rather, with inexorable consistency, it makes them – as if they were really only a single man – into accomplices in all actions undertaken and crimes committed by the totalitarian regime.[12]

The totalitarian rule of the Nazi regime historically arose on the basis of a mass democracy. This is one of the occasions that motivated Hannah Arendt to a vigorous critique of the privatism built into modern societies. Whereas the theorists of democratic elitism (following Schumpeter) commend representative government and the party system as channels for the political participation of a depoliticized mass, Arendt sees the danger precisely in this

situation. Mediatizing the population through highly bureaucra-
tized administrations, parties, and organizations just supplements
and fortifies those privatistic forms of life which provide the
psychological base for mobilizing the unpolitical, that is, for establishing totalitarian rule.[13] Thomas Jefferson, the radical democrat
among the fathers of the American constitution, already had

> at least a foreboding of how dangerous it might be to allow
> the people a share in public power without providing them at
> the same time with more public space than the ballot box and
> with more opportunity to make their voices heard in public
> than election day. What he perceived to be the mortal danger
> to the republic was that the Constitution had given all power
> to the citizens, without giving them the opportunity of *being*
> republicans and of *acting* as citizens. In other words, the
> danger was that all power had been given to the people in
> their private capacity, and that there was no space established
> for them in their capacity of being citizens.[14]

(b) Therein lies the motif that inspired Hannah Arendt to her
investigations of the bourgeois revolutions of the eighteenth century, the Hungarian uprising of 1956, and the civil disobedience
and student protests of the sixties. In connection with emancipatory
movements she is interested in the power of common conviction:
the withdrawal of obedience to institutions that have lost their
legitimacy; the confrontation of communicative power with the
means of force of a coercive but impotent state apparatus; the
beginnings of a new political order and the attempt – the pathos of
the new beginning – to hold fast to the initial revolutionary situation, to give institutional permanence to the communicative generation of power. It is fascinating to see how Hannah Arendt traces
the same phenomenon over and over. When revolutionaries seize
the power that lies in the streets; when a populace committed to
passive resistance confronts alien tanks with their bare hands; when
convinced minorities contest the legitimacy of existing laws and
organize civil disobedience; when the 'pure desire for action' manifests itself in the student movement – these phenomena confirm
again that no one really possesses power; it 'springs up between
men when they act together and vanishes the moment they disperse'.[15] This emphatic concept of praxis is more Marxist than
Aristotelian; Marx called it 'critical-revolutionary activity'.

Arendt identifies attempts to institutionalize direct democracy in
the American town meetings around 1776, in the *sociétés popu-*

laires in Paris between 1789 and 1793, in the sections of the Paris Commune of 1871, in the Russian soviets in 1903 and 1917, and in the *Rätedemokratie* in Germany in 1918. She sees in these different forms the only serious attempts at a constitution of liberty under the conditions of modern mass society. She traces their failure to the political defeats of the revolutionary labor movement and to the economic success of the unions and labor parties:

> with the transformation of a class society into a mass society and with the substitution of a guaranteed annual wage for daily or weekly pay ... the workers today are no longer outside of society; they are its members, and they are job-holders like everybody else. The political significance of the labor movement is now the same as that of any other pressure group.[16]

THE LIMITS OF CLASSICAL THEORY

In the context in which it stands, this thesis reads a bit too smoothly; it is not a result of well-balanced investigations but issues from a philosophical construction. So far I have tried to present what I take as strong aspects and promising applications of Arendt's concept of power. Now I would like to add some comments on its weaknesses.

Arendt stylizes the image she has of the Greek polis to the essence of politics as such. This is the background to her favored conceptual dichotomies between the public and the private, between state and economy, freedom and welfare, political-practical activity and production – rigid dichotomies which modern bourgeois society and the modern state, however, escape. Thus the mere fact that in modern times something characteristically new, a complementary relationship between state and economy, established itself with the development of the capitalist mode of production already counts as the mark of a pathology, of a destructive confusion:

> In the modern world the social and the political realms are much less distinct. . . . The functionalization [of politics] makes it impossible to perceive any serious gulf between the two realms; and this is not a matter of a theory or an ideology, since with the rise of society, that is, the rise of the 'household' (*oikia*) or of economic activities to the public realm, housekeeping and all matters pertaining formerly to the private sphere of the family have become a 'collective'

concern. In the modern world, the two realms indeed constantly flow into each other like the waves in the never-resting stream of the life process itself.[17]

Arendt rightly insists that the technical-economic overcoming of poverty is by no means a sufficient condition for the practical securing of political liberty. But she becomes the victim of a concept of politics that is inapplicable to modern conditions when she asserts that the

> intrusion of social and economic matters into the public realm, the transformation of government into administration, the replacement of personal rule by bureaucratic measures, and the attending transmutation of laws into decrees[18]

necessarily frustrate every attempt at a politically active public realm. She also views the French Revolution in this dim light; and she attributes the initial success of the foundation of liberty in America to the fact that 'the politically insoluble social question did not stand in the way'.[19] I cannot discuss this interpretion here.[20] I want only to indicate the curious perspective that Hannah Arendt adopts: a state which is relieved of the administrative processing of social problems; a politics which is cleansed of socio-economic issues; an institutionalization of public liberty which is independent of the organization of public wealth; a radical democracy which inhibits its liberating efficacy just at the boundaries where political oppression ceases and social repression begins – this path is unimaginable for any modern society.

Thus we are faced with a dilemma: on the one hand, the communications concept of power discloses important though extreme phenomena of the modern world to which political science has become more and more insensitive; on the other hand, it is linked with a conception of politics which, when applied to modern societies, leads to absurdities. Let us then return once more to the analysis of the concept of power. Arendt's concept of communicatively generated power can become a sharp instrument only if we extricate it from the clamps of an Aristotelian theory of action. In separating praxis from the unpolitical activities of working and laboring on the one side and of thinking on the other, Arendt traces back political power exclusively to praxis, to the speaking and acting together of individuals. Over against the production of material objects and theoretical knowledge, communicative action has to appear as the only political category. This narrowing of the political to the practical permits illuminating contrasts to the presently palpable elimination of essentially practical contents from the political process. But for this Arendt pays a certain price: (a) she screens all strategic elements, as force, out of politics; (b) she removes politics from its relations to the economic and social environment in which it is embedded through the administrative system; and (c) she is unable to grasp structural violence. Let me comment briefly on these three deficits.

STRATEGIC COMPETITION FOR POLITICAL POWER

War is the classic example of strategic action. For the Greeks it was something that took place outside the walls of the city. For Hannah Arendt too strategic action is essentially unpolitical, a matter for experts. The example of warfare is of course suited to demonstrating the contrast between political power and force. Waging war manifestly involves the calculated employment of means of force, whether for the sake of threatening or of physically overcoming an opponent. But the accumulation of means of destruction does not make superpowers more powerful; military strength is (as the Vietnam War showed) often enough the counterpart to impotence. Furthermore, the example of warfare seems suitable for subsuming strategic action under instrumental action. In addition to communicative action, the *vita activa* encompasses the essentially nonsocial activities of working and laboring. And since the purposive-rational employment of military means appears to have the same structure as the use of instruments to fabricate material objects or to work up nature, Arendt equates strategic with instrumental action. So she stresses that strategic action is instrumental as well as violent, and that action of this type falls outside of the domain of the political.

The matter looks different if we place strategic action alongside communicative action, as another form of social interaction (which is, to be sure, not oriented to reaching agreement but to success); and if we contrast it with instrumental action, as nonsocial action that can also be carried out by a solitary subject. It then becomes conceptually plausible that strategic action also took place *within* the walls of the city – thus in power struggles, in the competition for positions to which the exercise of legitimate power was tied. The *acquisition* and *maintenance* of political power must be distinguished from both the *employment* of political power – that is, rule – and the *generation* of political power. In the last case, but only in the last case, the concept of praxis is helpful. No occupant of a position of authority can maintain and exercise power, if these positions are not themselves anchored in laws and political institutions whose continued existence rests ultimately on common convictions, on 'an opinion upon which many are publicly in agreement'.

The elements of strategic action have undoubtedly increased in scope and importance in modern societies. With the capitalist mode of production this action type, which in pre-modern societies dominated above all in foreign relations, also became permissible within society as the normal case for economic relationships. Modern private law grants to all commodity owners formally equivalent spheres of strategic action. Moreover, in the modern state which supplements this economic society, the struggle for political power is normalized through the institutionalization of strategic action (through the admission of an opposition, through the competition of parties and associations, through the legalization of labor struggles, etc.). These phenomena of power acquisition and maintenance have misled political theorists from Hobbes to Schumpeter to identify power with a potential for successful strategic action. Against this tradition (in which Max Weber also stands), Arendt rightly urges that strategic contests for political power neither call forth nor maintain those institutions in which that power is anchored. Political institutions live not from force but from recognition.

Nevertheless, we cannot exclude the element of strategic action from the concept of the political. Let us understand the force exercised through strategic action as the ability to prevent other individuals or groups from realizing their interests.[21] In this sense force has always belonged to the means for acquiring and holding on to positions of legitimate power. In modern states this struggle for political power has even been institutionalized; it thereby became a normal component of the political system. On the other hand, it is not at all clear that someone should be able to *generate* legitimate power simply because he is in a position to prevent others from pursuing their interests. Legitimate power *arises* only among those who form common convictions in unconstrained communication.

THE EMPLOYMENT OF POWER IN THE POLITICAL SYSTEM

The communicative production of power and the struggle or strategic competition for political power can be grasped in terms of action-types; but for the employment of legitimate power the action structures through which it is exercised are not essential. Legitimate power permits the occupants of positions of authority to make binding decisions. This employment of power is of interest more from the vantagepoint of systems theory than from that of action theory. Hannah Arendt naturally resists leaving her action-theoretic framework in order to inject a functionalist analysis into it. In her view, the sphere of human affairs is not to be distantiated according to the standards of an objectivistic social science, because knowledge that is gained in this attitude cannot via enlightenment flow back into the commonsense world. In this respect, Arendt would not draw any distinction even between Hegel and Parsons; both investigate historical and social processes that pass over the heads of those involved.[22] She herself tries to capture this process aspect of social life in an action category by differentiating between work and labor. Labor differs from work not in the action structures themselves, but in the fact that the concept of 'labor' represents productive activity as an expenditure of labor power which has to be reproduced, and is thus located in the functional context of production, consumption, and reproduction. With her reservations, Arendt unnecessarily disadvantages herself vis-à-vis the systems analyses that are usual today. On the other hand, her mistrust is only too justified when systems theory is in turn cut off from action theory.

This can be seen in Parsons when, for instance, he discusses C. Wright Mills's zero-sum concept of power. Parsons wants to understand power as an augmentable good, like credit or buying power. If one side gains political power, the other side need not lose any. A zero-sum game results only when different parties struggle for available power positions, but not from the point of view of the rise and fall of the power of political institutions. Parsons and Arendt are in agreement on this point. But they have rather divergent ideas of the process of power generation. Parsons regards this process as a rise in activity; it might be roughly sketched as follows: in order that the output of the state apparatus can grow, the scope of action of the administrative system has to be expanded; this in turn requires a stronger input of rather unspecific support or mass loyalty. Thus the process of power enhancement begins on the input side. Political leaders must arouse new needs in the electorate in order that increasing demands arise which can be met only through heightened administrative activity.[23]

From the systems perspective, the production of power appears as a problem that can be solved by a stronger influence on the will of the population exerted by the political leadership. To the extent that this takes place by means of psychic constraint, by persuasion and manipulation, it amounts, in Hannah Arendt's view, to an increase in force but not in the power of the political system. For power can, on her assumption, arise only in the structures of unconstrained communication; it cannot be generated 'from above'. Parsons would have to dispute this hypothesis; given a set of cultural values, there can be for him no *structural* limits to the production of power. On the other hand, in the light of peculiar cases of power inflation and deflation, Parsons would very much like to be able to differentiate between serious and unserious power credits:

> There is a fine line between solid, responsible and constructive political leadership which in fact commits the collectivity beyond its capacities for instantaneous fulfillment of all obligations, and reckless overextendedness, just as there is a fine line between responsible banking and 'wildcatting'.[24]

But it is difficult to see how this 'fine line' could be conceived in terms of Parsons's own systems theory. Hannah Arendt offers a solution precisely to this problem. She attempts to derive from the structures of unimpaired intersubjectivity the conditions of the public-political realm that must be met if power is to be communicatively engendered or expanded.

THE COMMUNICATIVE PRODUCTION OF POWER — A VARIATION

Let us summarize the two points of criticism. The concept of the political must extend to the strategic competition for political power and to the employment of power within the political system. Politics cannot, as with Arendt, be identified with the praxis of those who talk together in order to act in common. Conversely, the dominant theory narrows this concept to phenomena of political competition and power allocation and does not do justice to the real phenomenon of the generation of power. At this point the distinction between power and force becomes sharp. It calls to mind that the political system cannot dispose of power at will. Power is a good *for* which political groups struggle and *with* which a political leadership manages things; but in a certain way both find this good already at hand; they don't produce it. This is the impotence of the powerful — they have to borrow their power from the producers of power. This is the credo of Hannah Arendt.

The objection thereto lies ready at hand: even if the leadership in modern democracies has to periodically procure legitimation, history is replete with evidence which shows that political rule must have functioned, and functions, otherwise than as Arendt claims. Certainly, it speaks *for* her thesis that political rule can last only so long as it is recognized as legitimate. It speaks *against* her thesis that basic institutions and structures which are stabilized through political rule could only in rare cases be the expression of an 'opinion on which many were publicly in agreement' – at least if one has, as Hannah Arendt does, a strong concept of the public realm. These two facts can be brought together if we assume that structural violence is built into political institutions (but not only into them). Structural violence does not manifest itself *as force*; rather, unperceived, it blocks those communications in which convictions effective for legitimation are formed and passed on. Such an hypothesis about inconspicuously working communication blocks can explain, perhaps, the formation of ideologies; with it one can give a plausible account of how convictions are formed in which subjects deceive themselves about themselves and their situation. Ideologies are, after all, illusions that are outfitted with the power of common convictions. This proposal is an attempt to render the communicative production of power in a more realistic version. In systematically restricted communications, those involved form convictions subjectively free from constraint, convictions which are, however, illusionary. They thereby communicatively generate a power which, as soon as it is institutionalized, can also be used against them.

If we wanted to accept this proposal, we would of course have to specify a critical standard and to distinguish between illusionary and non-illusionary convictions. Hannah Arendt doubts that this is possible. She holds fast to the classical distinction between theory and practice; practice rests on opinions and convictions that cannot be true or false in the strict sense:

> No opinion is self-evident. In matters of opinion, but not in matters of truth, our thinking is truly discursive, running as it were, from place to place, from one part of the world to the other through all kinds of conflicting views, until it finally ascends from all these particularities to some impartial generality.[25]

An antiquated concept of theoretical knowledge that is based on ultimate insights and certainties keeps Arendt from comprehending the process of reaching agreement about practical questions as rational discourse. If, by contrast, 'representative thought'[26] – which examines the generalizability of practical standpoints, that is, the legitimacy of norms – is not separated from argumentation by an abyss, then a cognitive foundation can also be claimed for the power of common convictions. In this case, such power is anchored in the de facto recognition of validity claims that can be discursively redeemed and fundamentally criticized. Arendt sees a yawning abyss between knowledge and opinion that cannot be closed with arguments. She has to look for another foundation for the power of opinion, and she finds it in the capability of responsible subjects to make and to keep promises.

> We mentioned before the power generated when people gather together and 'act in concert', which disappears the moment they depart. The force that keeps them together . . . is the force of mutual promise or contract.[27]

She regards as the basis of power the contract between free and equal parties with which they place themselves under mutual obligation. To secure the normative core of an original equivalence between power and freedom, Hannah Arendt finally places more trust in the venerable figure of the contract than in her own concept of a praxis, which is grounded in the rationality of practical judgement.[28] She retreats instead to the contract theory of natural law.

NOTES

1 Max Weber, *Wirtschaft und Gesellschaft*, 2 vols (J. C. B. Mohr, Tübingen, 1925), 1:. 16, 2: 1. Parsons distinguishes four types of exercise of power: persuasion, activation of commitments, inducement, coercion. Cf. Talcott Parsons, 'On the concept of political power', in his *Sociological Theory and Modern Society* (The Free Press, New York, 1967), pp. 310 ff.

2 Hannah Arendt, *On Violence* (Harcourt, Brace & World, New York, 1970), p. 44.

3 Talcott Parsons, 'Authority, legitimation and political action', in his *Structure and Process in Modern Societies* (The Free Press, Glencoe, Illinois, 1960), p. 181.

4 Talcott Parsons, 'Voting and the equilibrium of the American political system', in Parsons, *Sociological Theory and Modern Society*, pp. 224–5: 'The amount of its power is an attribute of the total system and is a function of several variables. These are the support that can be mobilized by those exercising power, the facilities they have access to (notably the control of the productivity of the economy), and the legitimation that can be accorded to the position of the holders of power. . . . '

5 Ibid., p. 193.

6 Hannah Arendt, *On Revolution* (Viking Press, New York, 1963), p. 71.

7 Arendt, *On Violence*, p. 41.

8 Hannah Arendt, *The Human Condition* (University of Chicago Press, Chicago, 1958), pp. 181 ff.

9 Ibid., p. 200.

10 Hannah Arendt, *The Origins of Totalitarianism* (Harcourt, Brace, New York, 1951); Arendt, *On Revolution*.

11 Hannah Arendt, *Elemente und Ursprünge totaler Herrschaft*, (Europäische Verlagsanstalt, Frankfurt, 1955), p. 745. Cf. Arendt, *The Origins of Totalitarianism*, part 3.

12 Arendt, *Elemente und Ursprünge totaler Herrschaft*, p. 749.

13 On this insight is based the thesis of the banality of evil which Arendt illustrated in the case of Eichmann (Hannah Arendt, *Eichmann in Jerusalem* (Viking Press, New York, 1963)). It can already be found in an essay on 'Organized guilt', written in 1944 and published immediately after the war in *Die Wandlung*; an English translation appeared in *Jewish Frontier*, January 1945: 'Heinrich Himmler does not belong to those intellectuals who come from the dark no-man's-land between bohemian and "five-penny" existence, and whose significance for the formation of the Nazi elite has recently been pointed out again and again. He is neither a bohemian like Goebbels, nor a sex criminal like Streicher, nor a perverted fanatic like Hitler, nor an adventurer like Göring. He is a "Babbitt" with all the appearance of respectability, with all the habits of the good family man, who does not cheat on his wife and who wants to secure a decent future for his children. And he consciously built up his newest organization of terror, which encompasses the entire country, on the assumption that most men are not bohemians, not fanatics, not adventurers, not sex criminals and not sadists, but in the first place "jobholders" and good family men. I think it was Péguy who called the family man the "grand adventurier du 20e siècle"; he died too soon to experience in him the great criminal of the century. We have been so accustomed to admiring or smiling at the good-natured solicitude of the family man, the serious concentration on the welfare of the family, the solemn commitment to devote his life to wife and children, that we scarcely perceived how the caring father, who was concerned above all for security, was transformed against his will, under the pressure of the chaotic economic conditions of our time, into an adventurer who with all his anxiety could never be sure of the next day. His pliability was already demonstrated in the homogenization at the start of the regime. It turned out that he was willing to sacrifice conscience, honor and human dignity for the sake of pension, life-insurance, the secure existence of wife and children' (Hannah Arendt, *Die verborgene Tradition* (Suhrkamp, Frankfurt, 1976), pp. 40 ff).
   It is this insight which turned both Hannah Arendt and her teacher, Karl Jaspers, in spite of their unmistakably elitist mentality, into intrepid radical democrats. How Arendt conceived the peculiar connection

of participatory democracy with the elitist structures that she regarded as necessary, is revealed in the following passage (in which she is speaking of the Rätesystem, the system of soviets or councils): 'It would be tempting to spin out further the potentialities of the councils, but it certainly is wiser to say with Jefferson, "Begin them only for a single purpose; they will soon show for what others they are the best instruments" – the best instruments, for example, for breaking up the modern mass society, with its dangerous tendency toward the formation of pseudo-political mass movements, or rather, the best, the most natural way for interspersing it at the grass roots with an "elite" that is chosen by no one, but constitutes itself. The joys of public happiness and the responsibilities for public business would then become the share of those few from all walks of life who have a taste for public freedom and cannot be "happy" without it. Politically, they are the best, and it is the task of good government and the sign of a well-ordered republic to assure them of their rightful place in the public realm. To be sure, such an "aristocratic" form of government would spell the end of general suffrage as we understand it today; for only those who as voluntary members of an "elementary republic" have demonstrated that they care for more than their private happiness and are concerned about the state of the world would have the right to be heard in the conduct of the business of the republic. However, this exclusion from politics should not be derogatory, since a political elite is by no means identical with a social or cultural or professional elite. The exclusion, moreover, would not depend on an outside body; if those who belong are self-chosen, those who do not belong are self-excluded. And such self-exclusion, far from being arbitrary discrimination, would in fact give substance and reality to one of the most important negative liberties we have enjoyed since the end of the ancient world, namely freedom from politics, which was unknown to Rome or Athens and which is politically perhaps the most relevant part of our Christian heritage' (*On Revolution*, pp. 283 ff).

14 Arendt, *On Revolution*, p. 256.
15 Arendt, *The Human Condition*, p. 200.
16 Ibid., p. 219.
17 Ibid., p. 33.
18 Arendt, *On Revolution*, p. 86.
19 Hannah Arendt, *Uber die Revolution*, (R. Piper, Munich, 1963), p. 85; cf. *On Revolution*, pp. 62 ff.
20 Cf. my review 'Die Geschichte von den zwei Revolutionen', in Jürgen Habermas, *Kultur und Kritik* (Suhrkamp, Frankfurt, 1973), pp. 365–70.
21 Cf. my elaboration of this concept in Jürgen Habermas and Niklas Luhmann, *Theorie der Gesellschaft oder Sozialtechnologie* (Suhrkamp, Frankfurt, 1971), pp. 250–7.
22 Arendt, *On Revolution*, pp. 45 ff.

23 Parsons, 'On the concept of political power', p. 340: 'Collective leader-
    ship may then be conceived as the bankers or 'brokers' who can
    mobilize the binding commitments of their constituents in such a way
    that the totality of commitments made by the collectivity as a whole can
    be enhanced. . . . The problem then is that of a basis for breaking
    through the circular stability of a zero-sum power system. The crucial
    point is that this can only happen if the collectivity and its members are
    ready to assume new binding obligations over and above those pre-
    viously in force. The crucial need is to justify this extension and to
    transform the 'sentiment' that something ought to be done into a
    commitment to implement the sentiment by positive action, including
    coercive sanctions if necessary. The crucial agency of this process seems
    to be leadership, precisely conceived as possessing a component analyti-
    cally independent of the routine power position of office, which defines
    the leader as the mobilizer of justification for policies.'
24 Ibid., p. 342.
25 Hannah Arendt, 'Truth and politics', in Peter Laslett and W. G.
    Runciman (eds), *Philosophy, Politics and Society*, 3rd series (Blackwell,
    Oxford, 1967), pp. 115 ff.
26 'Political thought is representative. I form an opinion by considering a
    given issue from different viewpoints, by making present to my mind
    the standpoints of those who are absent, that is, represent them. This
    process of representation does not blindly adopt the actual views of
    those who stand somewhere else and hence look upon the world from a
    different perspective; this is a question neither of empathy, as though I
    tried to be or feel like somebody else, nor of counting noses and joining
    a majority, but of being and thinking in my own identity where actually
    I am not. The more people's standpoints I have present in my mind
    while pondering a given issue and the better I can imagine how I would
    feel and think if I were in their place, the stronger will be my capacity
    for representative thinking and the more valid my final conclusions, my
    opinion. (It is this capacity for an "enlarged mentality" that enables men
    to judge; as such, it was discovered by Kant – in the first part of his
    Critique of Judgement – who, however, did not recognize the political
    and moral implications of his discovery.) The very process of opinion-
    formation is determined by those in whose places somebody thinks and
    uses his own mind, and the only condition for this exertion of imagina-
    tion is disinterestedness, the liberation from one's own private interests.
    Hence, even if I shun all company or am completely isolated while
    forming an opinion, I am not simply together only with myself in the
    solitude of philosophic thought; I remain in this world of mutual
    interdependence where I can make myself the representative of every-
    body else. To be sure, I can refuse to do this and form an opinion that
    takes only my own interest, or the interests of the group to which I
    belong, into account; nothing indeed is more common, even among
    highly sophisticated people, than this blind obstinacy which becomes
    manifest in lack of imagination and failure to judge. But the very

quality of an opinion as of a judgement depends upon its degree of impartiality' (Arendt, 'Truth and politics', p. 115).

27 Arendt, *The Human Condition*, pp. 244 ff.

28 Cf. R. J. Bernstein, 'H. Arendt: opinion and judgement', paper presented to the Annual Meeting of the American Political Science Association, Chicago, 1976.

6
Power and the Social System

TALCOTT PARSONS

Power is one of the key concepts in the great Western tradition of thought about political phenomena. It is at the same time a concept on which, in spite of its long history, there is, on analytical levels, a notable lack of agreement both about its specific definition, and about many features of the conceptual context in which it should be placed. There is, however, a core complex of its meaning having to do with the capacity of persons or collectivities 'to get things done' effectively, in particular when their goals are obstructed by some kind of human resistance or opposition. The problem of coping with resistance then leads into the question of the role of coercive measures, including the use of physical force, and the relation of coercion to the voluntary and consensual aspects of power systems.

The aim of this paper is to attempt to clarify this complex of meanings and relations by placing the concept of power in the context of a general conceptual scheme for the analysis of large-scale and complex social systems, that is of societies. In doing so I speak as a sociologist rather than as a political scientist, but as one who believes that the interconnections of the principal social disciplines, including not only these two, but especially their relations to economics as well, are so close that on matters of general theory of this sort they cannot safely be treated in isolation; their interrelations must be made explicit and systematic. As a sociologist, I thus treat a central concept of political theory by selecting among the elements which have figured prominently in political theory in terms of their fit with and significance for the general theoretical analysis of society as a whole.

There are three principal contexts in which it seems to me that the difficulties of the concept of power, as treated in the literature of the last generation, come to a head. The first of these concerns its

Talcott Parsons, 'On the concept of political power', is reprinted with permission from *Proceedings of the American Philosophical Society*, June 1963, pp. 232–62.

conceptual diffuseness, the tendency, in the tradition of Hobbes, to treat power as simply the generalized capacity to attain ends or goals in social relations, independently of the media employed or of the status of 'authorization' to make decisions or impose obligations.[1]

The effect of this diffuseness, as I call it, is to treat 'influence' and sometimes money; as well as coercion in various aspects, as 'forms' of power, thereby making it logically impossible to treat power as a *specific* mechanism operating to bring about changes in the action of other units, individual or collective, in the processes of social interaction. The latter is the line of thought I wish to pursue.

Secondly, there is the problem of the relation between the coercive and the consensual aspects. I am not aware of any treatment in the literature which presents a satisfactory solution of this problem. A major tendency is to hold that somehow 'in the last analysis' power comes down to one or the other, i.e., to 'rest on' command of coercive sanctions, *or* on consensus and the will to voluntary cooperation. If going to one or the other polar solution seems to be unacceptable, a way out, taken for example by Friedrich, is to speak of each of these as different 'forms' of power. I shall propose a solution which maintains that both aspects are essential, but that neither of the above two ways of relating them is satisfactory, namely subordinating either one to the other or treating them as discrete 'forms'.

Finally, the third problem is what, since the Theory of Games, has widely come to be called the 'zero-sum' problem. The dominant tendency in the literature, for example in Lasswell and C. Wright Mills, is to maintain explicitly or implicitly that power is a zero-sum phenomenon, which is to say that there is a fixed 'quantity' of power in any relational system and hence any gain of power on the part of A must by definition occur by diminishing the power at the disposal of other units, B, C, D. . . . There are, of course, restricted contexts in which this condition holds, but I shall argue that it does not hold for total systems of a sufficient level of complexity.

SOME GENERAL ASSUMPTIONS

The initial assumption is that, within the conception of society as a system, there is an essential parallelism in theoretical structure between the conceptual schemes appropriate for the analysis of the economic and the political aspects of societies. There are four respects in which I wish to attempt to work out and build on this parallel, showing at the same time the crucial substantive differences between the two fields.

First 'political theory' as here interpreted, which is not simply to be identified with the meaning given the term by many political scientists, is thought of as an abstract analytical scheme in the same sense in which economic theory is abstract and analytical. It is not the conceptual interpretation of any concretely complete category of social phenomena, quite definitely not those of government, though government is the area in which the political element comes nearest to having clear primacy over others. Political theory thus conceived is a conceptual scheme which deals with a restricted set of primary variables and their interrelations, which are to be found operating in all concrete parts of social systems. These variables are, however, subject to parametric conditions which constitute the values of other variables operating in the larger system which constitutes the society.

Secondly, following on this, I assume that the empirical system to which political theory in this sense applies is an analytically defined, a 'functional' subsystem of a society, not for example a concrete type of collectivity. The conception of the economy of a society is relatively well defined.[2] I should propose the conception of the *polity* as the parallel empirical system of direct relevance to political theory as here advanced. The polity of a given society is composed of the ways in which the relevant components of the total system are organized with reference to one of its fundamental functions, namely effective collective action in the attainment of the goals of collectivities. Goal-attainment in this sense is the establishment of a satisfactory relation between a collectivity and certain objects in its environment which include both other collectivities and categories of personalities, e.g. 'citizens'. A total society must in these terms be conceived, in one of its main aspects, as a collectivity, but it is also composed of an immense variety of sub-collectivities, many of which are parts not only of this society but of others.[3]

A collectivity, seen in these terms, is thus clearly not a concrete 'group' but the term refers to groups, i.e. systematically related pluralities of persons, seen in the perspective of their interests in and capacities for effective collective action. The political process then is the process by which the necessary organization is built up and operated, the goals of action are determined and the resources requisite to it are mobilized.

These two parallels to economic theory can be extended to still a third. The parallel to collective action in the political case is, for the economic, production. This conception in turn must be understood in relation to three main operative contexts. The first is adjustment to the conditions of 'demand' which are conceived to be external to the economy itself, to be located in the 'consumers' of the economic process. Secondly, resources must be mobilized, also from the environment of the economy, the famous factors of production. Thirdly, the intenal economic process is conceived as creatively combinatorial; it is, by the 'combination' of factors of production in the light of the utility of outputs, a process of creating more valuable facilities to meet the needs of consuming units than would be available to them without this combinatorial process. I wish most definitely to postulate that the logic of 'value added' applies to the political sphere in the present sense.[4]

In the political case, however, the value reference is not to utility in the economic sense but to effectiveness, very precisely, I think in the sense used by C. I. Barnard.[5] For the limited purposes of political analysis as such the givenness of the goal-demands of interest groups serves as the same order of factor in relation to the political system as has the corresponding givenness of consumer's wants for purposes of economic analysis – and of course the same order of qualifications on the empirical adequacy of such postulates.

Finally, fourth, political analysis as here conceived is parallel to economic in the sense that a central place in it is occupied by a generalized medium involved in the political interaction process, which is also a 'measure' of the relevant values. I conceive power as such a generalized medium in a sense directly parallel in logical structure, though very different substantively, to money as the generalized medium of the economic process. It is essentially this conception of power as a generalized medium parallel to money which will, in the theoretical context sketched above, provide the thread fur guiding the following analysis through the types of historic difficulty with reference to which the paper began.

THE OUTPUTS OF POLITICAL PROCESS AND THE FACTORS OF EFFECTIVENESS

The logic of the combinatorial process which I hold to be common to economic theory and the type of political theory advanced here, involves a paradigm of inputs and outputs and their relations. Again we will hold that the logic is strictly parallel to the economic case, i.e. that there should be a set of political categories strictly parallel to those of the factors of production (inputs) on the one hand, the shares of income (outputs) on the other.

In the economic case, with the exception of land, the remaining three factors must be regarded as inputs from the other three cognate functional subsystems of the society, labor from what we call the 'pattern-maintenance' system, capital from the polity and organization, in the sense of Alfred Marshall, from the integrative system.[6] Furthermore, it becomes clear that land is not, as a factor of production, simply the physical resource, but essentially the commitment, in value terms, of any resources to economic production in the system independent of price.

In the political case, similarly the equivalent of land is the commitment of resources to effective collective action, independent of any specifiable 'pay-off' for the unit which controls them.[7] Parallel to labor is the demands or 'need' for collective action as manifested in the 'public' which in some sense is the constituency of the leadership of the collectivity in question – a conception which is relatively clear for the governmental or other electoral association, but needs clarification in other connections. Parallel to capital is the control of some part of the productivity of the economy for the goals of the collectivity, in a sufficiently developed economy through financial resources at the disposal of the collectivity, acquired by earnings, gift, or taxation. Finally, parallel to organization is the legitimation of the authority under which collective decisions are taken.

It is most important to note that none of these categories of input is conceived as a form of power. In so far as they involve media, it is the media rooted in contiguous functional systems, not power as that central to the polity – e.g. control of productivity may operate through money, and constituents' demands through what I call 'influence'. Power then is the *means* of acquiring control of the factors in effectiveness; it is not itself one of these factors, any more than in the economic case money is a factor of production; to suppose it was, was the ancient mercantilist fallacy.

Though the analytical context in which they are placed is perhaps unfamiliar in the light of traditional political analysis, I hope it is clear that the actual categories used are well established, though there remain a number of problems of exact definition. Thus control of productivity through financing of collective action is very familiar, and the concept of 'demands' in the sense of what constituents want and press for, is also very familiar.[8] The concept legitimation is used in essentially the same sense in which I think Max Weber used it in a political context.[9]

The problem of what corresponds, for the political case, to the economist's 'shares of income' is not very difficult, once the essential distinction, a very old one in economic tradition, between monetary and 'real' income is clearly taken into account. Our concern is with the 'real' outputs of the political process – the analogue of the monetary here is output of power.

There is one, to us critically important revision of the traditional economic treatment of outputs which must be made, namely the bracketing together of 'goods and services', which then would be treated as outputs to the household as, in our technical terms, a part of the 'pattern-maintenance' system. The present position is that goods, i.e., more precisely property rights in the physical objects of possession, belong in this category, but that 'services', the commitment of human role-performances to an 'employer', or contracting agent constitute an output, not to the household, but to the polity, the type case (though not the only one) being an employing organization in which the role-incumbent commits himself to performance of an occupational role, a job,[10] as a contribution to the effective functioning of the collectivity.

There is, from this consideration, a conclusion which is somewhat surprising to economists, namely that service is, in the economic sense the 'real' counterpart of interest as monetary income from the use of funds. What we suggest is that the political control of productivity makes it possible, through combinatorial gains in the political context, to produce a surplus above the monetary funds committed, by virtue of which under specified conditions a premium can be paid at the monetary level which, though a result of the combinatorial process as a whole, is most directly related to the output of available services as an economic phenomenon, i.e. as a 'fluid resource'. Seen a little differently, it becomes necessary to make a clear distinction between labor as a factor of production in the economic sense and service as an output of the economic process which is utilized in a political context, that is one of organizational or collective effectiveness.

Service, however, is not a 'factor' in effectiveness, in the sense in which labor is a factor of production, precisely because it is a category of power. It is the point at which the economic utility of the human factor is matched with its potential contribution to effective collective action. Since the consumer of services is in principle the employing collectivity, it is its effectiveness for collective goals, not its capacity to satisfy the 'wants' of individuals, which is the vantage point from which the utility of the service is derived. The output of power which matches the input of services to the polity, I interpret to be the 'opportunity for effectiveness' which employment confers on those employed or contract offers to partners. Capital in the economic sense is one form of this opportunity for effectiveness which is derived from providing, for certain types of performances, a framework of effective organization.[11]

The second, particularly important context of 'real' output of the political process is the category which, in accord with much tradition, I should like to call capacity to assume leadership responsibility. This, as a category of 'real' output also is not a form of power, but this time of influence.[12] This is an output not to the economy but to what I shall call the integrative system, which in its relevance to the present context is in the first instance the sector of the 'public' which can be looked on as the 'constituencies' of the collective processes under consideration. It is the group structure of the society looked at in terms of their structured interests in particular modes of effective collective action by particular collectivities. It is only through effective organization that genuine responsibility can be taken, hence the implementation of such interest demands responsibility for collective effectiveness.[13] Again it should be made quite clear that leadership responsibility is not here conceived as an output of power, though many political theorists (e.g. Friedrich) treat both leadership and, more broadly influence, as 'forms' of power. The power category which regulates the output of leadership influence takes this form on the one side of binding policy decisions of the collectivity, on the other of political support from the constituency, in the type case through franchise. Policy decisions we would treat as a factor in integration of the system, not as a 'consumable' output of the political process.[14]

Finally, a few words need to be said about what I have called the combinatorial process itself. It is of course assumed in economic theory that the 'structures' of the factors of production on the one hand, the 'demand system' for real outputs on the other hand, are independent of each other. 'Utility' of outputs can only be enhanced, to say nothing of maximized, by processes of transformation of the factors in the direction of providing what is wanted as distinguished from what merely is available. The decision-making aspect of this transformative process, what is to be produced, how much and how offered for consumption, is what is meant by economic production, whereas the physical processes are not economic but 'technological'; they are controlled by economic considerations, but are not themselves in an analytical sense economic.

The consequence of successful adaptation of available resources to the want or demand system is an increment in the value of the resource-stock conceived in terms of utility as a type of value. But this means recombination of the components of the resource-stock in order to adapt them to the various uses in question.

The same logic applies to the combinatorial process in the political sphere. Here the resources are not land, labor, capital, and organization, but valuation of effectiveness, control of productivity, structured demands and the patterning of legitimation. The 'wants' are not for consumption in the economic sense, but for the solution of 'interest' problems in the system, including both competitive problems in the allocative sense and conflict problems, as well as problems of enhancement of the total effectiveness of the system of collective organization. In this case also the 'structure' of the available resources may not be assumed spontaneously to match the structure of the system of interest-demands. The increment of effectiveness in demand-satisfaction through the political process is, as in the economic case, arrived at through combinatorial decision-processes. The organizational 'technology' involved is not in the analytical sense political. The demand-reference is not to discrete units of the system conceived in abstraction from the system as a whole – the 'individual' consumer of the economist – but to the problem of the share of benefits and burdens to be allocated to subsystems of various orders. The 'consumption' reference is to the interest-unit's place in the allocative system rather than to the independent merits of particular 'needs'.

THE CONCEPT OF POWER

The above may seem a highly elaborate setting in which to place the formal introduction of the main subject of the paper, namely the concept of power. Condensed and cryptic as the exposition may have been, however, understanding of its main structure is an essential basis for the special way in which it will be proposed to combine the elements which have played a crucial part in the main intellectual traditions dealing with the problems of power.

Power is here conceived as a circulating medium, analogous to money, within what is called the political system, but notably over its boundaries into all three of the other neighboring functional subsystems of a society (as I conceive them), the economic, integrative, and pattern-maintenance systems. Specification of the properties of power can best be approached through an attempt to delineate very briefly the relevant properties of money as such a medium in the economy.

Money is, as the classical economists said, both a medium of exchange and a 'measure of value'. It is symbolic in that, though measuring and thus 'standing for' economic value or utility, it does not itself possess utility in the primary consumption sense – it has no 'value in use' but only 'in exchange', i.e. for possession of things having utility. The use of money is thus a mode of communication of offers, on the one hand to purchase, on the other to sell, things of utility, with and for money. It becomes an essential medium only when exchange is neither ascriptive, as exchange of gifts between assigned categories of kin, nor takes place on a basis of barter, one item of commodity or service directly for another.

In exchange for its lack of direct utility money gives the recipient four important degrees of freedom in his participation in the total exchange system. (1) He is free to spend his money for any item or combination of items available on the market which he can afford, (2) he is free to shop around among alternative sources of supply for desired items, (3) he can choose his own time to purchase, and (4) he is free to consider terms which, because of freedom of time and source he can accept or reject or attempt to influence in the particular case. By contrast, in the case of barter, the negotiator is bound to what his particular partner has or wants in relation to what he has and will part with at the particular time. The other side of the gain in degrees of freedom is of course the risk involved in the probabilities of the acceptance of money by others and of the stability of its value.

Primitive money is a medium which is still very close to a commodity, the commonest case being precious metal, and many still feel that the value of money is 'really' grounded in the commodity value of the metallic base. On this base, however, there is, in developed monetary systems, erected a complex structure of credit instruments, so that only a tiny fraction of actual transactions is conducted in terms of the metal – it becomes a 'reserve' available for certain contingencies, and is actually used mainly in the settlement of international balances. I shall discuss the nature of credit further in another connection later. For the moment suffice it to say that, however important in certain contingencies the availability of metallic reserves may be, no modern monetary system operates primarily with metal as the actual medium, but uses 'valueless' money. Moreover, the acceptance of this 'valueless' money rests on a certain institutionalized confidence in the monetary system. If the security of monetary commitments rested only on their convertibility into metal, then the overwhelming majority of them would be worthless, for the simple reason that the total quantity of metal is far too small to redeem more than a few.

One final point is that money is 'good', i.e. works as a medium, only within a relatively defined network of market relationships which to be sure now has become world-wide, but the maintenance of which requires special measures to maintain mutual convertibility of national currencies. Such a system is on the one hand a range of exchange-potential within which money may be spent, but on the other hand, one within which certain conditions affecting the protection and management of the unit are maintained, both by law and by responsible agencies under the law.

The first focus of the concept of an institutionalized power system is, analogously, a relational system within which certain categories of commitments and obligations, ascriptive or voluntarily assumed – e.g. by contract – are treated as binding, i.e. under normatively defined conditions their fulfillment may be insisted upon by the appropriate role-reciprocal agencies. Furthermore, in case of actual or threatened resistance to 'compliance', i.e. to fulfillment of such obligations when invoked, they will be 'enforced' by the threat or actual imposition of situational negative sanctions, in the former case having the function of deterrence, in the latter of punishment. These are events in the situation of the actor of reference which intentionally alter his situation (or threaten to) to his disadvantage, whatever in specific content these alterations may be.

Power then is generalized capacity to secure the performance of binding obligations by units in a system of collective organization when the obligations are legitimized with reference to their bearing on collective goals and where in case of recalcitrance there is a presumption of enforcement by negative situational sanctions – whatever the actual agency of that enforcement.

It will be noted that I have used the conceptions of generalization and of legitimation in defining power. Securing possession of an object of utility by bartering another object for it is not a monetary transaction. Similarly, by my definition, securing compliance with a wish, whether it be defined as an obligation of the object or not, simply by threat of superior force, is not an exercise of power. I am well aware that most political theorists would draw the line differently and classify this as power (e.g. Dahl's definition), but I wish to stick to my chosen line and explore its implications. The capacity to secure compliance must, if it is to be called power in my sense, be generalized and not solely a function of one particular sanctioning act which the user is in a position to impose,[15] and the medium used must be 'symbolic'.

Secondly, I have spoken of power as involving legitimation. This is, in the present context, the necessary consequence of conceiving power as 'symbolic', which therefore, if it is exchanged for something intrinsically valuable for collective effectiveness, namely compliance with an obligation, leaves the recipient, the performer of the obligation, with 'nothing of value'. This is to say, that he has 'nothing' but a set of expectations, namely that in other contexts and on other occasions, he can invoke certain obligations on the part of other units. Legitimation is therefore, in power systems, the factor which is parallel to confidence in mutual acceptability and stability of the monetary unit in monetary systems.

The two criteria are connected in that questioning the legitimacy of the possession and use of power leads to resort to progressively more 'secure' means of gaining compliance. These must be progressively more effective 'intrinsically', hence more tailored to the particular situations of the objects and less general. Furthermore in so far as they are intrinsically effective, legitimacy becomes a progressively less important factor of their effectiveness – at the end of this series lies resort, first to various types of coercion, eventually to the use of force as the most intrinsically effective of all means of coercion.[16]

I should like now to attempt to place both money and power in the context of a more general paradigm, which is an analytical classification of ways in which, in the processes of social interaction, the actions of one unit in a system can, intentionally, be oriented to bringing about a change in what the actions of one or more other units would otherwise have been – thus all fitting into the context of Dahl's conception of power. It is convenient to state this in terms of the convention of speaking of the acting unit of reference – individual or collective – as *ego*, and the object on which he attempts to 'operate' as *alter*. We may then classify the alternatives open to ego in terms of two dichotomous variables. On the one hand ego may attempt to gain his end from alter either by using some form of control over the situation in which alter is placed, actually or contingently to change it so as to increase the probability of alter acting in the way he wishes, or, alternatively, without attempting to change alter's situation, ego may attempt to change alter's intentions, i.e. he may manipulate symbols which are meaningful to alter in such a way that he tries to make alter 'see' that what ego wants is a 'good thing' for him (alter) to do.

The second variable then concerns the type of sanctions ego may employ in attempting to guarantee the attainment of his end from alter. The dichotomy here is between positive and negative sanctions. Thus through the situational channel a positive sanction is a change in alter's situation presumptively considered by alter as to his advantage, which is used as a means by ego of having an effect on alter's actions. A negative sanction then is an alteration in alter's situation to the latter's disadvantage. In the case of the intentional channel, the positive sanction is the expression of symbolic 'reasons' why compliance with ego's wishes is 'a good thing' independently of any further action on ego's part, from alter's point of view, i.e. would be felt by him to be 'personally advantageous', whereas the negative sanction is presenting reasons why noncompliance with ego's wishes should be felt by alter to be harmful to interests in which he had a significant personal investment and should therefore be avoided. I should like to call the four types of 'strategy' open to ego respectively (1) for the situational channel, positive sanction case, 'inducement'; (2) situational channel negative sanction, 'coercion'; (3) intentional channel, positive sanction, 'persuasion', and (4) intentional channel negative sanction, 'activation of commitments' as shown in the following table.

Sanction type	Channel			
	Intentional			Situational
Positive	Persuasion	3	1	Inducement
Negative	Activation of commitments	4	2	Coercion

A further complication now needs to be introduced. We think of a sanction as an intentional act on ego's part, expected by him to change his relation to alter from what it would otherwise have been. As a means of bringing about a change in alter's action, it can operate most obviously where the actual imposition of the sanction is made contingent on a future decision by alter. Thus a process of inducement will operate in two stages, first contingent offer on ego's part that, if alter will 'comply' with his wishes, ego will 'reward' him by the contingently promised situational change. If then alter in fact does comply, ego will peform the sanctioning act. In the case of coercion the first stage is a contingent threat that, unless alter decides to comply, ego will impose the negative sanction. If, however, alter complies, then nothing further happens, but, if he decides on non-compliance, then ego must carry out his threat, or be in a position of 'not meaning it'. In the cases of the intentional channel ego's first-stage act is either to predict the occurrence, or to announce his own intention of doing something which affects alter's sentiments or interests. The element of contingency enters in that ego 'argues' to alter, that if this happens, on the one hand alter should be expected to 'see' that it would be a good thing for him to do what ego wants – the positive case – or that if he fails to do it it would imply an important 'subjective cost' to alter. In the positive case, beyond 'pointing out' if alter complies, ego is obligated to deliver the positive attitudinal sanction of approval. In the negative case, the corresponding attitudinal sanction of disapproval is implemented only for noncompliance.

It is hence clear that there is a basic asymmetry between the positive and negative sides of the sanction aspect of the paradigm. This is that, in the cases of inducement and persuasion, alter's compliance obligates ego to 'deliver' his promised positive sanction, in the former case the promised advantages, in the latter his approval of alter's 'good sense' in recognizing that the decision wished for by ego and accepted as 'good' by alter, in fact turns out to be good from alter's point of view. In the negative cases, on the other hand, compliance on alter's part obligates ego, in the situational case, not to carry out his threat, in the intentional case by withholding disapproval to confirm to alter that his compliance did in fact spare him what to him, without ego's intervention, would have been the undesirable subjective consequences of his previous intentions, namely guilt over violations of his commitments.

Finally, alter's freedom of action in his decisions of compliance versus noncompliance is also a variable. This range has a lower limit at which the element of contingency disappears. That is, from ego's point of view, he may not say, if you do so and so, I will intervene, either by situational manipulations or by 'arguments' in such and such a way, but he may simply perform an overt act and face alter with a *fait accompli*. In the case of inducement a gift which is an object of value and with respect to the acceptance of which alter is given no option is the limiting case. With respect to coercion, compulsion, i.e. simply imposing a disadvantageous, alteration on alter's situation and then leaving it to alter to decide whether to 'do something about it' is the limiting case.

The asymmetry just referred to appears here as well. As contingent it may be said that the primary meaning of negative sanctions is as means of prevention. If they are effective, no further action is required. The case of compulsion is that in which it is rendered impossible for alter to avoid the undesired action on ego's part. In the case of positive sanctions of course ego, for example in making a gift to alter, cuts himself out from benefiting from alter's performance which is presumptively advantageous to him, in the particular exchange.

Both, however, may be oriented to their effect on alter's action in future sequences of interaction. The object of compulsion may have been 'taught a lesson' and hence be less disposed to noncompliance with ego's wishes in the future, as well as prevented from performance of a particular undesired act and the recipient of a gift may feel a 'sense of obligation' to reciprocate in some form in the future.

So far this discussion has dealt with sanctioning acts in terms of their 'intrinsic' significance both to ego and to alter. An offered inducement may thus be possession of a particular object of utility, a coercive threat, that of a particular feared loss, or other noxious experience. But just as, in the initial phase of a sequence, ego transmits his contingent intentions to alter symbolically through communication, so the sanction involved may also be symbolic, e.g. in place of possession of certain intrinsically valuable goods he may offer a sum of money. What we have called the generalized media of interaction then may be used as types of sanctions which may be analyzed in terms of the above paradigm. The factors of generalization and of legitimation of institutionalization, however, as discussed above, introduce certain complications which we must now take up with reference to power. There is a sense in which power may be regarded as the generalized medium of coercion in the above terms, but this formula at the very least requires very careful interpretation – indeed it will turn out by itself to be inadequate.

I spoke above of the 'grounding' of the value of money in the commodity value of the monetary metal, and suggested that there is a corresponding relation of the 'value', i.e. the effectiveness of power, to the intrinsic effectiveness of physical force as a means of coercion and, in the limiting case, compulsion.[17]

In interpreting this formula due account must be taken of the asymmetry just discussed. The special place of gold as a monetary base rests on such properties as its durability, high value in small bulk, etc., and high probability of acceptability in exchange, i.e. as means of inducement, in a very wide variety of conditions which are not dependent on an institutionalized order. Ego's primary aim in resorting to compulsion or coercion, however, is deterrence of unwanted action on alter's part.[18] Force, therefore, is in the first instance important as the 'ultimate' deterrent. It is the means which, again independent of any institutionalized system of order, can be assumed to be 'intrinsically' the most effective in the context of deterrence, when means of effectiveness which *are* dependent on institutionalized order are insecure or fail. Therefore, the unit of an action system which commands control of physical force adequate to cope with any potential counter threats of force is more secure than any other in a Hobbesian state of nature.[19]

But just as a monetary system resting entirely on gold as the actual medium of exchange is a very primitive one which simply cannot mediate a complex system of market exchange, so a power system in which the only negative sanction is the threat of force is a very primitive one which cannot function to mediate a complex system of organizational coordination – it is far too 'blunt' an instrument. Money cannot be only an intrinsically valuable entity if it is to serve as a generalized medium of inducement, but it must, as we have said, be institutionalized as a symbol; it must be legitimized, and must inspire 'confidence' within the system – and must also within limits be deliberately managed. Similarly power cannot be only an intrinsically effective deterrent; if it is to be the generalized medium of mobilizing resources for effective collective action, and for the fulfillment of commitments made by collectivities to what we have here called their constituents; it too must be both symbolically generalized, and legitimized.

There is a direct connection between the concept of bindingness, as introduced above, and deterrence. To treat a commitment or any other form of expectation as binding is to attribute a special importance to its fulfillment. Where it is not a matter simply of maintenance of an established routine, but of undertaking new actions in changed circumstances, where the commitment is thus to undertake types of action contingent on circumstances as they develop, then the risk to be minimized is that such contingent commitments will not be carried out when the circumstances in question appear. Treating the expectation or obligation as binding is almost the same thing as saying that appropriate steps on the other side must be taken to prevent nonfulfillment, if possible. Willingness to impose negative sanctions is, seen in this light, simply the carrying out of the implications of treating commitments as binding, and the agent invoking them 'meaning it' or being prepared to insist.

On the other hand there are areas in interaction systems where there is a range of alternatives, choice among which is optional, in the light of the promised advantageousness, situational or 'intentional', of one as compared to other choices. Positive sanctions as here conceived constitute a contingent increment of relative advantageousness, situational or intentional, of the alternative ego desires alter to choose.

If, in these latter areas, a generalized, symbolic medium, is to operate in place of intrinsic advantages, there must be an element of bindingness in the institutionalization of the medium itself – e.g. the fact that the money of a society is 'legal tender' which must be accepted in the settlement of debts which have the status of contractual obligations under the law. In the case of money, I suggest that, for the typical acting unit in a market system, what specific undertakings he enters into is overwhelmingly optional in the above sense, but whether the money involved in the transactions is or is not 'good' is not for him to judge, but his acceptance of it is binding. Essentially the same is true of the contractual obligations, typically linking monetary and intrinsic utilities, which he undertakes.

I would now like to suggest that what is in a certain sense the obverse holds true of power. Its 'intrinsic' importance lies in its capacity to ensure that obligations are 'really' binding, thus if necessary can be 'enforced' by negative sanctions. But for power to function as a generalized medium in a complex system, i.e. to mobilize resources effectively for collective action, it must be 'legitimized' which in the present context means that in certain respects compliance, which is the common factor among our media, is not binding, to say nothing of being coerced, but is optional. The range within which there exists a continuous system of interlocking binding obligations is essentially that of the internal relations of an organized collectivity in our sense, and of the contractual obligations undertaken on its behalf at its boundaries.

The points at which the optional factors come to bear are, in the boundary relations of the collectivity, where factors of importance for collective functioning other than binding obligations are exchanged for such binding commitments on the part of the collectivity and vice-versa, nonbinding outputs of the collectivity for binding commitments to it. These 'optional' inputs, I have suggested above, are control of productivity of the economy at one boundary, influence through the relations between leadership and the public demands at the other.[20]

This is a point at which the dissociation of the concept of polity from exclusive relation to government becomes particularly important. In a sufficiently differentiated society, the boundary-relations of the great majority of its important units of collective organization (including some boundaries of government) are boundaries where the overwhelming majority of decisions of commitment are optional in the above sense, though once made, their fulfillment is binding. This, however, is only possible effectively within the range of a sufficiently stable, institutionalized normative order so that the requisite degrees of freedom are protected, e.g. in the fields of employment and of the promotion of interest-demands and decisions about political support.

This feature of the boundary relations of a particular political unit holds even for cases of local government, in that decisions of residence, employment, or acquisition of property within a particular jurisdiction involve the optional element, since in all these respects there is a relatively free choice among local jurisdictions, even though, once having chosen, the citizen is, for example, subject to the tax policies applying within it – and of course he cannot escape being subject to any local jurisdiction, but must choose among those available.

In the case of a 'national' political organization, however, its territorial boundaries ordinarily coincide with a relative break in the normative order regulating social interaction.[21] Hence across such boundaries an ambiguity becomes involved in the exercise of power in our sense. On the one hand the invoking of binding obligations operates normally without explicit use of coercion within certain ranges where the two territorial collectivity systems have institutionalized their relations. Thus travellers in friendly foreign countries can ordinarily enjoy personal security and the amenities of the principal public accommodations, exchange of their money at 'going' rates, etc. Where, on the other hand, the more general relations between national collectivities are at issue, the power system is especially vulnerable to the kind of insecurity of expectations which tends to be met by the explicit resort to threats of coercive sanctions. Such threats in turn, operating on both sides of a reciprocal relationship, readily enter into a vicious circle of resort to more and more 'intrinsically' effective or drastic measures of coercion, at the end of which road lies physical force. In other words, the danger of war is endemic in uninstitutionalized relations between territorially organized collectivities.

There is thus an inherent relation between both the use and the control of force and the territorial basis of organization.[22] One central condition of the integration of a power system is that it should be effective within a territorial area, and a crucial condition of this effectiveness in turn is the monopoly of control of paramount force within the area. The critical point then, at which the institutional integration of power systems is most vulnerable to strain, and to degeneration into reciprocating threats of the use of force, is between territorially organized political systems. This, notoriously, is the weakest point in the normative order of human society today, as it has been almost from time immemorial.

In this connection it should be recognized that the possession, the mutual threat, and possible use of force is only in a most proximate sense the principal 'cause' of war. The essential point is that the 'bottleneck' of mutual regression to more and more primitive means of protecting or advancing collective interests is a 'channel' into which all elements of tension between the collective units in question may flow. It is a question of the many levels at which such elements of tension may on the one hand build up, on the other be controlled, not of any simple and unequivocal conception of the 'inherent' consequences of the possession and possible uses of organized force.

It should be clear that again there is a direct parallel with the economic case. A functioning market system requires integration of the monetary medium. It cannot be a system of N independent monetary units and agencies controlling them. This is the basis on which the main range of extension of a relatively integrated market system tends to coincide with the 'politically organized society', as Roscoe Pound calls it, over a territorial area. International transactions require special provisions not required for domestic.

The basic 'management' of the monetary system must then be integrated with the institutionalization of political power. Just as the latter depends on an effective monopoly of institutionally organized force, so monetary stability depends on an effective monopoly of basic reserves protecting the monetary unit and, as we shall see later, on centralization of control over the credit system.

THE HIERARCHICAL ASPECT OF POWER SYSTEMS

A very critical question now arises, which may be stated in terms of a crucial difference between money and power. Money is a 'measure of value', as the classical economists put it, in terms of a continuous linear variable. Objects of utility valued in money are more or less valuable than each other in numerically statable terms. Similarly, as medium of exchange, amounts of money differ in the same single dimension. One acting unit in a society has more money – or assets exchangeable for money – than another, less than, or the same.

Power involves a quite different dimension which may be formulated in terms of the conception that A may have power over B. Of course in competitive bidding the holder of superior financial assets has an advantage in that, as economists say, the 'marginal utility of money' is less to him than to his competitor with smaller assets. But his 'bid' is no more binding on the potential exchange partner than is that of the less affluent bidder, since in 'purchasing power' all dollars are 'created free and equal'. There may be auxiliary reasons why the purveyor may think it advisable to accept the bid of the more affluent bidder; these, however, are not strictly economic, but concern the interrelations between money and other media, and other bases of status in the system.

The connection between the value of effectiveness – as distinguished from utility – and bindingness, implies a conception in turn of the focussing of responsibility for decisions, and hence of authority for their implementation.[23] This implies a special form of inequality of power which in turn implies a priority system of commitments. The implications of having assumed binding commitments, on the fulfillment of which spokesmen for the collectivity are prepared to insist to the point of imposing serious negative sanctions for noncompliance, are of an order of seriousness such that matching the priority system in the commitments themselves there must be priorities in the matter of which decisions take precedence over others and, back of that, of which decision-making agencies have the right to make decisions at what levels. Throughout this discussion the crucial question concerns bindingness. The reference is to the collectivity, and hence the strategic significance of the various 'contributions' on the performance of which the effectiveness of its action depends. Effectiveness for the collectivity as a whole is dependent on hierarchical ordering of the relative strategic importance of these contributions, and hence of the conditions governing the imposition of binding obligations on the contributors.

Hence the power of A over B is, in its legitimized form, the 'right' of A, as a decision-making unit involved in collective process, to make decisions which take precedence over those of B, in the interest of the effectiveness of the collective operation as a whole.

The right to use power, or negative sanctions on a barter basis or even compulsion to assert priority of a decision over others, I shall, following Barnard, call authority. Precedence in this sense can take different forms. The most serious ambiguity here seems to derive from the assumption that authority and its attendant power may be understood as implying opposition to the wishes of 'lower-order' echelons which hence includes the prerogative of coercing or compelling compliance. Though this is implicit, it may be that the higher-order authority and power may imply the prerogative is primarily significant as 'defining the situation' for the performance of the lower-order echelons. The higher 'authority' may then make a decision which defines terms within which other units in the collectivity will be expected to act, and this expectation is treated as binding. Thus a ruling by the Commissioner of Internal Revenue may exclude certain tax exemptions which units under his jurisdiction have thought taxpayers could claim. Such a decision need not activate an overt conflict between commissioner and taxpayer, but may rather 'channel' the decisions of revenue agents and taxpayers with reference to performance of obligations.

There does not seem to be an essential theoretical difficulty involved in this 'ambiguity'. We can say that the primary function of superior authority is clearly to define the situation for the lower echelons of the collectivity. The problem of overcoming opposition in the form of dispositions to noncompliance then arises from the incomplete institutionalization of the power of the higher authority holder. Sources of this may well include overstepping of the bounds of his legitimate authority on the part of this agent. The concept of compliance should celarly not be limited to 'obedience' by subordinates, but is just as importantly applicable to observance of the normative order by the high echelons of authority and power. The concept of constitutionalism is the critical one at this level, namely that even the highest authority is bound in the strict sense of the concept bindingness used here, by the terms of the normative order under which he operates, e.g. holds office. Hence binding obligations can clearly be 'invoked' by lower-order against higher-order agencies as well as vice-versa.

This of course implies the relatively firm institutionalization of the normative order itself. Within the framework of a highly differentiated polity it implies, in addition to constitutionalism itself, a procedural system for the granting of high political authority, even in private, to say nothing of public organizations, and a legal framework within which such authority is legitimized. This in turn includes another order of procedural institutions within which the question of the legality of actual uses of power can be tested.

POWER AND AUTHORITY

The institutionalization of the normative order just referred to thus comes to focus in the concept of authority. Authority is essentially the institutional code within which the use of power as medium is organized and legitimized. It stands to power essentially as property, as an institution, does to money. Property is a bundle of rights of possession, including above all that of alienation, but also at various levels of control and use. In a highly differentiated institutional system, property rights are focussed on the valuation of utility, i.e. the economic significance of the objects, e.g. for consumption or as factors of production, and this factor comes to be differentiated from authority. Thus, in European feudalism the 'landlord' had both property rights in the land, and political jurisdiction over persons acting on the same land. In modern legal systems these components are differentiated from each other so the landowner is no longer the landlord; this function is taken over mainly by local political authority.

Precisely with greater differentiation the focus of the institution becomes more generalized and, while specific objects of possession of course continue to be highly important, the most important object of property comes to be monetary assets, and specific objects are valued as assets, i.e., in terms of potentials of marketability. Today we can say that rights to money assets, the ways in which these can be legitimately acquired and disposed of, the ways in which the interests of other parties must be protected, have come to constitute the core of the institution of property.[24]

Authority, then, is the aspect of a status in a system of social organization, namely its collective aspect, by virtue of which the incumbent is put in a position legitimately to make decisions which are binding, not only on himself but on the collectivity as a whole and hence its other member-units, in the sense that so far as their implications impinge on their respective roles and statuses, they are bound to act in accordance with these implications. This includes the right to insist on such action though, because of the general division of labor, the holder of authority very often is not himself in a position to 'enforce' his decisions, but must be dependent on specialized agencies for this.

If, then, authority be conceived as the institutional counterpart of power, the main difference lies in the fact that authority is not a circulating medium. Sometimes, speaking loosely, we suggest that someone 'gives away his property'. He can give away property rights in specific possessions but not the institution of property. Similarly the incumbent of an office can relinquish authority by resigning, but this is very different from abolishing the authority of the office. Property as institution is a code defining rights in objects of possession, in the first instance physical objects, then 'symbolic' objects, including cultural objects such as 'ideas' so far as they are valuable in monetary terms, and of course including money itself, whoever possesses them. Authority, similarly, is a set of rights in status in a collectivity, precisely in the collectivity as actor, including most especially right to acquire and use power in that status.

The institutional stability, which is essential to the conception of a code, then for property inheres in the institutional structure of the market. At a higher level the institution of property includes rights, not only to use and dispose of particular objects of value, but to participate in the system of market transactions.

It is then essentially the institutionalized code defining rights of participation in the power system which I should like to think of as authority. It is this conception which gives us the basis for the essential distinction between the internal and the external aspects of power relative to a particular collectivity. The collectivity is, by our conception, the definition of the range within which a system of institutionalized rights to hold and use power can be closed. This is to say, the implications of an authoritative decision made at one point in the system can be made genuinely binding at all the other relevant points through the relevant processes of feed-back.

The hierarchical priority system of authority and power, with which this discussion started can, by this criterion, only be binding within a given particular collectivity system. In this sense then a hierarchy of authority — as distinguished from the sheer differences of power of other coercive capacities — must be internal to a collectivity organized system in this sense. This will include authority to bind the collectivity in its relations to its environment, to persons and to other collectivities. But bindingness, legitimized and enforced through the agency of this particular collectivity, cannot be extended beyond its boundaries. If it exists at all it must be by virtue of an institutionalized normative order which transcends the particular collectivity, through contractual arrangements with others, or through other types of mutually binding obligation.

POWER, INFLUENCE, EQUALIZATION AND SOLIDARITY

It is on this basis that it may be held that at the boundaries of the collectivity the closed system of priorities is breached by 'free' exercise, at the constituency or integrative boundary, of influence. Status in the collectivity gives authority to settle the terms on which power will be exchanged with influence over this boundary. The wielder of influence from outside, on the collectivity, is not bound in advance to any particular terms, and it is of the essence of use of power in the 'foreign relations' of the collectivity, that authority is a right, within certain limits of discretion, to spend power in exchange for influence. This in turn can, through the offer of accepting leadership responsibility in exchange for political support, replenish the expenditure of power by a corresponding input.

By this reasoning influence should be capable of altering the priority system within the collectivity. This is what I interpret policy decision as a category of the use of power as a medium to be, the process of altering priorities in such a way that the new pattern comes to be binding on the collectivity. Similarly, the franchise must be regarded as the institutionalization of a marginal, interpenetrating status, between the main collectivity and its environment of solidary groupings in the larger system. It is the institutionalization of a marginal authority, the use of which is confined to the function of selection among candidates for leadership responsibility. In the governmental case, this is the inclusion in a common collectivity system of both the operative agencies of government and the 'constituencies' on which leadership is dependent, a grant not only in a given instance of power to the latter but a status of authority with respect to the one crucial function of selection of leadership and granting them the authority of office.

In interpreting this discussion it is essential to keep in mind that a society consists, from the present point of view, not in one collectivity, but in a ramified system of collectivities. Because, however, of the basic imperatives of effective collective action already discussed, these must in addition to the pluralistic cross-cutting which goes with functional differentiation, also have the aspect of a 'Chinese box' relation. There must be somewhere a paramount focus of collective authority and with it of the control of power – though it is crucial that this need not be the top of the total system of normative control, which may for example be religious. This complex of territoriality and the monopoly of force are central to this, because the closed system of enforceable bindingness can always be breached by the intervention of force.[25]

The bindingness of normative orders other than those upheld by the paramount territorial collectivity must be defined within limits institutionalized in relation to it. So far as such collectivities are not 'agencies' of the state, in this sense, their spheres of 'jurisdiction' must be defined in terms of a normative system, a body of law, which is binding both on government and on the nongovernmental collectivity units, though in the 'last analysis' it will, within an institutionalized order either have to be enforced by government, or contrariwise, by revolutionary action against government.

Since independent control of serious, socially organized force cannot be given to 'private' collectivities, their ultimate negative sanctions tend to be expulsion from membership, though many other types of sanction may be highly important.

Considerations such as these thus do not in any way eliminate or weaken the importance of hierarchical priorities within a collective decision-system itself. The strict 'line' structure of such authority is, however, greatly modified by the interpenetration of other systems with the political, notably for our purposes the importance of technical competence. The qualifications of the importance of hierarchy apply in principle at the boundaries of the particular collective system analytically considered – rather than internally to it. These I would interpret as defining the limits of authority. There are two main contexts in which norms of equality may be expected to modify the concrete expectations of hierarchical decision-systems, namely on the one hand, the context of influence over the right to assume power, or decision-making authority and, on the other hand, the context of access to opportunity for status as a contributing unit in the specific political system in question.

It is essential here to recall that I have treated power as a circulating medium, moving back and forth over the boundaries of the polity. The 'real' outputs of the political process, and the factors in its effectiveness – in the sense corresponding to the real outputs and factors of economic production – are not in my sense 'forms' of power but, in the most important cases, of financial control of economic resources, and of influence, in the meaning of the category of influence, defined as a generalized mechanism of persuasion. These are very essential elements in the total political process, but it is just as important to distinguish them from power as it is to distinguish financially valuable outputs and factors of production from money itself. They may, in certain circumstances, be exchangeable for power, but this is a very different thing from being forms of power.

The circulation of power between polity and integrative system I conceive to consist in binding policy decisions on the one hand, which is a primary factor in the integrative process, and political support on the other, which is a primary output of the integrative process. Support is exchanged, by a 'public' or constituency, for the assumption of leadership responsibility, through the process of persuading those in a position to give binding support that it is advisable to do so in the particular instance – through the use of influence or some less generalized means of persuasion. In the other political 'market' *vis-à-vis* the integrative system, policy decisions are given in response to interest-demands in the sense of the above discussion. This is to say that interest groups, which, it is most important to note as a concept says nothing about the moral quality of the particular interest, attempt to persuade those who hold authority in the relevant collectivity, i.e. are in a position to make binding decisions, that they should indeed commit the collectivity to the policies the influence-wielders want. In our terms this is to persuade the decision makers to use and hence 'spend' some of their power for the purpose in hand. The spending of power is to be thought of, just as the spending of money, as essentially consisting in the sacrifice of alternative decisions which are precluded by the commitments undertaken under a policy. A member of the collectivity we conceive as noted to have authority to 'spend' power through making binding decisions through which those outside acquire claims against the collectivity. Its authority, however, is inalienable; it can only be exercised, not 'spent'.

It has been suggested that policies must be hierarchically ordered in a priority system and that the power to decide among policies must have a corresponding hierarchical ordering since such decisions bind the collectivity and its constituent units. The imperative of hierarchy does not, however, apply to the other 'market' of the power system in this direction, that involving the relations between leadership and political support. Here on the contrary it is a critically important fact that in the largest-scale and most highly differentiated systems, namely the leadership systems of the most 'advanced' national societies, the power element has been systematically equalized through the device of the franchise, so that the universal adult franchise has been evolved in all the Western democracies.[26] Equality of the franchise which, since the consequences of its exercise are very strictly binding,[27] I classify as in fact a form of power, has been part of a larger complex of its institutionalization, which includes in addition the principle of universality – its extension to all responsible adult citizens in good standing and the secrecy of the ballot, which serves to differentiate this context of political action from other contexts of involvement, and protect it against pressures, not only from hierarchical superiors but, as Rokkan points out, from status-peers as well.

Of course the same basic principle of one member, one vote, is institutionalized in a vast number of voluntary associations, including many which are subassociations of wider collectivities, such as faculties in a university, or boards and committees. Thus the difference between a chairman or presiding officer, and an executive head is clearly marked with respect to formal authority, whatever it may be with respect to influence, by the principle that a chairman, like any other member, has only one vote. Many collectivities are in this sense 'truncated' associations, e.g. in cases where fiduciary boards are self-recruiting. Nevertheless the importance of this principle of equality of power through the franchise is so great empirically that the question of how it is grounded in the structure of social systems is a crucial one.

It derives, I think, from what I should call the universalistic component in patterns of normative order. It is the value-principle that discriminations among units of a system, must be grounded in intrinsically valued differences among them, which are, for both persons and collectivities, capacities to contribute to valued societal processes. Differences of power in decision-making which mobilizes commitments, both outward in relation to the environment of the collectivity and internally, to the assignment of tasks to its members, are ideally grounded in the intrinsic conditions of effectiveness. Similarly, differences on the basis of technical competence to fulfill essential roles are grounded in the strategic conditions of effective contribution.

These considerations do not, however, apply to the functions of the choice of leadership, where this choice has been freed from ascriptive bases of right, e.g. through kinship status or some imputed 'charismatic' superiority as in such a case as 'white supremacy'. There is a persistent pressure of the sufficiently highly valued functions or outcomes, and under this pressure there seems to have been a continual, though uneven, process of erosion of discriminations in this critical field of the distribution of power.

It may be suggested that the principle of universalistic normative organization which is immediately superordinate to that of political democracy in the sense of the universal equal franchise, is the principle of equality before the law; in the case of the American Constitution, the principle of equal protection of the laws. I have emphasized that a constitutional framework is essential to advanced collective organization, given of course levels of scale and complexity which preclude purely 'informal' and traditional normative regulation. The principle in effect puts the burden of proof on the side of imposing discriminations, either in access to rights or in imposition of obligations, on the side that such discriminations are to be justified only by differences in sufficiently highly valued exigencies of operation of the system.

The principle of equality both at the level of application of the law and of the political franchise, is clearly related to a conception of the status of membership. Not all living adults have equal right to influence the affairs of all collectivities everywhere in the world, nor does an American have equal rights with a citizen of a quite different society within its territory. Membership is in fact the application to the individual unit of the concept of boundary of a social system which has the property of solidarity, in Durkheim's sense. The equal franchise is a prerogative of members, and of course the criteria of membership can be very differently institutionalized under different circumstances.

There is an important sense in which the double interchange system under consideration here, which I have called the 'support' system linking the polity with the integrative aspect of the society, is precisely the system in which power is most directly controlled, both in relation to more particularized interest-elements which seek relatively particularized policies – which of course includes wanting to prevent certain potential actions – and in relation to the more general 'tone' given to the directionality of collective action by the character of the leadership elements which assume responsibility and which, in exchange, are invested, in the type case by the electoral process, with authority to carry out their responsibilities. One central feature of this control is coming to terms with the hierarchical elements inherent in power systems in the aspects just discussed. Certain value systems may of course reinforce hierarchy, but it would be my view that a universalistically oriented value system inherently tends to counteract the spread of hierarchical patterns with respect to power beyond the range felt to be functionally necessary for effectiveness.[28]

There is, however, a crucial link between the equality of the franchise and the hierarchical structure of authority within collectivities, namely the all-or-none character of the electoral process. Every voter has an equal vote in electing to an office, but in most cases only one candidate is in fact elected – the authority of office is not divided among candidates in proportion to the numbers of votes they received, but is concentrated in the successful candidate, even though the margin be very narrow, as in the US presidential election of 1960. There are, of course, considerable possible variations in electoral rules, but this basic principle is as central as is that of the equality of the franchise. This principle seems to be the obverse of the hierarchy of authority.

The hierarchical character of power systems has above been sharply contrasted with the linear quantitative character of wealth and monetary assets. This has in turn been related to the fundamental difference between the exigencies of effectiveness in collective action, and the exigencies of utility in providing for the requirements of satisfying the 'wants' of units. In order to place the foregoing discussion of the relations between power and influence in a comparable theoretical context, it is necessary to formulate the value-standard which is paramount in regulating the integrative function which corresponds to utility and effectiveness in the economic and political functions respectively.

This is, with little doubt, the famous concept of solidarity as formulated by Durkheim.[29] The two essential points of reference for present purposes concern the two main aspects of membership, as outlined above, the first of which concerns claims on executive authority for policy decisions which integrate the total collective interest on the one hand, the 'partial' interest of a sub-group on the other. The second concerns integration of rights to a 'voice' in collective affairs with the exigencies of effective leadership and the corresponding responsibility.

The principle is the 'grounding' of a collective system in a consensus in the sense of the above discussion, namely an 'acceptance' on the part of its members of their belonging together, in the sense of sharing, over a certain range, common interests, interests which are defined both by type, and by considerations of time. Time becomes relevant because of the uncertainty factor in all human action, and hence the fact that neither benefits nor burdens can be precisely predicted and planned for in advance; hence an effective collectivity must be prepared to absorb unexpected burdens, and to balance this, to carry out some sort of just distribution of benefits which are unexpected and/or are not attributable to the earned agency of any particular subunit.

Solidarity may then be thought of as the implementation of common values by definition of the requisite collective systems in which they are to be actualized. Collective action as such we have defined as political function. The famous problem of order, however, cannot be solved without a common normative system. Solidarity is the principle by virtue of which the commitment to norms, which is 'based' in turn on values, is articulated with the formation of collectivities which are capable of effective collective action. Whereas, in the economic direction, the 'problem' of effective action is coping with the scarcity of available resources, including trying to facilitate their mobility, in the integrative direction it is orderly solution of competing claims, on the one hand to receive benefits – or minimize losses – deriving from memberships, on the other to influence the processes by which collective action operates. This clearly involves some institutionalization of the subordination of unit-interest to the collective in cases where the two are in conflict, actual or potential, and hence the justification of unit interests as compatible with the more extensive collective interest. A social system then possesses solidarity in proportion as its members are committed to common interests through which discrete unit interests can be integrated and the justification of conflict resolution and subordination can be defined and implemented. It defines, not the modes of implementation of these common interests through effective agency, but the standards by which such agency should be guided and the rights of various constituent elements to have a voice in the interpretation of these standards.

POWER AND EQUALITY OF OPPORTUNITY

We may now turn to the second major boundary of the polity, at which another order of modifications of the internal hierarchy of authority comes to focus. This is the boundary *vis-à-vis* the economy where the 'political' interest is to secure control of productivity and services, and the economic interest lies in the collective control of fluid resources and in what we may call opportunity for effectiveness. I shall not attempt here to discuss the whole interchange complex, but will confine myself to the crucial problem of the way that here also the hierarchical structure of power can, under certain conditions, be modified in an egalitarian direction.

Productivity of the economy is in principle allocable among collective (in our sense political) claimants to its control as facilities, in linear quantitative terms. This linear quantification is achieved through the medium of money, either allocation of funds with liberty to expend them at will, or at least monetary evaluation of more specific facilities.

In a sufficiently developed system, services must be evaluated in monetary terms also, both from the point of view of rational budgeting and of the monetary cost of their employment. In terms of their utilization, however, services are 'packages' of performance-capacity, which are qualitatively distinct and of unequal value as contributions to collective effectiveness. Their evaluation as facilities must hence involve an estimate of strategic significance which matches the general priority scale which has been established to regulate the internal functioning of the collectivity.

Services, however, constitute a resource to be acquired from outside the collectivity, as Weber puts it through a 'formally free' contract of employment. The contracts thus made are binding on both sides, by virtue of a normative system transcending the particular collectivity, though the obligation must articulate with the internal normative order including its hierarchical aspect. But the purveyors of service are not, in advance, bound by this internal priority system and hence an exchange, which is here interpreted to operate in the first instance as between strategic significance expressed as power-potential, and the monetary value of the service, must be arrived at.

Quite clearly, when the purveyor of service has once entered into such a contract, he is bound by the aspect of its terms which articulates the service into this internal system, including the level of authority he exercises and its implications for his power position in the collectivity. If the collectivity is making in any sense a rational arrangement, this must be tailored to an estimate of the level of the value of his strategic contribution, hence his performance-capacity.

Since, however, the boundary interchange is not integral to the internal system of bindingness, the hierarchical imperatives do not apply to the opportunity aspect of this interchange on the extra-political side. This is to say that the same order of pressures of a higher-order universalistic normative system can operate here that we suggested operated to bring about equality in the franchise. Again the principle is that no particularistic discriminations are to be legitimized which are not grounded in essential functional exigencies of the system of reference.

In the case of the franchise there seems to be no inherent stopping place short of complete equality, qualified only by the minimum consideration of competence attached to fully responsible membership – excluding only minors, 'defectives', through retardation and mental illness, and those morally disqualified through crime. In the service case, on the other hand, given commitments to optimum performance which in the present context can be taken for granted, the limit to the equating of universalism and equality lies in the concept of competence. Hence the principle arrived at is the famous one of equality of opportunity, by which there is equalization of access to opportunity for contribution, but selection on criteria of differential competence, both quantitative and qualitative.

Whereas the equalization of the franchise is a control on differential power 'from above' in the hierarchy of control and operates mainly through the selection of leadership, equality of opportunity is (in the corresponding sense) a control from below, and operates to check particularistic tendencies which would tend to exclude sources of service which are qualified by competence to contribute, and/or to check tendencies to retain services which are inferior to those available in competition with them.

It is the combination of these two foci of universalization, the equalitarianism of upper rights to control through the franchise, and of rights to participate through service on the basis of competence, which account for the extent to which the 'cumulative advantage',[30] which might seem to be inherent in the hierarchical internal structure of power systems, often in fact fails either to materialize at all, or to be as strong as expected.

Long and complex as it is, the above discussion may be summed up as an attempted solution of the second of the three main problems with which this paper began, namely that of the relation between the coercive and the consensual aspects of the phenomenon of power. The answer is first premised on the conception of power as a specific but generalized medium of the functioning of social relationships in complex, differentiated systems of social interaction.

Power is secondly specifically associated with the bindingness of obligations to performance within a range of circumstances which may arise in a varying and changing situation. The obligations concerned are hence in some important degree generalized so that particularities under them are contingent on circumstances. The bindingness of obligations implies that they stand on a level of seriousness such that the invoking agent, ego, may be put in the position of asserting that, since he 'means it' that alter must comply, he is prepared to insist on compliance. Partly then as a symbolic expression of this seriousness of 'meaning it' and partly as an instrument of deterrence of noncompliance,[31] this insistence is associated with command of negative situational sanctions the application of which is frequently contingent on noncompliance, and in certain cases deterrence is achieved by compulsion. We would not speak of power where situational negative sanctions or compulsion are in no circumstances attached to noncompliance in cases where a legitimate agent insists on compliance.

Thirdly, however, power is here conceived as a generalized medium of mobilizing commitments or obligation for effective action. As such it ordinarily does not itself possess intrinsic effectiveness, but symbolizes effectiveness and hence the bindingness of the relevant obligations to contribute to it. The operative validity of the meaningfulness of the symbolization is not a function of any one single variable but, we argue, of two primary ones. One of these is the willingness to insist upon compliance, or at least to deter noncompliance, a line of reasoning which leads to the understanding of willingness to resort to negative sanctions, the nature of which will vary, as a function of the seriousness of the question, on the dimension of their progressively more drastic nature, in the last analysis force.

The other variable concerns the collective reference and hence the justification[32] of invoking the obligations in question in the situation. This aspect concerns the dependence of power on the institutionalization of authority and hence the rights of collective agents to mobilize performances and define them as binding obligations. This justification inherently rests on some sort of consensus among the members of the collectivity of reference, if not more broadly, with respect to a system of norms under which authority and power are legitimized on a basis wider than this particular collectivity by the values of the system. More specifically, authority is the institutionalized code within which the 'language of power' is meaningful and, therefore, its use will be accepted in the requisite community, which is in the first instance the community of collective organization in our sense.

Seen in this light the threat of coercive measures, or of compulsion, without legitimation or justification, should not properly be called the use of power at all, but is the limiting case where power, losing its symbolic character, merges into an intrinsic instrumentality of securing compliance with wishes, rather than obligations. The monetary parellel is the use of a monetary metal as an instrument of barter where as a commodity it ceases to be an institutionalized medium of exchange at all.

In the history of thought there has been a very close connection between emphasis on the coercive element in power systems and on the hierarchical aspect of the structure of systems of authority and power. The above discussion has, I hope, helped to dissociate them by showing that this hierarchical aspect, important as it is, is only part of the structure of power systems. The view advanced is that it is an inherent aspect of the internal structure of collectivities. No collectivity, even the nation, however, stands alone as a total society since it is integrated with norms and values; sub-collectivities can even less be claimed to be societies. The collectivity aspect of total social structure may in a particular case be dominant over others, but always in principle it impinges on at least two sorts of boundary-problems, namely that involved in its 'support' system and that involved in the mobilization of services as sources of contribution to its functioning.

In both these cases, we have argued, quite different principles are operative from that of the hierarchy of authority, namely the equality of franchise on the one hand, equality of opportunity on the other. In both cases I envisage an interchange of power, though not of authority, over the boundary of the polity, and in neither case can the principle governing the allocation of power through this interchange be considered to be hierarchical in the line authority sense. The empirical problems here are, as elsewhere, formidable, but I definitely argue that it is illegitimate to hold that, from serious consideration of the role of power as a generalized medium, it can be inferred that there is a general trend to hierarchization in the total empirical social systems involved.[33]

THE ZERO-SUM PROBLEM

We are now in a position to take up the last of the three main problems with which the discussion started, namely whether power is a zero-sum phenomenon in the sense that, in a system, a gain in power by a unit *A* is in the nature of the case the cause of a corresponding loss of power by other units, *B, C, D.* . . . The parallel with money on which we have been insisting throughout should give us clues to the answer, which clearly is, under certain circumstances yes, but by no means under all circumstances.

In the monetary case it is obvious that in budgeting the use of a fixed income, allocation to one use must be at the expense of alternative uses. The question is whether parallel limitations apply to an economy conceived as a total system. For long this seemed to many economists to be the case; this was the main burden of the old 'quantity theory of money'. The most obvious political parallel is that of the hierarchy of authority within a particular collectivity. It would seem to be obvious that, if *A*, who has occupied a position of substantial power, is demoted, and *B* takes his place, *A* loses power and *B* gains it, the total in the system remaining the same. Many political theorists like Lasswell and C. Wright Mills, generalized this to political systems as a whole.[34]

The most important and obvious point at which the zero-sum doctrine breaks down for money is that of credit-creation through commercial banking. This case is so important as a model that a brief discussion here is in order. Depositors, that is, entrust their money funds to a bank, not only for safe keeping, but as available to the bank for lending. In so doing, however, they do not relinquish any property rights in these funds. The funds are repayable by the bank in full on demand, the only normal restrictions being with respect to banking hours. The bank, however, uses part of the balances on deposit with it to make loans at interest, pursuant to which it not only makes the money available to the borrower, but in most cases assumes binding obligations not to demand repayment except on agreed terms, which in general leave the borrower undisturbed control for a stipulated period – or obligates him to specified installments of amortization. In other words, the same dollars come to do 'double duty', to be treated as possessions by the depositors, who retain their property rights, and also by the banker who preempts the rights to loan them, as if they were 'his'. In any case there is a corresponding net addition to the circulating medium, measured by the quantity of new bank deposits created by the loans outstanding.[35]

Perhaps the best way to describe what happens is to say that there has occurred a differentiation in the functions of money and hence there are two ways of using it in the place of one. The ordinary deposit is a reserve for meeting current expenses, whether 'private' or 'business', which is mainly important with respect to the time element of the degrees of freedom mentioned above. From the point of view of the depositor the bank is a convenience, giving him safekeeping, the privilege of writing checks rather than using cash, etc., at a cost which is low because the bank earns interest through its loaning operations. From the point of view of the borrower, on the other hand, the bank is a source of otherwise unavailable funds, ideally in the economist's sense, for investment, for financing operations promising future increments of economic productivity, which would not otherwise have been feasible.

The possibility of this 'miracle of loaves and fishes' of course rests on an empirical uniformity, namely that depositors do in fact, under normal circumstances, keep sufficient balances on hand – though they are not required to – so that it is safe for the bank to have substantial amounts out on loan at any given time. Underlying this basic uniformity is the fact that an individual bank will ordinarily also have access to 'reserves', e.g. assets which, though earning interest, are sufficiently liquid to be realized on short notice, and in the last analysis such resources as those of a federal reserve system. The individual bank, and with it its depositors, is thus ordinarily relatively secure.

We all know, however, that this is true only so long as the system operates smoothly. A particular bank can meet unusual demands for withdrawal of deposits, but if this unusual demand spreads to a whole banking system, the result may be a crisis, which only collective action can solve. Quite clearly the expectation that all depositors should be paid, all at once, in 'real' money, e.g. even 'cash' to say nothing of monetary metal, cannot be fulfilled. Any monetary system in which bank credit plays an important part is in the nature of the case normally 'insolvent' by that standard.

Back of these considerations, it may be said, lies an important relation between bindingness and 'confidence' which is in certain respects parallel to that between coercion and consensus in relation to power, indeed one which, through the element of bindingness, involves a direct articulation between money and power. How is this parallel to be defined and how does the articulation operate?

First the banking operation depends on mutual confidence or trust in that depositors entrust their funds to the bank, knowing, if they stop to think about it, that the bank will have a volume of loans outstanding which makes it impossible to repay all deposits at once. It is well known with what hesitation, historically, many classes have been brought to trust banks at all in this simple sense – the classical case of the French peasant's insistence on putting his savings in cash under the mattress is sufficient illustration. The

other side of the coin, however, is the bank's trust that its depositors will not panic to the point of in fact demanding the complete
fulfillment of their legal rights.

The banker here assumes binding obligations in two directions,
the honoring of both of which depends on this trust. On the one
hand he has loaned money on contract which he cannot recover on
demand, on the other he is legally bound to repay deposits on
demand. But by making loans on binding contractual terms he is
enabled to create money, which is purchasing power in the literal
sense that, as noted above, the status of the monetary unit is
politically guaranteed – e.g. through its position as 'legal tender' –
and hence the newly created dollars are 'as good as' any other
dollars. Hence I suggest that what makes them good in this sense is
the input of power in the form of the bindingness of the contractual
obligation assumed by the banker – I should classify this as opportunity for effectiveness. The bank, as collectivity, thus enjoys a
'power position' by virtue of which it can give its borrowers
effective control of certain types of opportunity.

It is, however, critically important that in general this grant of
power is not unconditional. First it is power in its form of direct
convertibility with money, and second, within that framework, the
condition is that, per unit of time, there should be a surplus of
money generated, the borrower can and must return more money
than he received, the difference being 'interest'. Money, however, is
a measure of productivity, and hence we may say that increasing
the quantity of money in circulation is economically 'functional'
only if it leads after a sequence of operations over a period of time
to a corresponding increase in productivity – if it does not the
consequence is inflationary. The process is known as investment,
and the standard of a good investment is the expected increment of
productivity which, measured in money terms, is profitability. The
organizational question of allocation of responsibility for decisions
and payments should of course not be too directly identified with
the present level of analytical argument.

It may help round out this picture if the concept of investment is
related to that of 'circular flow' in Schumpeter's sense.[36] The
conception is that the routine functioning of economic processes is
organized about the relation between producing and consuming
units, we may say firms and households. So long as a series of
parametric constants such as the state of demand and the coeffi-
cients of cost of production hold, this is a process in equilibrium
through which money mediates the requisite decisions oriented to
fixed reference points. This is precisely the case to which the zero-

sum concept applies. On the one hand a fixed quantity and 'velocity of circulation' of the monetary medium is an essential condition of the stability of this equilibrium, whereas on the other hand, there is no place for banking operations which, through credit expansion, would change the parametric conditions.

These decisions are governed by the standard of solvency, in the sense that both producing and consuming units are normally expected to recoup their monetary expenditures, on the one hand for factors of production, on the other for consumers' goods, from monetary proceeds, on the producing side, sale of output, on the consuming, sale of factors of production, notably labor. Solvency then is a balance between monetary cost and receipts. Investment is also governed by the standard of solvency, but over a longer time period, long enough to carry out the operations necessary to bring about an increase of productivity matching the monetary obligations assumed.

There is here a crucial relation between the time-extension of the investment process and use of power to make loan contracts binding. Only if the extension of control of resources through loans creates obligations can the recipients of the loans in turn assume further obligations and expect others to assume them.

The essential principle here is that, in the sense of the hierarchy of control, a higher-order medium is used as a source of leverage to break into the 'circle' of the Schumpeterian flow, giving the recipients of this power effective control of a share of fluid resources in order to divert them from the established routine channels to new uses. It is difficult to see how this could work systematically if the element of bindingness were absent either from loan contracts or from the acceptance-status of the monetary medium.

One further element of the monetary complex needs to be mentioned here. In the case of investment there is the element of time, and hence the uncertainty that projected operations aiming at increase in productivity will in fact produce either this increase or financial proceeds sufficient to repay loans plus interest in accordance with contract. In the case of the particular borrower-lender relationship this can be handled on an individual contract-solvency basis with a legally determined basis of sharing profits and/or losses. For the system, however, it creates the possibility of inflation, namely that the net effect of credit-extension may not be increase in productivity but decline in the value of the monetary unit. Furthermore, once a system involves an important component of credit, the opposite disturbance, namely deflation with a rearrangement of the meaning of the whole network of financial and credit expectations and relationships, is also a possibility. This suggests that there is, in a ramified credit economy, a set of mechanisms which, independently of particular circular flow, and credit-extension and repayment transactions, regulates the total volume of credit, rates of interest, and price-level relations in the economy.

ZERO-SUM: THE CASE OF POWER

Let us now attempt to work out the parallel, and articulating, analysis for power sysems. There is, I suggest, a circular flow operating between polity and economy in the interchange between factors in political effectiveness – in this case a share of control of the productivity of the economy – and an output to the economy in the form of the kind of control of resources which a loan for investment provides – though of course there are various other forms. This circular flow is controlled by the medium of power in the sense that the input of binding obligations, in particular through commitment to perform services, broadly balances the output of offer of opportunity for effective performance.

The suggestion is that it is a condition of the stability of this circulation system that the inputs and outputs of power on each side should balance. This is another way of saying that it is ideally formulated as a zero-sum system, so far as power is concerned, though because it includes the investment process, the same is not true for the involvement of monetary funds in the interchanges. The political circular flow system then is conceived as the locus of the 'routine' mobilization of performance expectations either through invoking obligations under old contractual – and in some cases, e.g. citizenship, ascriptive – relations, or through a stable rate of assumption of new contractual obligations, which is balanced by the liquidation, typically through fulfillment, of old ones. The balance applies to the system, of course, not to particular units.

Corresponding to utility as the value-pattern governing economic function I have put forward effectiveness as that governing political function. If it is important to distinguish utility, as the category of value to which increments are made by the combinatorial process of economic production, from solvency as the standard of satisfactory performance in handling money as the medium of economic process, then we need to distinguish effectiveness as the political value category, from a corresponding standard for the satisfactory handling of power. The best available term for this standard seems to be the success of collective goal-attainment. Where the polity is sufficiently differentiated so that power has become genuinely a generalized medium we can say that collective units are expected to be successful in the sense that the binding obligations they undertake in order to maintain and create opportunities for effectiveness, are balanced by the input of equally binding commitments to perform service, either within the collectivity in some status of employment, or for the collectivity on a contractual basis.

The unit of productive decision-making, however, is, in a sense corresponding to that applying to the household for the economic case, also expected to be successful in the sense that its expenditure of power through not only the output of services but their commitment to utilization by particular collectivities, is balanced by an input of opportunity which is dependent on collective organization, that is a unit in a position to undertake to provide opportunities which are binding on the unit.

In the light of this discussion it becomes clear that the business firm is in its aspect as collectivity in our technical sense, the case where the two standards of success and solvency coincide. The firm uses its power income primarily to maintain or increase its productivity and, as a measure of this, its money income. A surplus of power will therefore in general be exchanged for enhancement of its control of economic productivity. For a collectivity specialized in political function the primary criterion of success would be given in its power position, relative that is to other collectivities. Here there is the special problem of the meaning of the term power position. I interpret it here as relative to other collectivities in a competitive system, not as a position in an internal hierarchy of power. This distinction is of course particularly important for a pluralistic power system where government is a functionally specialized subsystem of the collectivity structure, not an approximation to the totality of that structure.[37] In somewhat corresponding fashion a collectivity specialized in integrative function would measure its success in terms of its 'level of influence' – for example, as a political interest group in the usual sense, its capacity to influence public policy decisions. A consequence of this reasoning is that such an influence group would be disposed to 'give away' power, in the sense of trading it for an increment of influence. This could take the form of assuring political support, without barterlike conditions, to leadership elements which seemed to be likely to be able to exercise the kind of influence in question.

Is there then a political equivalent of the banking phenomenon, a way in which the circular flow of power comes to be broken through so as to bring about net additions to the amount of power in the system? The trend of the analytical argument indicates that there must be, and that its focus lies in the support system, that is the area of interchange between power and influence, between polity and integrative system.

First I suggest that, particularly conspicuous in the case of democratic electoral systems, political support should be conceived as a generalized grant of power which, if it leads to electoral success, puts elected leadership in a position analogous to that of the banker. The 'deposits' of power made by constituents are revocable, if not at will, at the next election – a condition analogous to regularity of banking hours. In some cases election is tied to barterlike conditions of expectation of carrying out certain specific measures favored by the strategically crucial voters and only these. But particularly in a system which is pluralistic not only with reference to the composition of political support, but also to issues, such a leadership element acquires freedom to make certain types of binding decision, binding in the nature of the case on elements of the collectivity other than those whose 'interest' is directly served. This freedom may be conceived to be confined to the circular flow level, which would be to say that the input of power through the channel of political support should be exactly balanced by the output through policy decisions, to interest groups which have specifically demanded these decisions.

There is, however, another component of the freedom of elected leadership which is crucial here. This is the freedom to use influence – for example through the 'prestige' of office as distinguished from its specified powers – to embark on new ventures in the 'equation' of power and influence. This is to use influence to create additions to the total supply of power. How can this be conceived to work?

One important point is that the relation between the media involved with respect to positive and negative sanctions is the obverse of the case of creating money through banking. There it was the use of power embodied in the binding character of loan contracts which 'made the difference'. Here it is the optional capacity to exert influence through persuasion. This process seems to operate through the function of leadership which, by way of the involvements it possesses with various aspects of the constituency structure of the collectivity, generates and structures new 'demands' in the specific sense of demands for policy decision.

Such demands then may be conceived, in the case of the deciders, to justify an increased output of power. This in turn is made possible by the generality of the mandate of political support, the fact that it is not given on a barter basis in exchange for specific policy decisions, but once the 'equation' of power and influence has been established through election, it is a mandate to do, within constitutional limits, what seems best, in the governmental case 'in the public interest'. Collective leadership may then be conceived as the bankers or 'brokers' who can mobilize the binding commitments of their constituents in such a way that the totality of commitments made by the collectivity as a whole can be enhanced. This enhancement must, however, be justified through the mobilization of influence; it must, that is, both be felt to be in accordance with valid norms and apply to situations which 'call for' handling at the level of binding collective commitments.

The critical problem of justification is, in one direction, that of consensus, of its bearing on the value-principle of solidarity as we have outlined this above. The standard therefore which corresponds to the value principle of solidarity is consensus in the sense in which that concept has been used above.

The problem then is that of a basis for breaking through the circular stability of a zero-sum power system. The crucial point is that this can only happen if the collectivity and its members are ready to assume new binding obligations over and above those previously in force. The crucial need is to justify this extension and to transform the 'sentiment' that something ought to be done into a commitment to implement the sentiment by positive action, including coercive sanctions if necessary. The crucial agency of this process seems to be leadership, precisely conceived as possessing a component analytically independent of the routine power position of office, which defines the leader as the mobilizer of justifications for policies which would not be undertaken under the circular flow assumptions.

It may be suggested that the parallel to credit creation holds with respect to time-extension as well as in other respects. The increments of effectiveness which are necessary to implement new binding policies which constitute an addition to the total burden on the collectivity cannot simply be willed into being; they require organizational changes through recombinations of the factors of effectiveness, development of new agencies, procurement of personnel, new norms, and even changes in bases of legitimation. Hence leadership cannot justifiably be held responsible for effective implementation immediately, and conversely, the sources of political support must be willing to trust their leadership in the sense of not demanding immediate – by the time of the next election – 'pay-off' of the power-value of their votes in their decisions dictated by their own interests.[38]

It is perhaps legitimate to call the responsibility assumed in this connection specifically leadership responsibility and distinguish it in these terms from administrative responsibility which focuses on the routine functions. In any case I should like to conceive this process of power-enhancement as strictly parallel to economic investment, in the further sense that the pay-off should be an increment to the level of collective success in the sense outlined above, i.e. enhanced effectiveness of collective action in valued areas which could not have been expected without risk-taking on the part of leadership in a sense parallel to entrepreneurial investment.

The operation of both governmental and nongovernmental collectivities is full of illustrations of the kind of phenomenon I have in mind, though because this type of formal analysis is somewhat unfamiliar, it is difficult to pin them down exactly. It has, for example, often been pointed out that the relation of executive responsibility to constituency-interests is very different in domestic and in foreign affairs. I suggest that the element of 'political banking' in the field of foreign affairs is particularly large and that the sanction of approval of policy decisions, where it occurs, cannot infallibly be translated into votes, certainly not in the short run. Similar considerations are very frequently involved in what may be called 'developmental' ventures, which cannot be expected to be 'backed' by currently well-structured interests in the same sense as maintenance of current functions. The case of support of research and training is a good one since the 'community of scholars' is not a very strong 'pressure group' in the sense of capacity directly to influence large blocks of votes.

It would follow from these considerations that there is, in developed polities, a relatively 'free-floating' element in the power system which is analogous to a credit-system. Such an element should then be subject to fluctuations on a dimension of inflation–deflation, and be in need of controls for the system as a whole, at a level above that of the activities of particular units.

The analogue of inflation seems to me to touch the credibility of the assertion of the bindingness of obligations assumed. Power, as a symbolic medium, is like money in that it is itself 'worthless', but is accepted in the expectation that it can later be 'cashed in', this time in the activation of binding obligations. If, however, 'power-credit' has been extended too far, without the necessary organizational basis for fulfillment of expectations having been laid, then attempting to invoke the obligations will result in less than a full level of performance, inhibited by various sorts of resistance. In a collectivity undergoing disintegration the same formal office may be 'worth less' than it otherwise would have been because of attrition of its basis of effectiveness. The same considerations hold when it is a case of overextension of new power-expectations without adequate provision for making them effective.

It goes without saying that a power-system in which this credit-like element is prominent is in a state analogous to the 'insolvency' of a monetary system which includes an important element of actual credit, namely its commitments cannot be fulfilled all at once, even if those to whom they have been made have formally valid rights to such fulfillment. Only a strict zero-sum power system could fulfill this condition of 'liquidity'. Perhaps the conservation of political ideologies makes it even more difficult to accept the legitimacy of such a situation – it is all too easy to define it as 'dishonest' – than in the corresponding economic case.

There is, however, a fine line between solid, responsible and constructive political leadership which in fact commits the collectivity beyond its capacities for instantaneous fulfillment of all obligations, and reckless overextendedness, just as there is a fine line between responsible banking and 'wild-catting'.

Furthermore, under unusual pressures, even highly responsible leadership can be put in situations where a 'deflationary' spiral sets in, in a pattern analogous to that of a financial panic. I interpret, for instance McCarthyism as such a deflationary spiral in the political field. The focus of the commitments in which the widest extension had taken place was in the international field – the United States had very rapidly come into the position of bearing the largest share of responsibility for maintenance of world political order against an expansionist Communist movement. The 'loss of China' was in certain quarters a particularly traumatic experience, and the Korean war a highly charged symbol of the costs of the new stewardship.

A pluralistic political system like the American always has a large body of latent claims on the loyalty of its citizens to their government, not only for the 'right sentiments' but for 'sacrifices', but equally these are expected to be invoked only in genuine emergencies. The McCarthy definition of the situation was, however, that virtually anyone in a position of significant responsibility should not only recognize the 'in case' priority – not necessarily by our basic values the highest – of national loyalty, but should explicitly renounce all other loyalties which might conceivably compete with that to the nation, including those to kith and kin. This was in effect a demand to liquidate all other commitments in favor of the national, a demand which in the nature of the case could not be met without disastrous consequences in many different directions. It tended to 'deflate' the power system by undermining the essential basis of trust on which the influence of many elements bearing formal and informal leadership resonsibilities, and which in turn sustained 'power-credit', necessarily rested. Perhaps the most striking case was the allegation of communist infiltration and hence widespread 'disloyalty' in the army, which was exploited to try to force the army leadership to put the commitments of all associated personnel, including e.g. research scientists, in completely 'liquid' form. Two features of the McCarthy movement particularly mark it as a deflationary spiral, first the vicious circle of spreading involvement with the casting of suspicion on wider and wider circles of otherwise presumptively loyal elements in the society and secondly the surprisingly abrupt end of the spiral once the 'bubble was pricked' and 'confidence restored', events associated particularly with the public reaction to McCarthy's performance in the televised army hearings, and to Senator Flanders' protest on the floor of the Senate.[39]

The focus of the McCarthy disturbance may be said to have been in the influence system, in the relation between integrative and pattern-maintenance functions in the society. The primary deflationary effect was on the 'credit' elements of pluralistic loyalties. This in turn would make leadership elements, not only in government but private groups, much less willing to take risks in claiming loyalties which might compete with those to government. Since, however, in the hierarchy of control the influence system is superordinate to the power system, deflation in the former is necessarily propagated to the latter. This takes in the first instance the form of a rush to withdraw political support – which it will be remembered is here treated as a form of power – from leadership elements which could in any sense be suspected of 'disloyalty'. The extreme perhaps was the slogan propagated by McCarthy and played with by more responsible Republican leaders like Thomas E. Dewey, of 'twenty years of treason' which impugned the loyalty of the Democratic Party as a whole. The effect was, by depriving opposition leadership of influence, to make it unsafe even to consider granting them power.

The breaking through of the zero-sum limitations of more elementary power systems opens the way to altogether new levels of collective effectiveness, but also, in the nature of the case, involves new levels of risk and uncertainty. I have already dealt briefly with this problem at the level of the particular collectivity and its extension of commitments. The problem of course is compounded for a system of collectivities because of the risk not only of particular

failures, but of generalized inflationary and deflationary distur-
bances. There are, as we have noted, mechanisms of control which
operate to regulate investment, and similarly extension of the commitments of particular collectivities, both of which have to do with
the attempt to ensure responsibility, on the one hand for solvency
over the long run, on the other for success of the larger 'strategy' of
extension. It is reasonable to suppose that beyond these, there must
be mechanisms operating at the level of the system as a whole in
both contexts.

In the monetary case it was the complex of central banking,
credit management and their relations to governmental finance
which has been seen to be the focus of these highest-level controls.
In the case of power it is of course the first crucial point that there
was to be some relatively paramount apex of control of the power
and authority system, which we think of as in some sense the
'sovereign' state.[40] This has mainly to do with the relations between
what we have called justification and legitimacy, in relation to
government as the highest-order tightly integrated collectivity
structure — so far. This is the central focus of Weber's famous
analysis of authority, but his analysis is in need of considerable
extension in our sense. It seems, among other things, that he posed
an unduly sharp alternative between charismatic and 'routine'
cases, particularly the rational–legal version of the latter. In particular it would be my view that very substantial possibilities of regulated extension of power-commitments exist within the framework
of certain types of 'legal' authority, especially where they are
aspects of a political system which is pluralistic in general terms.
These problems, however, cannot further be explored at the end of
what is already a very long paper.

CONCLUSION

This paper has been designed as a general theoretical attack on the
ancient problem of the nature of political power and its place, not
only in political systems, narrowly conceived, but in the structure
and processes of societies generally. The main point of reference for
the attack has been the conception that the discussion of the
problem in the main traditions of political thought has not been
couched at a sufficiently rigorously analytical level, but has tended
to treat the nation, the state, or the lower-level collectively organized 'group', as the empirical object of reference, and to attempt to
analyze its functioning without further basic analytical breakdown.

The most conspicuous manifestation of this tendency has been the treatment of power.

The present paper takes a radically different position, cutting across the traditional lines. It takes its departure from the position of economic theory and, by inference, the asymmetry between it and the traditional political theory,[41] which has treated one as the theory of an analytically defined functional system of society – the economy – and the other as a concrete substructure, usually identified with government. Gradually the possibility has opened out both the extension of the analytical model of economic theory to the political field and the direct articulation of political with economic theory within the logical framework of the theory of the social system as a whole, so that the *polity* could be conceived as a functional subsystem of the society in all its theoretical fundamentals parallel to the economy.

This perspective necessarily concentrated attention on the place of money in the conception of the economy. More than that, it became increasingly clear that money was essentially a 'symbolic' phenomenon and hence that its analysis required a frame of reference closer to that of linguistics than of technology, i.e. it is not the intrinsic properties of gold which account for the value of money under a gold standard any more than it is the intrinsic properties of the sounds symbolized as 'book' which account for the valuation of physically fixed dissertations in linguistic form. This is the perspective from which the conception of power as a *generalized symbolic medium* operating in the processes of social interaction has been set forth.

This paper has not included a survey of the empirical evidence bearing on its ramified field of problems, but my strong conviction is not only that the line of analysis adopted is consistent with the broad lines of the available empirical evidence, but that it has already shown that it can illuminate a range of empirical problems which were not well understood in terms of the more conventional theoretical positions – e.g. the reasons for the general egalitarian pressure in the evolution of the political franchise, or the nature of McCarthyism as a process of political deflationary spiral.

It does not seem necessary here to recapitulate the main outline of the argument. I may conclude with the three main points with which I began. I submit, first, that the analytical path entered upon here makes it possible to treat power in conceptually specific and precise terms and thus gets away from the theoretical diffuseness called to attention, in terms of which it has been necessary to include such a very wide variety of problematical phenomena as 'forms' of power. Secondly, I think it can advance a valid claim to present a resolution of the old dilemma as to whether (in the older terms) power is 'essentially' a phenomenon of coercion or of consensus. It is both, precisely because it is a phenomenon which integrates a plurality of factors and outputs of political effectiveness and is not to be identified with any one of them. Finally, light has been thrown on the famous zero-sum problem, and a definite position taken that, though under certain specific assumptions the zero-sum condition holds, these are not constitutive of power systems in general, but under different conditions systematic 'extension' of power spheres without sacrifice of the power of other units is just as important a case.

These claims are put forward in full awareness that on one level there is an inherent arbitrariness in them, namely that I have defined power and a number of related concepts in my own way, which is different from many if not most of the definitions current in political theory. If theory were a matter only of the arbitrary choice of definitions and assumptions and reasoning from there, it might be permissible to leave the question at that and say simply, this is only one more personal 'point of view'. Any claim that it is more than that rests on the conception that the scientific understanding of societies is arrived at through a gradually developing organon of theoretical analysis and empirical interpretation and verification. My most important contention is that the line of analysis presented here is a further development of a main line of theoretical analysis of the social system as a whole, and of verified interpretation of the empirical evidence presented to that body of theory. This body of theory must ultimately be judged by its outcomes both in theoretical generality and consistency, over the whole range of social system theory, and by its empirical validity, again on levels which include not only conventionally 'political' references, but their empirical interrelations with all other aspects of the modern complex society looked at as a whole.

NOTES

1 Thus E. C. Banfield, *Political Influence* (The Free Press, New York, 1962), p. 348, speaks of control as the ability to cause another to give or withhold action, and power as the ability to establish control over another. Similarly Robert Dahl, 'The concept of power', *Behavioral Scientist*, 2 (July, 1957), says that *A* has power over *B* to the extent that he can get *B* to do something that B would not otherwise do. C. J.

Friedrich takes a similar position in his forthcoming book, the tentative title of which is 'Man and his Government'.

2 Cf. Talcott Parsona and Neil J. Smelser, *Economy and Society* (The Free Press, Glencoe, Ill., 1956), chapter I, for a discussion of this conception.

3 E.g. the American medical profession is part of American society, but also it is part of a wider medical profession which transcends this particular society, to some extent as collectivity. Interpenetration in membership is thus a feature of the relations among collectivities.

4 For discussions of the concept of 'value added' in spheres of application broader than the economic alone, cf. Neil J. Smelser, *Social Change in the Industrial Revolution* (The Free Press, Glencoe, Ill., 1959), chapter II, pp. 7–20, and Neil J. Smelser, *Theory of Collective Behavior* (The Free Press, New York, 1963), chapter II, pp. 23–47.

5 C. I. Barnard, *The Functions of the Executive* (Harvard University Press, Cambridge, Mass., 1938), chapter V, pp. 46–64.

6 On the rationale of these attributions, see *Economy and Society*, chapter II.

7 'Pay-off' may be a deciding factor in choice between particular contexts of use, but not as to whether the resource shall be devoted to collective effectiveness at all.

8 I have in fact adopted the term 'demands' from the usage of David Easton, 'An approach to the analysis of political systems', *World Politics*, 9 (1957), pp. 383–400.

9 Cf. Max Weber, *The Theory of Social and Economic Organization* (Oxford University Press, New York, 1947), p. 124. Translation by A. M. Henderson and Talcott Parsons; edited by Talcott Parsons.

10 The cases of services concretely rendered to a household will be considered as a limiting case where the roles of consumer and employer have not become differentiated from each other.

11 In the cases treated as typical for economic analysis the collective element in capital is delegated through the *bindingness* of the contracts of loan of financial resources. To us this is a special case, employment being another, of the binding obligation assumed by an organization, whether it employs or loans, by virtue of which the recipient can be more effective than would otherwise be the case. It is not possible to go further into these complex problems here, but they will, perhaps, be somewhat illuminated by the later discussion of the place of the concept of bindingness in the theory of power.

12 See my paper 'On the concept of influence', *Public Opinion Quarterly*, 27 (Spring, 1963), pp. 37–62.

13 Here again Barnard's usage of the concept of responsibility seems to me the appropriate one. See Barnard, *Functions of the Executive*.

14 In order not to complicate things too much, I shall not enter into the problem of the interchange system involving legitimation here. See my paper 'Authority, legitimation, and political process', in *Nomos* 1, reprinted as chapter V of my *Structure and Process in Modern Societies* (The Free Press, Glencoe, Ill., 1960), chapter V, pp. 170–98.

15 There is a certain element of generality in physical force as a negative sanction, which gives it a special place in power systems. This will be taken up later in the discussion.

16 There are complications here deriving from the fact that power is associated with *negative* sanctions and hence that, in the face of severe resistance, their effectiveness is confined to deterrence.

17 I owe the insight into this parallel to Professor Karl W. Deutsch of Yale University (personal discussion).

18 'Sadistic' infliction of injury without instrumental significance to ego does not belong in this context.

19 I have attempted to develop this line of analysis of the significance of force somewhat more fully in 'Some reflections of the role of force in social relations', in Harry Eckstein (ed.), *The Problems of Internal War* (Princeton University Press, New Jersey, 1963).

20 Thus, if control of productivity operates through monetary funds, their possessor cannot 'force' e.g. prospective employees to accept employment.

21 This, of course, is a relative difference. Some hazards increase the moment one steps outside his own home, police protection may be better in one local community than the next, and crossing a state boundary may mean a considerable difference in legal or actual rights.

22 Cf. my paper 'The principal structures of community', *Nomos* 2 and *Structure and Process*, chapter 8. See also W. L. Hurst, *Law and Social Process in the United States* (University of Michigan Law School, Ann Arbor, 1960).

23 As already noted, in this area, I think the analysis of Chester I. Barnard, in *The Function of the Executive*, is so outstandingly clear and cogent that it deserves the status of a classic of political theory in my specific sense. See especially chapter X.

24 Two particularly important manifestations of this monetization of property are, first the general legal understanding that executors of estates are not obligated to retain the exact physical inventory intact pending full statement, but may sell various items – their fiduciary obligation is focussed on the money value of the estate. Similarly in the law of contract increasing option has been given to compensate with money damages in lieu of the specific 'performance' originally contracted for.

25 Since this sytem is the territorially organized collectivity, the state with its government, these considerations underlie the critical importance of foreign relations in the sense of the relations to other territorially organized, force-controlling collectivities, since, once internal control of force is effectively institutionalized, the danger of this kind of breach comes from the outside in this specific sense of outside. The point is cogently made by Raymond Aron.

26 See, on this process, Stein Rokkan, 'Mass suffrage, secret voting, and political participation', *European Journal of Sociology*, 2 (1961), pp. 132–52.

27 I.e., the aggregate of votes, evaluated by the electoral rules, determines the incumbency of office.

28 Of course where conditions are sufficiently simple, or where there is sufficient anxiety about the hierarchial implications of power, the egalitarian element may penetrate far into the political decision-making system itself, with, e.g. insistence that policy-decisions, both external and internal in reference, by made by majority vote of all members, or even under a unanimity rule. The respects in which such a system — which of course realistically often involves a sharply hierarchical stratification of influence — is incompatible with effectiveness in many spheres, can be said to be relatively clear, especially for *large* collectivities.

29 It is the central concept of *The Division of Labor in Society*. For my own relatively recent understanding of its significance, see 'Durkheim's contribution to the theory of integration of social systems', in Kurt Wolff (ed.), *Émile Durkheim, 1858–1917* (Ohio State University Press, Ohio, 1960), pp. 118–53.

30 Cf. C. Wright Mills, *The Power Elite* (Oxford University Press, New York, 1956) and my commentary in *Structure and Process in Modern Societies*, chapter 6.

31 Cf. Durkheim's famous essay, 'Deux lois de l'evolution pénale', *L'Année Sociologique*, 4 (1899–1900), pp. 65–95.

32 Cf. my paper 'On the concept of influence', for a discussion of the concept of justification and its distinction from legitimation.

33 Failure to see this seems to me to be a major source of the utopian strain in Marxist theory, expressed above all by the expectation of the 'withering away of the state'. There is perhaps a parallel to the confusion connected for many centuries with the Aristotelian doctrine of the 'sterility' of money.

34 H. D. Lasswell and A. Kaplan, *Power and Society* (Yale University Press, New Haven, 1950) and Mills, *The Power Elite*.

35 Whether this be interpreted as net addition to the medium or as increase in the velocity of circulation of the 'slow' deposit funds, is indifferent, because its economic effects are the same.

36 Joseph Schumpeter, *The Theory of Economic Development* (Harvard University Press, Cambridge, Mass., 1955), translated by Redvers Opie.

37 If very carefully interpreted, perhaps the old term 'sovereignty' could be used to designate this standard somewhat more definitely than success.

38 Perhaps this is an unusually clear case of the relativity of the formal legal sense of the bindingness of commitments. Thus the populistic component in democratic government often ties both executive and legislative branches rather rigidly in what they can formally promise. However, there are many *de facto* obligations assumed by Government which are very nearly binding. Thus legally Congress could withdraw the totality of funds recently granted to universities for the support of scientific research and training, the formal appropriations being made

year by year. Universities, however, plan very much in the expectation of maintenance of these funds and this maintenance is certainly something like a *de facto* obligation of Congress.

39 I have dealt with some aspects of the McCarthy episode in 'Social strains in America', *Structure and Process*, chapter 7, pp. 226–49. The inherent impossibility of the demand for 'absolute security' in a pluralistic system is very cogently shown by Edward Shils in *The Torment of Secrecy* (The Free Press, New York, 1956), especially in chapter VI.

40 In saying this I am very far from maintaining that 'absolute' sovereignty is an essential condition of the minimal integration of political systems. On the contrary, first it is far from absolute internally, precisely because of the pluralistic character of most modern political systems and because of the openness of their boundaries in the integrative economic and other directions. Externally the relation of the territorial unit to norms and values transcending it is crucial and steadily becoming more so. See my paper 'Polarization of the world and international order', in Quincy Wright, William M. Evan and Morton Deutsch (eds), *Preventing World War III* (Simon and Schuster, New York, 1962), pp. 310–31.

41 I myself once accepted this. Cf. *The Social System* (Free Press, Glencoe, Ill., 1951), chapter V, pp. 161–63.

7
Class Power

NICOS POULANTZAS

By power, we shall designate *the capacity of a social class to realize its specific objective interests*. This concept is not without difficulties, especially in so far as it introduces the concept of 'interests'; and we know the importance of this concept in Marx and Lenin, for whom the Marxist conception of classes and power is linked to that of 'class interests'. But it is important briefly to locate this definition of power relative to some others which have had important repercussions on political theory.

1 This definition differs from Lasswell's[1] conception of power as 'the fact of taking part in decision-making' and from the definitions common to the whole series of theories of the *decision-making process*. The fundamental defect of this conception, at least in the framework of a society characterized by class conflict, is that (i) it succumbs to a voluntarist conception of the decision-making process, through disregarding the effectiveness of the structures, and it is not able exactly to locate beneath the appearances the effective centres of decision inside which the distribution of power works; and (ii) it takes as a principle the 'integrationist' conception of society, from which the concept of 'participation' in decision-making is derived.

2 This definition of power is different from that of Weber, for whom power (*Herrschaft*) is 'the probability that a command with a given specific content will be obeyed by a given group of persons'.[2] This is because Weber's definition is located in the historicist perspective of a society/subject, a product of the normative behaviour of subjects/agents, a view which is at the basis of his conception of 'probability' and of 'specific command'. This command is conceived as being practised inside an 'authoritarian association', a

Reprinted with permission from Nicos Poulantzas, *Political Power and Social Classes*, translation editor Timothy O'Hagan, London: New Left Books and Sheed and Ward, 1973, pp. 104–14.

crystallization of the values—ends of these agents. Thus, in the Weberian problematic the concept of power is reduced to that of legitimacy.

3 This definition is distinguished from that of Parsons,[3] for whom power is 'the capacity to carry on certain functions to the profit of the social system considered in its entirety'. Such a definition is expressly bound up with the 'functionalist-integrationist' conception of the social system.

It is, of course, impossible to undertake a detailed critique of the many concepts of power to be found in political science: these few references aim only at showing the complexity of the problem. If the proposed concept of power is accepted, it will be seen to be capable of accounting for the whole range of Marxist analyses of this problem.

A This concept is related precisely to the field of 'class' practices and of relations of class practices, i.e. to the field of class struggle: its *frame of reference* is the class struggle of a society divided into classes. That means that in these societies the effects of the structure are concentrated in the practices of those particular ensembles constituted by social classes. An initial clarification is necessary here: the concept of power is related to that precise type of social relation which is characterized by class *'conflict'* and struggle; that is, to a field inside which, precisely because of the existence of classes, the capacity of one class to realize its own interests through its practice is in *opposition* to the capacity and interests of other classes. This determines a *specific* relation of *domination* and *subordination* of class practices, which is exactly characterized as a relation of power. Thus, starting from this opposition, the relation of power implies the possibility of demarcating a clear line between the *places* of domination and subordination. In the context of societies where this division into classes is non-existent (and it would be interesting to examine to what extent this is also applicable to non-antagonistic class relations in the transition from socialism to communism) and where therefore these relations cannot be specified by this struggle as relations of domination or subordination of classes, a different concept should be used, which would ultimately be that of *authority*.[4]

The concept of power cannot be applied to 'inter-individual'[5] relations or to relations whose constitution in given circumstances is presented as independent of their place in the process of production, i.e. in societies divided into classes, as independent of the class struggle: for example, relations of friendship, relations between members of a sports club, etc. In their case the concept of *might* *(puissance)*[6] can be used: this concept has been especially used in political science to indicate the element of 'force', while the concept of power *(pouvoir)* has been used in the case of a *legitimate* force, that is, exercised in a frame of reference of a minimum of 'consent' on the part of those over whom this power is exercised.[7] Yet this distinction, while it can be very useful, is in fact a distinction concerning the *forms of power*, the forms of domination–subordination implied in the relations of power. It should be remembered that the distinction between power and might concerns the frame of reference within which these phenomena are located: that of power is placed in the framework of the class *struggle*, which reflects the effects of the unity of the structures of a formation on the supports. In this sense, we can say that power is a typical phenomenon, traceable from the structures, while that of might is a phenomenon characterized by a sociological amorphy.

B This concept of power refers to the *capacity* of a class to realize specific objective interests. This element of the concept of power has particular reference to Marx and Lenin's analyses of *class organization.*

As the problem is important, we should stop here in order to introduce some distinctions which will prevent confusion. It has been pointed out in the chapter on classes that a class can exist in a social formation as a *distinct class*, even in the case when it is *under-determined*, i.e. even when it does not possess what is normally called *its own* political and ideological organization. The condition for this is that its existence at the economic level is expressed at the levels of its political and ideological practices by a specific presence, namely that of 'pertinent effects'. This *presence* of a class as a *social force* in fact presupposes a certain organizational *threshold*, in the broadest sense of the term. For example, in the case of the smallholding peasants, Marx refuses to assign to them in general the character of a distinct class; this is because of their isolation, which excludes any possibilities of organization, in so far as these are conditions of their existence as a distinct class. They were given this organization, in the broad sense of the term, by Louis Bonaparte in the Second Empire. In this broad sense, the term organization covers simply the conditions of a class practice with 'pertinent effects'. However, the theory of organization, in the strict sense of the term found in Marx and especially in Lenin, involves not simply class practices, conditions of existence of a class as a distinct class (social force), *but the conditions of class power, that is, the conditions of a practice leading to class power.* For example, Marx's texts concerning a class's 'own' political and ideological organization do not in fact refer to its functioning as a distinct class. But they are still valuable concerning class power and organization as a condition of this power, which Marx expresses in these terms: '. . . a political movement . . . [is] a movement of the class, *with the object of enforcing its interests in* a general form, *in a form possessing general, socially coercive force'.*[8]

It is clear that this theoretical line governs Lenin's analyses of organization, and especially his analyses of the organization of the working-class party. The fact that politico-ideological class practice is not identical with an organized practice as a condition of class power was registered by Lenin in his concept of open or declared action, which is not coterminous with that of practice. The *organization of the power* of a class often appears in Lenin *as a condition of its open action.* But the contrary is not necessarily true, since the organization of the power of a class may not lead to a declared action if its power depends on its political eclipse; as is the case of the bourgeoisie under the Second Empire. So we note an essential difference and some important dislocations between class organization in the broad sense, which coincides with the concept of practice-with-'pertinent-effects', and *the organization of power*: for example, the small-holding peasants of *The Eighteenth Brumaire* had, through Louis Bonaparte, an organization which gave them existence as a distinct class, without thereby having any power, since Bonaparte did not satisfy any of their class interests.

On the other hand, though this specific organization of a class is the *necessary condition* of its power, it is not the sufficient condition. This observation allows us better to understand the reasons for distinguishing between a class's practice-with-'pertinent-effects' and the organization of its power. The organization of the power of a class is not a sufficient condition of its power since this power is obtained in the limits (*qua* effects) of the structures in the field of practices: in contrast to the 'voluntarist' conception, the effective realization of interests depends on these limits. But there is also another factor which shows us, in other respects, the basis of the distinction between practice-with-'pertinent-effects' and organization of power: the concept of power specifies as limits the effects of the structure *in the relations between the various practices of the classes in conflict.* In this sense, power reveals relations not directly determined by the structure, and depends on the exact relation of the social forces present in the class struggle. The capacity of a class to realize its interests, of which the organization of its power is the necessary condition, depends on the capacity of other classes to realize their interests. The degree of effective power of a class depends directly on the degree of power of the other classes, in the framework of the determination of class practices in the limits set by the practices of the other classes. Strictly speaking, *power is identical with these limits in the second degree.* It does not show the mode of intervention of the practice of one level of a class directly on the practices of *other* levels of the same class; but rather it shows the mode of intervention of the practice of one level of a class on practices of the *same* level of the *other* classes, within the limits which each class practice sets for that of the others. This *precise meaning* of limits is particularly important and has results for problems other than that of power. For example, concerning the political level and the problem of strategy, it shows itself in the specific effects which the political practice of one class has on that of another class, in short, the *strategy of the opponent.*

C   The question of a class's 'interests' and 'objective interests' must now be discussed. Owing to the breadth of this problem, I shall now only give some pointers. My discussion will concentrate on the following theme: what are the relations of class 'interests' to structures and practices? What is the meaning of the term 'objective interests' of a class? My aim will be to arrive at an adequate concept of 'interest'.

At the outset certain mistaken interpretations must be eliminated. Class interests are situated in the field of practices, in the field of the class struggle. We cannot locate interests in the structures without falling into an anthropological interpretation of Marxism, not simply into that of individuals-subjects, but even into that of class-subjects. In fact, though they are in no way a 'psychological' notion, interests can be located only in the proper field of practices and classes. In the structures, for example, wages or profit do not express the interest of the worker, nor of the capitalist with his 'lure of gain', but constitute economic categories related to forms of combination. However, in saying that interests can be conceived only by theoretical reference to a practice, we are not thereby attributing to interests a relation with 'individual behaviour'; as a first step, we are excluding interests from being located in structures.

This exclusion is important. It is true that there are some analyses of the classics of Marxism which, at a first reading, seem to locate class interests in the relations of production. This is the type of reading which identifies structures and practices, and which sees in relations of production the class-in-itself (class interests), as opposed to the political and ideological levels consisting of the practice (i.e. organization) of the class-for-itself. Marx goes so far as to say that class interests, in the class struggle, have an existence somehow prior to the formation itself, to the practice of a class. Concerning the interests of the proletariat he says, in *The German Ideology*, that the German bourgeoisie is in opposition to the proletariat even before the proletariat is organized as a class.

Nevertheless, by reference to the above analyses, it should be possible to see that, in fact, with respect to the relation between class interests and practices, class interests are not identical with the class struggle, in a relation of structures to practices. This leads us to pose the problem of the relations between interests and structures. It might be useful to point out that this preoccupation has been of prime importance in the 'functionalist' school of contemporary sociology: it is one of its merits to have posed the problem. This school goes back in the last analysis to a historicist problematic of the subject, and so leads to a view which defines practice as the behaviour or conduct of agents. It has posed the problem in the following way: the place of agents in relation to structure is determined by *objective interests* which constitute the *agents' role*.[9] The concept of interest is thus at first sight without psychological connotations. However, since the structure is here conceived as the substratum and product of the agents' behaviour or conduct, the interests-structures, the *role*-situation, consist of expectations (probabilities) of certain conducts on the part of agents as a function of their structural role. What is most important for us to note here is that this location of objective interests in the structures (the 'situation') is totally dependent on a problematic of the subject, which sees in the structures the product of agents. These interests are 'objective' to the extent that they are located in the structures, while practices are reduced to conduct or behaviour.

As soon as the functionalist school attempted to pose the problem of structures in a rigorous way, this way of posing the problem of interests led them to an impasse. Since interests cannot effectively be grasped except in the field of supports (agents), the school readily introduces the notions of 'latent interests', determining the agents' structural role, and of 'manifest interests', located, say, in the field of practices.[10] The group has the following theoretical status: latent interests are seen as giving rise to 'quasi-groups' (groups-in-themselves), manifest interests to 'interest groups' (groups-for-themselves).[11] Disregarding the use of the term 'group' (for class), the consequences of this perspective are very precisely the same as for the economist-historicist perspective in Marxism. This latter sees in the economic structure the economic interests (the 'situation') of the class-in-itself. Similar to the economist-historicist division of social 'class' into two conceptually delimited parts is the functionalist division between (a) class-in-itself: class situation, latent interests, quasi-groups, and (b) groups-for-themselves: status groups, political elites, manifest interests, interest groups.

It is therefore obvious that these attempts to locate class interests in the structures are incompatible with a scientific conception. The concept of interests can only be related to the field of practices, in so far as interests are always interests of a class, of supports distributed in social classes. But this does not mean that interests consist of behavioural motivations, any more than the fact of locating practices in social relations means a return to a problematic of the subject. While the concept of class indicates the effects of the structure on the supports and while the concept of practice covers not behaviour but an operation carried on within the limits imposed by the structure, interests certainly indicate these limits, but at a particular level as the *extension of the field* of the practice of one class in relation to those of the other classes, i.e. the extension of the 'action' of classes in relations of power. This is not any kind of metaphorical play on the terms of limits and field, but a result of the complexity of the relations covered by these terms.

We find an indication of the problem in connection with the political conjuncture in Lenin's analyses. In fact, his concept of the present moment is characterized by: (a) *social classes*, political class practices, the social forces, and (b) *relations of interests*: that which, seen from the viewpoint of the political practice of the working class, is expressed as 'the deeper interest-relationship of the proletariat'.[12] These two terms, social forces and interests, although found in the field of political class practices, *are not identical*. Social forces concern the specific presence of a class, through 'pertinent effects', on the plane of political class practice. In other words, the effects of structures on the field of the class struggle are reflected here as a class's *threshold of existence* as a distinct class, as a social force. But these effects are reflected also as an *extension of the ground* which this class can cover according to the stages of specific organization attainable by it (organization of power); and this ground extends as far as its objective interests. If we refer in this way to this double limit of the field (every field having a 'near side' and a 'far side'), a class's objective interests do not appear directly as the *threshold* of its existence as a distinct class, as some kind of 'situation' of the class-'in-itself', but as the horizon of its action as a social force. This holds true for all the particular levels of practices in the field of the class struggle. So, just as economic interests do not constitute the 'situation' of a class-in-itself at the economic level, but the horizon of its economic action, so political interests cannot be grasped as the 'finality' of the 'praxis' of a class-for-itself: they are, at the level of political practice, the horizon which delimits the ground of a class's political practice.

Class interests, as limits of extension of a specific class practice, *are displaced* according to the interests of the other classes present. We are dealing always with relations, strictly speaking with strategic oppositions of class interests. It is in this perspective that the strategic distinction (in the proper sense of the term) between *long- and short-term interests* is located. In other words, these limits of extension constitute both limits-effects of the structure, and limits-effects at one remove, imposed by the intervention of the practices of different classes (class struggle) at a particular level of practices. In this sense, the extent or degree to which a class practice actually covers the ground outlined by its class interests also depends on the extent or degree to which it is covered by the opponent. The capacity of a class to realize its objective interests, and so its class power, depends on the capacity, and so on the power, of its opponent.

I have mentioned that class interests are 'objective' interests so as to rule out any question of behavioural motivations. In this sense, Marx says in *The German Ideology*: 'This communal interest . . . [of a class] . . . does not exist merely in the imagination, as the "general interest", but first of all in reality, as the mutual interdependence of the individuals among whom the labour is divided.'[13] But it is obvious that, in the field of practices, owing to the functioning of ideology in this respect, these interests *qua* limits can differ from the *representation* that agents or even classes make of them. This does not mean that when dislocated from (real) interests as limits, these interests as imagined or experienced are 'subjective' limits: because the effectiveness of the ideological (in the present case in the masking of these limits from the agents) cannot be grasped by the category of the 'subjective'. In this respect, the use of the term 'objective' can in fact be considered as superfluous, and it is only retained here in order clearly to show that the concept of interests can and must be stripped of all psychological connotations. However, there is no doubt that in this field of interests, ideology as it functions can give rise to numerous forms of illusion.

Power, as capacity to realize interests, refers not to imaginary interests, in a situation where, on account of ideology, they are dislocated from interests-limits, but to these latter themselves.

Ⓓ The last element in the concept of power is that of the *specificity* of the class interests to be realized. Indeed, if interests are located not in the structures, as the class 'situation' in the relations of production, but rather as limits of the levels in the field of practices, the possibility of speaking of relatively autonomous interests of a class in the economic, political and ideological spheres is clear. Power is located at the level of the *various* class practices, in so far as there are class interests concerning the economic, the political and the ideological. In particular, in a capitalist formation characterized by the specific autonomy of the levels of structures and practices, and of the respective class interests, we can clearly see the distinction between *economic power, political power, ideological power*, etc., according to the capacity of a class to realize its relatively autonomous interests at each level.[14] In other words, relations of power are not located at the political level alone any more than class interests are located at the economic level alone. The relations of these various powers (their index of effectiveness, etc.) themselves relate to the articulation of the various class practices (class interests) which, in a dislocated manner, reflect the articulation of the various structures of a social formation or of one of its stages or phases.

In short, power relations do not constitute a simple expressive totality, any more than structures or practices do; but they are complex and dislocated relations, determined in the last instance by economic power. Political or ideological power is not the simple expression of economic power. Numerous examples of a class which is economically but not politically dominant,[15] ideologically but not economically or politically dominant, etc., can be cited. A class may have the capacity to realize economic interests (the problem of trade-unionism) without having the capacity to realize political interests. It can have an economic power without having a 'corresponding' political power or even a political power without having a 'corresponding' ideological power, etc.

One last remark should be made in connection with the problem of decentration of places of domination at the various levels, places which can be occupied by different classes. This does not mean that we cannot rigorously define which is or are the dominant class(es) in a formation, or, in other words, *which place of domination has dominance over the others*. If we take into account the ensemble of these complex relations, we shall see that in the case of a decentration of this kind, the dominant class(es) in a formation is, in the last analysis, that which occupies the dominant place(s) at that level of the class struggle which maintains the dominant role in the complex whole of that formation. They are therefore that class or those classes which maintain the *dominant power*. For example, in the dissociation of the places of domination in Britain before 1688, the bourgeoisie which has the economically dominant place is often treated as the 'dominant class', although it does not have 'direct domination', in the sense of political domination. This is because, in the concrete case of Britain, the economic appears as maintaining the dominant role. On the other hand, in the dissociation of the places of domination in Prussia at the end of Bismarck's regime, the landed nobility (through its political dominance) is generally treated as the dominant class: it appears that the political there maintains the dominant role.[16]

NOTES

1 H. D. Lasswell and A. Kaplan, *Power and Society, a Framework for Social Enquiry* (New Haven, Conn., 1950), pp. 70 ff; Lasswell, Politics: who gets what, when, how (New York, 1936), pp. 40 ff.

2 M. Weber, The Theory of Social and Economic Organization (Glencoe, 1964), p. 152.

3 T. Parsons, Structure and Process in Modern Societies (Glencoe, 1960), pp. 199 ff.; 'On the concept of Power', *Proceedings of the American Philosophical Society*, 107(3), 1963.

4 We should note here that the problematic of the concept of 'power' related to that of a specific relation characterized by a demarcation of places of subordination and domination in particular conditions of a 'conflict' was pointed out by M. Weber, op. cit., pp. 152–3 and 130 ff. He designates this relation as a '*Herrschaftsverband*', which produces *legitimacy* capable of engendering relations of 'power'; and he distinguishes it from the general relation 'rulers-ruled', a relation which is found in every social organization and which is grasped not by the same concept as the *specific* relation of domination-subordination, but by the concept of '*Macht*'. It is important to add here that that which marks out the domination-subordination relation and locates the 'conflict' is in fact originally situated in a *place exterior* to this relation itself: this 'conflict' is delimited by the structure. In this sense, not every 'rulers–ruled' relation implies by its very intrinsic nature a 'conflict' or, in Marxist terms, a class 'struggle': on the other hand, only a conflict traceable from the structures (in Marxist terms a class struggle) can create a particular relation of domination-subordination grasped by the concept of power.

5 It is unnecessary to point out how mistaken are the different ideologies which locate power as an 'inter-personal' phenomenon; these include the whole range of psycho-sociological-style definitions (see R. Dahl and K. Lewin). These are of the type: 'The power of a person *A* over a person *B* is the capacity of *A* to get *B* to do something he would not have done without the intervention of *A*' (see especially R. Dahl, 'the concept of power' in *Behavioral Science*, 2 (1957), pp. 201–15. F. Bourricaud probably belongs in the same theoretical line).

6 Throughout this section, *pouvoir* is translated *power*; *puissance* is translated *might*. The distinction between the two terms is made clear in the text. [trans.]

7 Amongst others, see R. Aron, 'Macht, power, puissance: prose démocratique ou poésie démoniaque?' in *AES*, No. 1 (1964); G. Lavau, 'La dissociation du pouvoir' in *Esprit*, June 1953 (special number devoted to the question of 'political power and economic power').

8 Letter to Bolte, 23 November 1871, concerning the Gotha programme, *MESW* (1970), p. 673.

9 This general line is found in Parsons, Merton, Dahrendorf, etc.

10 This is particularly clear in R. Merton's application of the concepts of 'manifest functions' and 'latent functions' in his analysis of 'boss-politics' in the United States. See *Social Theory and Social Structures* (Glencoe, 1957), pp. 73 ff.

11 See in particular M. Ginsberg, *Sociology* (London, 1953), pp. 40 ff.

12 See 'Letters from afar – first letter', *Selected Works* (Moscow, n.d.), vol. 2, p. 6.

13 *The German Ideology*, p. 44.

14 It is unnecessary to insist on the clear distinction in Marx, Lenin and Gramsci between economic interests (Lenin), economic-corporate interests (Gramsci), private economic interests (Marx) on the one hand, and political interests on the other. This distinction is connected to the distinction indicated above, between economic struggle and political struggle.

15 The classic case is that of the bourgeoisie in England before 1688. It is the *economically dominant* class, while the landed aristocracy remains the *politically dominant* class despite the revolution of 1640. Yet in 1688 the English bourgeoisie, without becoming the hegemonic class, a subject to which we shall return later, enters the power bloc: its hegemony is confirmed thereafter. The particular case of England is dealt with by Marx, and also by Engels, especially in the 1892 Preface to the first English edition of *Socialism, Utopian and Scientific* (*MESW*, London (1970), pp. 385 ff.). On this subject in general, we also possess Engels's numerous texts on the absolutist state, which he sees as reflecting the 'equilibrium' between two classes, the landed nobility and the bourgeoisie. Marx refines this analysis in showing that England during the period in question is characterized not by a political equilibrium between these two classes, as in France during the period preceding the Revolution, but by the fact that 'political power and economic

strength are not united in the same hands'. Then again we have the case of Prussia towards the end of the Bismarckian state: on this subject, see Engels, *The Housing Question* (1872), II.2., concerning economic domination of the bourgeoisie and political domination of the landed nobility. I note in passing that Engels's articles in the *New York Daily Tribune* of 1851–2, which are known under the title *Revolution and Counter-Revolution in Germany*, concern a different phenomenon. On the subject under discussion, see also the remarks of R. Miliband, 'Marx and the State', *Socialist Register* (London, 1964), pp. 283 ff.

16 See the texts of Marx and Engels cited above.

8
Toward a Theory of Social Power

ALVIN I. GOLDMAN

The concept of power has long played a significant role in political thought, and recent decades have witnessed many attempts to analyze power and provide criteria for its measurement.[1] In spite of this impressive literature, however, our understanding of power remains inadequate. Specifically, no fully comprehensive conceptual framework exists within which questions about power can be formulated precisely and dealt with systematically. In the absence of such a framework it is difficult to investigate empirical questions, such as the extent to which a country is dominated by a 'power elite', and it is hard to discuss normative issues, such as the relationship between power and freedom, or the relationship between equality of power and justice.

In this paper I shall outline a theory of power the ultimate aim of which is to shed light on empirical and normative questions in the political domain. To achieve this aim, however, it is wise to broaden our perspective. The domain of power is not confined to the political realm, narrowly conceived: employers have power over employees and teachers over students. Nor is power purely an inter-personal matter: men have power over nature as well as over other men. Although I am primarily interested in social and political power, I shall construe the notion of power broadly enough to cover all of these areas. There is an even wider sense of 'power' with which I shall not be concerned, the sense in which we speak of the power of an engine or a machine. I shall confine my attention to the sense in which a man or a *group* of men are said to have power. In this endeavor I shall be in the spirit of Hobbes, who wrote: 'The power of a man, to take it universally, is his present means to obtain some future apparent good.'

A theory of power must enable us to account for the fact that

Alvin I. Goldman, 'Towards a theory of social power', *Philosophical Studies*, 23, 4 (1972), pp. 221–68, is reprinted by permission of the publisher.

Nelson Rockefeller is, on the whole, an extremely powerful person. This does not imply that he has power over every man or every issue. There are many issues over which Rockefeller lacks power completely, e.g., what grade a student receives in my course. Nevertheless, a person's total power is clearly related to his power over particular issues. Thus, in the first section of the paper, I shall explain what it is for an individual to have power with respect to a given issue, for example, who obtains a certain appointment, or whether it rains on Wednesday. Social theory does not restrict its interest to the power of individuals, however; of equal significance is the power of groups. In the second section, therefore, I shall turn to the nature of collective power. An analysis of collective power is needed to appraise the power of a nation, of the Pentagon, or of groups such as automobile manufacturers and ethnic minorities. Moreover, to the extent that a person's power is a function of his membership in groups that have collective power, an understanding of collective power is necessary to complete our account of the power of an individual. The first two sections of the paper primarily concern the conditions in which a person or group has at least *some* power on a given issue. A full-fledged theory, however, must enable us to make comparisons of power. While the Secretary of Defense has considerable power over military policy, the President has even more power. In the third and fourth sections, then, I shall address myself to the problem of comparisons of power and degrees of power. Finally, in the fifth section I shall discuss the nature of power over a *person* (as opposed to an *issue*) and to the nature of *overall* power.

Throughout the paper I shall of course try to capture common-sense intuitions and judgements about power (ones that would be shared by people of different political persuasions). My primary concern, however, is not to canvass every use of 'power' in every-day speech, but rather to embark on the construction of a theory. Perhaps it is an inevitable feature of philosophical theorizing that certain intuitions and usages are emphasized while others receive merely passing attention. But the benefits of theory construction can make this price well worth paying.

I   INDIVIDUAL POWER

The central idea in the concept of power, I suggest, is connected with *getting what one wants*. An all-powerful being is a being whose every desire becomes reality. An all-powerful dictator is one whose every desire for state policy becomes the policy of the state.

One man X has another man Y 'in his power' if what happens to Y is a function of what X wants to happen to him. The central notion, in all of these cases, is that a powerful man is a man whose desires are actualized, i.e., a man who gets what he wants.

It would be wrong to conclude that whenever one gets what he wants one must have power in the matter. A farmer may want rain on a particular occasion and may happen to get what he wants, but it does not follow that he has power or control over the weather. Even a person who *regularly* gets what he wants need not be powerful. The Stoics, and Spinoza as well, recommended that one form one's desires to accord with what can realistically be expected to happen in any case; they regarded freedom as conformity of events with actual desires, or rather, as conformity of desires with events. But as an account of power this is inadequate. To take an extreme example, consider Robert Dahl's case of the 'chameleon' legislator who always correctly predicts beforehand what the legislature is going to decide, and then forms a desire or preference to accord with this outcome.[2] The chameleon always gets what he wants, but he is not one of the more powerful members of the assembly.

What these cases show — and what is probably clear from the outset — is that an analysis of power cannot simply concern itself with what an agent actually wants and actually gets, but must concern itself with what he *would* get on the assumption of various *hypothetical* desires. To day that S is powerful is not to say that he usually gets what he in fact wants, but that whatever he wanted he would get, no matter what he might happen to want. To explicate the concept of power, we must appeal therefore to subjunctive conditionals. Although we shall later discuss what it is for a person to be powerful in general, we begin by asking what it is for a person to have power over, or with respect to, a single issue or event. The following notation will be used. 'E' stands for an issue, e.g., whether or not it rains at a particular time and place; 'e' and 'not-e' stand for possible outcomes of that issue, e.g., the occurrence of rain and the non-occurrence of rain, respectively. To assess the claim that person S has power with respect to (henceforth to be written: 'w.r.t.') an issue E, let us ask what would happen (a) if S wanted e to occur, (b) if S wanted not-e to occur, and (c) if S were neutral between e and not-e. If E is the issue of whether or not it rains (at a particular time and place), we would consider whether or not it would rain (a) if S wanted rain, (b) if S wanted non-rain, and (c) if S were neutral between rain and non-rain. For any issue E, there are eight (logically) possible situations S might be in w.r.t. E, each represented by a function that maps attitudes of S vis-à-vis E onto outcomes of E. These eight situations are shown in the table below, in which the following notation is used: '$N(S, e)$' stands for 'S is neutral between e and not-e', '$W(S, e)$' stands for 'S wants e', and '$W(S, -e)$' stands for 'S wants not-e'. The if-thens are subjunctive conditionals. Situation (4), for example, is a situation in which outcome e would occur if S were neutral on the issue, or if S wanted e to occur, but outcome not-e would occur if S wanted not-e to occur.

	If $N(S, e)$ then	If $W(S, e)$ then	If $W(S, -e)$ then
(1)	e	e	e
(2)	e	$-e$	e
(3)	e	$-e$	$-e$
(4)	e	e	$-e$
(5)	$-e$	$-e$	$-e$
(6)	$-e$	$-e$	e
(7)	$-e$	e	e
(8)	$-e$	e	$-e$

In two of these possible cases, viz. (1) and (5), S is impotent w.r.t. the issue. In (1) it would rain no matter how S might feel about it. In other words, S's attitude would make no difference to the outcome, though if he happens to have the 'right' desire, he will get what he wants. In cases (2) and (6) S is even worse off than impotent; he is 'counter-potent'. In these possible cases it would rain if S wanted non-rain and it would not rain if S wanted rain. Cases (3) and (7) are rather anomalous, and I have no name for them. But, like the four previous cases, they are not ones in which S has power w.r.t. the rain. Turning finally to (4) and (8), we find cases in which S does have power w.r.t. the rain. In these cases S would get his way on the issue no matter which outcome he might prefer. A desire for rain would lead to rain and a desire for non-rain would lead to non-rain. The difference between (4) and (8) is that in the former, rain would occur if S were neutral on the issue, whereas in the latter, non-rain would occur if S were neutral. In both cases, however, a desire by S for either outcome would lead to the occurrence of that outcome.

The following analysis of power is suggested by the foregoing.

S has power w.r.t. issue E if and only if

I   1 If S wanted outcome e, then e would occur, and
      2 If S wanted outcome not-e, then not-e would occur.

This analysis, I believe, is very much on the right track. But the following difficulty presents itself. Suppose that S is totally paralyzed and incapable of action. Another person, S^*, has the ability to control the weather; but S does not know of S^*'s existence, and even if he did, he would have no idea how to communicate with him. Unbeknownst to S, however, S^* can detect S's desires by ESP (or by appropriate gadgetry attached to his central nervous system), and S^* has freely decided to make the weather conform with whatever desire S has vis-à-vis the weather. In this case S satisfies (I) w.r.t. the weather, but it is doubtful that we would credit S with power w.r.t. the weather. Although S would get what he wants vis-à-vis the weather, this is not because of anything *he* would *do*.

A refinement in our analysis seems to be called for, a refinement that incorporates the element of action. To formulate this refinement, let us introduce the notion of a *basic act-type*. There are certain types of acts, e.g., raising one's hand, taking a step, and uttering certain sounds, which have the following properties: (a) in ordinary circumstances, if a person wanted to perform such an act, he would perform it, and (b) his ability to perform it is independent of knowledge or information concerning other acts that would have to be performed in order to perform it.[3] In short, a basic act-type is one that a person can do 'at will', an act-type that is 'directly' under his control. Now frequently, in order to achieve a desired outcome, a person has to perform an appropriate sequence of basic acts, and these acts have to be performed at appropriate times. It is necessary, therefore, to attend to temporal matters. First, the issue in question must be clearly specified by indicating its time (i.e., the time of its outcomes). Who will be elected mayor in 1972 is a different issue from who will be elected mayor in 1974; S may have power w.r.t. one of these issues but not the other. Similarly, whether or not it will rain in Ann Arbor on Tuesday is a different issue from whether or not it will rain in Ann Arbor on Wednesday; S's having power w.r.t. one of these issues does not ensure his having power w.r.t. the other. We shall be concerned, then, with the issues that have 'built in' times.[4] This will be indicated by placing the temporal reference in parentheses. Secondly, we need to specify the time at which a person has power w.r.t. an issue. If, at t_1, there are sequences of acts available to S that would lead to each of the outcomes of $E(\text{at } t_{10})$, then S may have power, at t_1, w.r.t. $E(\text{at } t_{10})$. But if S fails to act appropriately between t_1 and t_5, he may no longer have power, at t_5, w.r.t. $E(\text{at } t_{10})$. With these points in mind, we may propose the following analysis of (individual) power.

S has power, at t_1, w.r.t. issue E(at t_n) if and only if

I' 1 There is a sequence of basic act-types such that

   a if S wanted e, then he would perform these acts at appropriate times between t, and t_n, and

   b if S performed these acts at these appropriate times, then e would occur (at t_n);

   2 There is a sequence of basic act-types such that

   a if S wanted not-e, then he would perform these acts at appropriate times between t_1, *and* t_n, and

   b if S performed these acts at these appropriate times, then not-e would occur (at t_n).[5]

Let us see how (I') would apply to the rain example. The issue here is whether or not rain occurs (at t_n). Let us assume that the state of the world (in particular, the meteorological conditions) at t_1 is such that it is going to rain at t_n unless S does certain things between t_1 and t_n. (I assume that the occurrence or nonoccurrence of rain is *determined* by antecedent events, including the acts of S. Determinism will be assumed throughout the paper.) In order to prevent rain, S must disperse the clouds, or evaporate them, and this must be done before t_n. Now there are two possible cases to consider.

Case 1 S is an ordinary fellow who has no way to disperse or evaporate the clouds; in other words, no basic acts of his would lead to the dispersion or evaporation of the clouds prior to t_n. In this case, S does not satisfy (I'). Of course S trivially satisfies the first conjunct of (I'), assuming, at any rate, that he can perform some basic acts. For no matter what sequence of basic acts he performs between t_1 and t_n, it *will* rain at t_n (the rain will not be *caused* by any of his acts, however). But S does not satisfy the second conjunct of (I'), for, *ex hypothesi*, no basic acts S could perform would lead to non-rain at t_n.

Case 2 S possesses a chemical that evaporates rain clouds, and S has an airplane at his disposal that would enable him to spray the chemical onto the clouds (before t_n). Moreover, S knows that the chemical would evaporate the clouds, knows how to fly the plane, and has other requisite pieces of information. In this case, S satisfies the second conjunct of (I') in addition to the first conjunct. There is a sequence of basic acts – viz., acts by which S would place the chemical into the plane, acts by which he would fly the plane into the atmosphere, and acts by which he would spray the chemical onto the clouds – such that (a) if S wanted non-rain he would perform this sequence of acts (at appropriate times), and (b) if S performed them, non-rain would occur (at t_n).

It must be stressed that the conditionals in (I′) are subjunctive conditionals, not *causal* subjunctive conditionals. If they were construed as *causal* conditionals, then even in Case 2 S could not be credited with power w.r.t. E. This is because there is no sequence of basic acts S can perform that would *cause* the occurrence of rain at t_n (although there are many sequences of basic acts he can perform such that, if he performed them, rain would occur at t_n).

It might be argued that the use of causal subjunctives could simplify our analysis; instead of requiring that S be able to obtain *both* outcomes of E, we could merely require that S be able to *cause* (at least) *one* outcome of E. (As long as ordinary subjunctives are employed rather than causal subjunctives, the requirement that *two* outcomes be achievable must be retained; otherwise S would qualify for having power w.r.t. the rain even in Case 1. Using causal conditionals, however, it might be sufficient to require that S be able to cause *one* outcome.) Although reliance on causal conditionals probably would simplify the analysis, I believe it would also prove less illuminating. By relying on ordinary subjunctives only, we shall be forced to take a careful look at problems which might be neglected if we allowed ourselves the luxury of the causal idiom. Causal terminology is especially unhelpful in dealing with the kinds of cases of paramount interest to a theory of power, i.e., cases in which an outcome is a function of the actions of numerous agents. In thinking about distributions of power and degrees of power among many persons and many groups, the use of causal terminology is likely to obscure the crucial questions rather than illuminate them. It seems advisable, therefore, to avoid all reliance on the concept of causation from the outset.

A different possible objection to our analysis of power is that it seems to neglect the most important ingredients of power. In most of the literature on power, such things as wealth, authority, status and similar 'resources' play a crucial role; but they make no appearance whatever in (I′). Is this not a devastating omission? Now although such resources are not explicitly mentioned in our analysis, it should be clear that the satisfaction of (I′) in any particular case depends on precisely such factors. Our analysis makes no reference to the existence of certain chemicals, or the availability of an airplane, but it is just such things that make it true that S has power w.r.t. the rain (at t_n). Similarly, although our analysans makes no explicit reference to institutional hierarchies or to positions of influence, it is just these sorts of things that determine whether a person has power w.r.t. the granting of a government contract. If S has control over a defense contract, this is not simply because he has a certain basic act repertoire; it must be because he occupies a position of authority in the governmental structure, or perhaps because he is in a position to influence officials through credible threats or offers. That these are the sorts of resources that give rise to power, however, does not imply that they ought to be mentioned explicitly in the analysis of power. Indeed, it would be foolish to try to construct an analysis that itemizes relevant resources. For even a single issue, the number and variety of potentially relevant resources is endless; and it is surely wholly impossible to say what resources are necessary and sufficient for issues *in general*. What is important, then, is that an analysans imply the *existence* of an appropriate set of resources, without necessarily characterizing these resources 'intrinsically'. This is what we accomplish in our analysans by the use of subjunctive conditionals.

Our analysis of power may be compared to a conditional analysis of disposition terms like 'soluble' or 'fragile'. In analyzing 'X is soluble in water' as 'If X were immersed in water, it would dissolve', we say nothing specific about the internal structure of X, the structure in virtue of which it is true that X would dissolve if immersed in water. Nevertheless, there must be some actual structure which makes this conditional true. Moreover, we may construe the hypothetical statement 'If X were immersed in water, it would dissolve' as asserting the existence of such a structure.[6] That is, we may construe it as asserting: 'The structure of X (and the structure of water) is such that if X were immersed in water, it would dissolve'. The case of power is quite analogous. In saying that outcome e would occur if S were to perform certain acts, we do not indicate which facts about the world, which resources possessed by S, make this conditional true. Nevertheless, there must be some such facts or resources. Indeed, we may construe our subjunctive conditionals as asserting their existence. That is, we may construe the force of (1)(b) as follows: 'The state of S's resources (or the state of the world) is such that if S performed the indicated sequence of basic acts at appropriate times, then outcome e would occur (at t_n)'. We may say, therefore, that resources such as wealth, authority, reputation, attractiveness, friendship and physical location play the same sort of role vis-à-vis power as molecular structure plays vis-à-vis solubility. It is the possession of such resources that confers power, or, if you like, that *is* power.

The preceding remarks give us insight into the kinds of conditions that must obtain in order that certain outcomes would occur if S performed certain sequences of basic acts. In other words, we gain some insight into the conditions underlying clauses (1)(b) and (2)(b) of (I'). But what of (1)(a) and (2)(a)? What conditions must hold in order that S would select an appropriate sequence of basic acts if he wanted outcome e and in order that S would select an appropriate sequence of basic acts if he wanted outcome not-e? The answer is: S must have appropriate items of knowledge or belief. In order that S select appropriate sequences of basic acts – i.e. sequences that would really lead to the desired outcome – it is not sufficient that S simply *want* that outcome. Unless he has knowledge, or belief, concerning *which* acts would lead to the desired outcome, he might select acts which do not lead to it at all. We can imagine cases, indeed, in which there *are* sequences of basic acts which, if performed by S at appropriate times, would lead to whichever outcome he might desire, and yet where S is *counter-potent* w.r.t. the issue! S might be so confused or misinformed that if he wanted e he would perform acts that would lead to not-e, and if he wanted not-e he would perform acts that would lead to e. Under these circumstances, we would hardly say that S has power w.r.t. E. We may conclude, therefore, that the possession of power w.r.t. an issue depends not only on the possession of physical or social resources, but also on the possession of informational resources. Hence the maxim 'Knowledge is power'.

It must be acknowledged that there are certain uses of the term 'power' – especially as a count-noun – in which informational resources seem irrelevant. To take an example of Rogers Albritton's, a man who is endowed with a capacity to strike people dead by uttering a magic formula can be said to possess this special '*power*' even though he does not know that he has this power, and even though he has no idea what the formula is. Similarly, we may speak of an officer of an organization as having certain powers even if he happens to be ignorant of the fact that he has these powers. In this use of the term 'power', a power simply seems to be a resource of a crucial sort, though not necessarily a resource which is sufficient, by itself, to ensure any particular desired outcome.

Having noted this use, however, I propose henceforth to ignore it. I am interested primarily in the conditions under which a person has power over, or w.r.t., an issue, and the possession of power w.r.t. an issue *does* seem to require informational resources. Suppose S is standing in a large mansion which contains, unknown to S, a hidden button; if this button is pressed, New York City will be destroyed. Suppose, moreover, that there is a sequence of basic acts which, if performed by S, would uncover the button and place him in a position to destroy the city. Does it follow that S has power w.r.t. the destruction of the city (say, in the next ten minutes)? If S has no idea whatever where the button is, and if S has no way of finding out where the button is (in the next ten minutes), then I think it is clear that S does not have power w.r.t. this issue. Thus, the absence of relevant information implies the absence of power.[7]

A precise statement of the required information, however, is difficult to formulate. It is not necessary that S *know*, for each outcome e and not-e, which sequence of basic acts would be appropriate; it is not even necessary that he *believe* – in the sense of *believe it to be more probable than not* – of any sequence that it would lead to the desired outcome. It is sufficient for S to believe, of a certain sequence which happens to be appropriate, that it is *more likely* than any other sequence to lead to the given outcome; this is sufficient even if he thinks that the chances of its leading to that outcome are very small. To introduce some terminology to cover this possibility, we may say that it is sufficient that S '*epistemically* favors' that sequence as a means to that outcome.

Further complications are introduced by temporal considerations. In order for S to have power at t_1 it is not necessary that S be able at t_1 to select an entire sequence of basic acts. If, at t_1, S has a kit for assembling a harpsichord, then he may have power, at t_1, w.r.t. the issue of whether or not there will be a harpsichord in his house at t_n (say, two months later). But there certainly is no entire sequence of basic acts which S epistemically favors, at t_1, as a means to obtaining the outcome of there being a harpsichord in his house at t_n. There are certain basic acts which S epistemically favors as *initial* members of such a sequence, viz., acts that would enable him to read the instruction manual. Moreover, once he performs these initial acts, his reading of the instruction manual will lead him to form beliefs concerning further basic acts to perform. But at no point does he have the entire sequence of appropriate basic acts in mind. Extrapolating from this case, we can say that S would obtain an outcome e, if he wanted it, as long as the following is true:

There is a sequence of basic acts $A_1 \ldots, A_i, \ldots, A_n$ such that

A at t_1 S epistemically favors A_1 as the first act to perform as a means to e,

B for every $i(1 \leq i \leq n-1)$, if S performed the first i members of the sequence from t_1 through t_i (assuming that each act is performed at a single moment), then S would epistemically favor, at t_{i+1}, act A_{i+1} as the next act to perform as a means to e, and

C   if S performed each of the acts A_i at time t_i $(1 \leqslant i \leqslant n)$, then e would occur (at t_n).

In the foregoing discussion I have talked as if the only factors that determine which basic acts S performs are, first, his desire for a particular outcome of E, and, second, his beliefs concerning the various means available to him to secure this outcome. In general, however, other desires and aversions come into play as well, not just S's attitude vis-à-vis the outcomes of E. For example, although S wants e to occur, and although he epistemically favors sequence A^* as a means to e, he may choose a different sequence of basic acts because he expects A^* to be very *costly*, that is, because he thinks A^* will have consequences he wants to avoid. In short, an agent's choice of action normally depends on more than one desire, and since more than one desire is involved, the relative strength of these desires is also an important factor. In the present section, however, I am intentionally neglecting these complications. I am assuming that S's desire for e (or for not-e) is the *only* motivating factor in his selection of a course of action. Since it is the only motivating factor, its strength or intensity is of no significance. If S wants e he will perform whatever acts he epistemically favors as a means to e, and if he wants not-e he will perform whatever acts he epistemically favors as a means to not-e. In section IV I shall drop these simplifying assumptions, but they will be retained until then.

Since our analysis makes central use of subjunctive conditionals, several remarks on their interpretation are in order. My approach to subjunctive conditionals follows the general lines of the analysis proposed by Robert Stalnaker.[8] On this analysis we assess the truth of any conditional 'If A then B' by considering a possible world in which A is true and which otherwise differs minimally from the actual world. A conditional of this form is true if and only if B is true in that possible world. Now if A is true in the actual world, the possible world we select is the actual world; but if A is contrary to fact, we must select some non-actual possible world. The tricky matter here is to select the respects in which this possible world should resemble the actual world and the respects (other than A itself) in which it may differ. In other words, we must decide what, in addition to A, is to be counterfactualized and what is to be held constant.[9] One constraint is that the possible world must be a nomologically consistent world (using the laws of nature of the actual world); but more must be said about the selection of a possible world.

When we are interested in S's power, at t_1, w.r.t. E (at t_n), we begin by counterfactualizing S's desire vis-à-vis E, more specifically, his desire vis-à-vis E *from t_1 through t_n*. While counterfactualizing this desire, however, the following three things are held constant: (1) the basic act repertoire of S, (2) the set of beliefs that S has at t_1, and (3) S's resources at t_1. The notion of resources is here construed very broadly, to include not only physical conditions, such as the presence of clouds, but also the acts and inclinations of other persons (*at t_1*). Thus, to say that we hold constant the *resources S* has at t_1 is to say, roughly, that we hold constant *the state of the entire world at t_1* – with the exception, of course, of S's own desire vis-à-vis E and whatever is nomologically implied by that desire (e.g., the state of his brain). Now once we have counterfactualized S's desire vis-à-vis E, other counterfactualizations will have to be made in order to obtain a nomologically consistent world. In particular, if S's desire from t_1 through t_n is different from his desire vis-à-vis E in the actual world, the basic acts he performs from t_1 through t_n will presumably be different (at least many of these acts). Moreover, if these acts are different, various other events that are causally connected with these acts will be different. Thus, once we have been forced to counterfactualize the basic acts S performs, we shall also have to counterfactualize numerous other events, including, perhaps, the acts of other agents and the beliefs S himself forms after t_1 (which in turn influence his subsequent acts). Of paramount importance is a possible change in the outcome of E. Since we are interested in S's power w.r.t. E, the crucial question is whether the counterfactual hypothesis that S desires, say, outcome e nomologically implies the performance of basic acts which nomologically imply the occurence of outcome e (at t_n).

Our discussion of individual power has heretofore assumed that every issue has exactly two possible outcomes; and, working on this assumption, we have maintained that a person has power w.r.t. an issue only if he can obtain *each* of these possible outcomes. Both of these assumptions, however, are too restrictive. Most of the interesting issues in the social or political arena admit of more than two possible outcomes, and when this is so, it is not necessary, in order for a person to have power, that he be able to obtain *each* of the various possible outcomes. Suppose, for example, that money is to be allocated for a certain project, and there are 50 possible amounts that might be allocated: $1 million, $2 million, . . . , $49 million, $50 million. Now suppose that although S is not able to ensure *whichever* of these 50 allocations he might desire, he is in a position to ensure any of the first 20 of these allocations. In this case, S clearly has power w.r.t. the issue of how much money is to be allocated for the project. On the other hand, if S is in a position to ensure any of the first 40 of these allocations, rather than any of the first 20, then S has even more power w.r.t. this issue.

To accommodate this sort of case, we proceed as follows. First, instead of *defining* an issue in terms of a partition of outcomes, we think of a *single* issue as subject to a *variety* of different possible partitions. For example, we may take the single issue of *the weather* (at a particular time and place) and partition it into any of the following partitions, where each partition contains outcomes that are mutually exclusive and jointly exhaustive:

1 (a) rain, (b) non-rain;
2 (a) rain, (b) snow, (c) hail, (d) anything else;
3 (a) sunny, (b) cloudy, (c) precipitation;
4 (a) to precipitation, (b) less than an inch of precipitation, (c) an inch or more of precipitation; etc.[10]

Once we have the idea of different partitions of the same issue, we can make the following generalizations. If there is any partition of E into two or more mutually exclusive and jointly exhaustive outcomes such that S can obtain the occurrence of *at least two* of the outcomes of this partition, then S has at least *some* power w.r.t. E. Moreover, consider any partition P of E into possible outcomes $e_1, e_2, \ldots, e_n$, where $n \geq 2$. (For simplicity, I confine our attention to finite partitions.) Call the set of these n possible outcomes E^*. If we wish to compare S's power w.r.t. E in one possible world (where S possesses certain resources) with S's power w.r.t. E in another possible world (where he possesses different resources), we proceed as follows. We consider subsets E' and E'' of E^*, where E'' contains at least two members. Then if the following three conditions are satisfied, S has *more power* w.r.t. E in possible world W_2 than he has w.r.t. E in W_1: (a) in W_1 subset E' is the largest subset of E^* such that S can obtain whichever member he chooses, (b) in W_2 subset E'' is the largest subset of E^* such that S can obtain whichever member he chooses, and (c) E' is a proper subset of E''.[11]

II   COLLECTIVE POWER

I have focused until now on the power of a single person, but this barely touches the more important complexities in the topic of power. Most issues of interest in the social arena are issues in which many persons and many groups have some degree of power. Moreover, we are usually inclined to say, in such cases, that some of these people or groups have more power than others. Nothing I have said thus far, however, sheds light on these matters. I have said nothing concerning the power of groups of people, nor anything about comparisons of power between two or more persons (or groups). An adequate theory of power, obviously, must deal with these matters.

The problems that lurk in these areas can be conveniently introduced by a brief passage from an article in *New York Magazine* entitled 'The ten most powerful men in New York'. Having listed his choice for the ten most powerful men in New York, the author, Dick Schaap, writes as follows:

> I offer only one theory in defense of the above list: if all ten men agreed upon the wisdom and necessity of a single, specific act affecting New York City, that act would take place, no matter how the rest of the city's eight million people felt.[12]

In passing, we may note two obvious deficiencies in Schaap's suggestion, at least if it is regarded as a criterion for determining the ten most powerful men. First, it is too strong. It is not necessary that the ten most powerful men would *always* get their way despite the attitudes of *all* other New Yorkers. Secondly, the test does not ensure uniqueness. A number of different groups of ten men might each satisfy the test.

But let us reflect on other features of the test. It is noteworthy that Schaap's test does not require any one of the ten to be able to obtain outcomes *by himself*; that is, it does not require that there be any issue such that at least one of the ten would obtain different outcomes of that issue if he wanted them. The test can be satisfied even if each of the ten is only a *member* of a group whose *joint* preferences would determine the outcomes of issues. This seems perfectly appropriate if we are considering the power of the *group*. But by calling these men 'the ten most powerful', Schaap also implies that *each* of them has considerable power. This raises an interesting question for the account of power given in section I. If neither of two persons can *individually* get what he wants, but if the two of them can *jointly* get what they want, can either of them be credited *as a single person* with power w.r.t. the issue? This point requires an investigation both into the nature of group or collective power and into the relationship between collective power and individual power.

Another noteworthy feature of Schaap's 'theory' is the phrase 'no matter how the rest of the city's eight million people felt'. To complete Schaap's test of a proposed list of ten men, we must not only hypothesize that all ten agree in supporting a given outcome, but we must also hypothesize that all other New Yorkers oppose that outcome. Only if the ten men would achieve their outcome despite everyone else's opposition would it be true that they would achieve it 'no matter how the rest of the city's eight million people felt', and only then would they qualify, on Schaap's test, as the ten most powerful. Schaap's requirement is reminiscent of a similar stipulation made by Max Weber, who defined 'power' as 'the probability that one actor within a social relationship will be in a position to carry out his own will *despite resistance* . . . ',[13] and of C. Wright Mills's definition, 'By the powerful we mean, of course, those who are able to realize their will, *even if others resist it*'.[14] Our own analysis of power has made no reference to the resistance or opposition, either actual or hypothetical, of other persons. The place of this idea in an account of power must therefore be explored.

In this section, however, we confine our attention to collective power. Suppose that you and I, both healthy and reasonably normal men, are standing behind a stalled Buick. If either of us alone pushes at it, the car will not budge; but if we both push simultaneously, it will move. Let E be the issue of the movement of the Buick (in the next several seconds) and let E be partitioned into two outcomes: (e) it moves, and (not-e) it does not move. If both of us want outcome e to occur, then we shall both push at the car and outcome e will take place. If both of us want not-e, neither of us will push and not-e will take place. Thus, if we jointly desire either outcome, that outcome will occur. This is a good reason to conclude that the two of us have *collective power* w.r.t. issue E. It appears, however, that neither of us has individual power w.r.t. E. True enough, if one of us wanted not-e, he would ensure that not-e would occur even if the other wanted e (or was neutral on the issue). But if only one of us wanted outcome e, while the other wanted not-e, the one who preferred e would not succeed in getting his way. It does not seem to be true of either of us, therefore, that for at least *two* outcomes of E, he would get his way on each outcome if he wanted that outcome. Actually, this conclusion is too hasty, as we shall see below. There is no doubt, however, that we must distinguish between collective power and individual power, and that collective power deserves study in its own right.

An analysis of collective power can easily be constructed along the lines of our analysis of individual power. For simplicity we confine our attention to two-outcome partitions.

A group of persons $S_1, \ldots, S_i, \ldots, S_m$ have collective power, at t_1, w.r.t. issue E (at t_n) if and only if

II 1 There is a set of sequences of basic act-types, a sequence for each person S_i, such that

      a if each person S_i wanted outcome e to occur, each would perform his respective sequence of acts at appropriate times between t_1 and t_n, and

      b if each person S_i performed his sequence at appropriate times, then e would occur (at t_n);

II 2 There is a set of sequences of basic act-types, a sequence for each person S_i such that

      a if each person S_i wanted outcome not-e to occur, each would perform his respective sequence of acts at appropriate times between t_1 and t_n, and

      b if each person S_i performed his sequence at appropriate times, then not-e would occur (at t_n).

Paralleling the case of individual power, there are two kinds or classes of resources that are relevant to the possession of collective power. First, informational resources are needed to satisfy clauses (1)(a) and (2)(a) of the analysis. Secondly, non-informational resources of various sorts are needed to satisfy clauses (1)(b) and (2)(b). Nothing especially distinctive is true of the class of non-informational resources, but some attention to informational (or epistemic) resources should be instructive.

In collective action toward a common goal, coordination is usually required in the selection of mutually supportive sequences of acts. For me to choose an appropriate sequence I may have to know what other members of the group are going to do; and similarly for each of them. Without information of this sort we may act discordantly despite good intentions. Often, therefore, acts performed in order to achieve a given outcome are designed to acquire information about future acts of partners in the undertaking. The nature of coordinative activity is a fascinating subject, which need not be expanded upon here.[15] It is (partly) the need for coordination, however, that makes the degree of organization or structural delineation of a group contribute to its power. An established pattern of division of labor facilitates the mutual selection of appropriate courses of action. The political power of lobbies and pressure groups, as opposed to that of random collections of individuals (e.g., until recently, consumers), is partly a function of this factor.

Two aspects of the problem of coordination should be distinguished. First, I may need information about the acts of others to decide *which* acts would be appropriate for me to perform. Secondly, even if I know which acts of mine are the ones most likely to lead to the desired outcome, I may need to know what others are going to do in order to assess *how likely* it is that the performance of these acts will be followed by the outcome. In particular, if I believe that others will not 'do their part', and if I believe that it will be very costly for me to perform my most appropriate sequence of acts, then even if I know which sequence of acts would be most appropriate for me to perform (as a means to the desired outcome), I may choose not to perform them. Admittedly, this consideration introduces the element of cost, which we resolved to abstract from until section IV. Nevertheless, it is sufficiently important in this context that it should not be ignored.

Suppose that a small group of bandits are holding up a train containing a large number of passengers. How shall we assess the collective power of the passengers w.r.t. the issue of whether or not they will be robbed? Suppose that the bandits 'have the drop' on the passengers, but that there is a set of sequences of acts, a sequence for each passenger, such that if they performed these sequences of acts, they would disarm the bandits (with no harm to themselves) and foil the robbery. Assume further that each passenger knows which acts would be the most appropriate ones for him to perform as a means to foiling the robbery. This is not enough to ensure that all would perform these acts if all wanted the robbery to be foiled. The rub, of course, is that each passenger has little reason to believe (indeed, has strong reason to disbelieve) that enough other passengers will do their part. Since, for each passenger, it would be very costly if he did his part (e.g., started to disarm the bandit nearest him) while few others did theirs, each passenger would refrain from doing these acts, and the robbery would succeed. A similar problem arises in assessing the power of a large group of slaves over a small group of masters. If all the slaves acted in unison, they would overwhelm their masters. But it does not follow that they have much (or any) collective power over their masters. Like the train passengers, the problem for the slaves is that each is insufficiently confident that rebellious action on his part would be supported by others. There is an important respect, then, in which 'faith is power'. To the extent that members of a group have greater confidence in the reliability of their partners (and hence greater confidence in the efficacy of their own acts as part of the larger group) the group itself has more power, or is more likely to have at least *some* power w.r.t. a selected issue.

With a clearer grasp of the notion of collective power, let us next look more closely at the relationship between collective and individual power. In our discussion of the Buick example it was said that this is a case where you and I have collective power w.r.t. its movement but where neither of us has individual power w.r.t. its movement. Closer examination shows, however, that this is not unconditionally true: it depends on further specification of the example. Suppose, first, that you are not going to push at the Buick in the next few seconds, and that there are no acts I could perform that would induce you to push. In that case, there is no sequence of basic acts I could perform that would lead to the car's moving (in the next few seconds). Hence, it is correct to say that I lack individual power w.r.t. the issue. But suppose now that, as a matter of fact, you *are* going to push at the Buick in the next few seconds (and suppose that you have no inclination *not* to push in case I push). In that case, (I') licenses us to say that I *do* have individual power w.r.t. the issue, for your act of pushing serves as a 'resource' of mine. If I wanted the car to move I would push at it, and, given your pushing as a resource, this would lead to the car's moving. If I wanted the car not to move, I would not push it, and in this case, despite your pushing, it would not move. Thus, whichever outcome I wanted would occur.

This example brings out the true contrast between collective power and individual power (as we have defined these notions). The difference between them lies in the conditions that we counterfactualize in each case. In making a judgement about the individual power of a person S at t_1, we begin by counterfactualizing his desire (from t_1 through t_n) and his desire only. The only other counterfactualizations that we allow are ones that follow from, or are necessitated by, this initial counterfactualization. In particular, we do not counterfactualize the desires or acts of other persons unless those desires and acts would be affectred by the difference in S's desire. In making a judgement about the collective power at t_1 of a *group* of persons, we begin differently. We begin by counterfactualizing *at the outset* the desires of all of the members of the group. We ask what would happen if they *all* wanted outcome e (from t_1 through t_n) and what would happen if they *all* wanted outcome not-e (from t_1 through t_n). Thus, in individual power we consider all persons other than S purely as 'resources' (or liabilities) of his; in collective power we consider all persons outside the *group* purely as resources.

Let us return to the case where you and I have collective power w.r.t. the movement of the Buick but neither of us has individual power (this is the case where neither of us is *in fact* going to push, but where the car would move if we both wanted it to move). According to the analysis of section I it should be concluded that neither of us has any power w.r.t. the issue; for it was implied in section I that a person has power w.r.t. an issue only if he has *individual* power w.r.t. it. This assumption, however, must now be called into question. As noted earlier, Schaap's formula implicitly denies it; for Schaap's formula allows a person to be one of the ten most powerful men in New York simply by being a member of a group that has collective power. What Schaap's formula suggests, then, is some sort of *distributive* principle: if a group of persons has collective power w.r.t. an issue, then every member of the group has power w.r.t. the issue. This formulation, however, is too strong. If group G has collective power w.r.t. E, another group G' can always be formed by adding to G some randomly selected, irrelevant person; and this new group, G', will also have collective power w.r.t. E. But we do not want to say of any randomly selected person that he has power w.r.t. E. A qualification is needed, therefore, to the effect that each member must be *non-dispensable* w.r.t. E. This notion can be explained as follows. If there is at least one outcome of E such that (a) if all members of G wanted that outcome it would occur, and (b) if all members of G except S wanted that outcome, whereas S opposed it, it would not occur, then S is a non-dispensable member of .G w.r.t. E. In the Buick case, for example, you and I have collective power w.r.t. the issue, and each of us is a non-dispensable member of this group (w.r.t. this issue). We can now formulate the following principle.

A person S has some power w.r.t. issue E if there is some group G such that S is a non-dispensable member of G w.r.t. E and the members of G have collective power w.r.t. E.

This principle proves useful in a variety of cases. In the Buick case, for example, although neither of us has individual power w.r.t. the issue, it seems plausible to say that each of us has some power, i.e. that neither of us is powerless w.r.t. it. The new principle licenses us to say this.

The principle also permits us to account for the power of each member of a legislature. To illustrate, consider an assembly of 100 legislators, in which 51 votes are required to pass a proposal and 50 to defeat it. Let E be the issue of whether a particular bill is passed and let us assume that the actual vote is 75 in favor and 25 opposed. Consider legislator S who in fact voted for the bill. Did he have power w.r.t. E? Assume that S did not have individual power, for the bill would have passed even if he had opposed it. Was *S* a non-dispensable member of a group which had collective power w.r.t. *E*? Yes. Let group *G* consist of 25 members of the assembly, including *S*, each of whom actually voted for the bill. Then, holding *constant* the attitudes of the 25 original opponents of the bill and the remaining 50 supporters, we can say that if all members of *G* (including *S*) wanted the bill to be passed, it would have been passed, and if all members of *G* (including *S*) wanted the bill to be defeated, it would have been defeated. Thus, *G* had collective power w.r.t. *E*. But if all members of *G except for S* wanted the bill defeated, whereas *S* wanted it passed, then it would *not* have been defeated. thus, *S* was a non-dispensable member of *G* w.r.t. *E*, and hence he had some power w.r.t. *E*.

Consider next a rather different case. Let E be the issue of whether Brown will be alive at noon today. At 11:00 a.m. Smith has a loaded gun in his hand, aimed at Brown, and Smith has the requisite beliefs such that he would kill Brown before noon if he wanted Brown dead and he would not kill Brown if he wanted him alive. A third man, Jones, is also in a position to kill Brown by noon. Moreover, Jones is resolved to kill Brown before noon if (and only if) Smith does not kill Brown. Finally, asume that Smith cannot influence Jones's action in this matter. Now in this situation we are surely inclined to say that Smith has some power w.r.t. *E*. According to the account of individual power, though, Smith does not have individual power (at 11:00) w.r.t. *E*.[16] Given the facts concerning Jones, it turns out that there is nothing Smith can do that would lead to Brown's being alive at noon; so Smith is impotent w.r.t. *E*, for Brown will be dead at noon no matter what Smith wants or does about it.

Using the new principle, however, we can account for the intuition that Smith does have at least some power w.r.t. *E*. For Smith is a non-dispensable member of a group (viz., Smith and Jones) which has collective power w.r.t. *E*. Smith and Jones have collective power w.r.t. *E* because if they both wanted Brown dead at noon that outcome would ensue, and if they both wanted Brown to be alive at noon they would perform acts leading to that outcome. Smith is a non-dispensable member of this group w.r.t. *E* because if Jones wanted Brown to be alive while Smith opposed it, then Brown would not be alive (at noon).

III   CONFLICT AND COMPARISONS OF POWER

We turn now to the significance of conflict or opposition in the criteria of power offered by Schaap, Weber and Mills. Schaap, it will be recalled, characterized the ten most powerful men in New York as the ten that would get their way no matter how the rest of the city's people felt about it. Whether or not this criterion is adequate, its rationale is clear. To determine relative amounts of power between people (or groups), it is appropriate to ask who would 'get his way', i.e. who would get his preferred outcome, in case of conflict. Schaap does not suggest (nor do Weber and Mills) that power is present only in situations of actual conflict or opposition. What is suggested, though, is that comparisons of power can be made by ascertaining what would happen *if* there were conflict or opposition. Since comparisons of power are of central concern, let us reflect on this matter. I shall not try to deal with the relative power of groups, nor with the relative power of three or more individuals. I shall confine my attention to comparisons between two individuals (although third-parties will have to be mentioned to clarify the nature of the two-person case).

Let us begin with an example. Jones and I are both standing next to an open door. Jones is a muscular 250-pounder and I a 145-pounder. Let E be the issue of whether or not the door remains open. If both Jones and I can rely on raw strength alone, it is pretty clear that he has more power than I do w.r.t. E. For there is a sequence of basic acts Jones can perform to ensure, no matter what basic acts I perform, that the door will stay open; and there is a sequence of acts Jones can perform that would ensure that the door will be closed, no matter what basic acts I perform. (Here we rely on the fact that Jones's basic act repertoire exceeds mine: he can exert a greater amount of pressure on the door than I can.) Thus, assuming Jones has the requisite beliefs, the door would stay open if Jones wanted it open, no matter how I felt about it; and the door would be closed if Jones wanted it closed, no matter how I might feel about it. Should Jones and I have opposing preferences, then, Jones's preferred outcome would be the one to occur.

In this example Jones can perform a certain sequence of basic acts such that, no matter what basic acts I perform, the door will stay open; and similarly for the door being closed. Is this sort of relationship generally necessary in order that one person have more power than another w.r.t. an issue? Restricting our attention to partitions with two outcomes, this would be generalized as follows: S_1 has more power than S_2 w.r.t. E only if, for each of the two outcomes, there exists a sequence of basic acts S_1 can perform such that, for *any* sequence of basic acts S_2 might perform, the performance of the sequence by S_1 would lead to this outcome. Such a requirement is clearly too strong. It demands the existence of a single course of action for S_1 that would 'win' in the face of all possible responses from S_2. A weaker requirement is therefore needed. The condition that naturally suggests itself next is this: For each of the two outcomes, no matter what basic acts S_2 might perform, there is a sequence of basic acts S_1 could perform that would lead to this outcome. This condition is *too weak*. The statement that for any course of action by S_2 there is a 'winning' course of action for S_1 is compatible with the statement that for any course of action by S_1 there is a 'winning' course of action for S_2.[17] So this requirement would not provide even prima facie grounds for thinking that S_1 has more power than S_2.

The next natural suggestion is to appeal to the game-theoretic notion of a winning strategy. What would be required is that for each outcome, *e* and not-*e*, there be a strategy or function F which assigns to S_1 an initial move and which, for every set of possible moves of S_2, assigns to S_1 a succeeding move (or moves), such that if S_1 were to abide by this function, that outcome would occur. In fact, however, even this requirement is too strong. The existence of a winning strategy for S_1 implies that S_1 can win no matter what S_2 does, in other words, even if S_2 adopts the best strategy available to him. But suppose that S_2 does not have information that would lead him to adopt (what is in fact) his best strategy. Then S_1 may be in a position to 'beat' S_2 even if S_1 lacks a *winning* strategy (i.e. a strategy that would win for S_1 against *all* possible strategies of S_2). In fact, S_2 might even have a winning strategy against S_1; yet if S_2 does not know what this strategy is, and has no way to find out, then S_1 may have more power than S_2 in spite of this. His having more power would simply consist in the fact that he would get his preferred outcome (by an appropriate course of action) if the two of them had opposing preferences.

Let us abandon the attempt to specify in detail what combinations of strategy-and-information would be necessary and sufficient for S_1 to have more power than S_2. Instead, we can give a simple analysis of this notion that parallels our earlier analyses of individual power and collective power.

At t_1 S_1 has more power than S_2 w.r.t. issue E (at t_n) if and only if:

III   1   There is a pair of sequences of basic act-types, Σ_1 and Σ_2, such that
         a   if S_1 wanted outcome *e* and if S_2 wanted outcome not-*e*, then S_1 would perform Σ_1 at certain times between t_1 and t_n and S_2 would perform Σ_2 at certain times between t_1 and t_n, and

b if S_1 were to perform Σ_1 at these times and if S_2 were to perform Σ_2 at these times, then outcome e would occur (at t_n);

2 There is a pair of sequences of basic act-types, Σ'_1 and Σ'_2, such that

a if S_1 wanted outcome not-e and if S_2 wanted outcome e, then S_1 would perform Σ'_1 at certain times between t_1 and t_n and S_2 would perform Σ'_2 at certain times between t_1 and t_n, and

b if S_1 were to perform Σ'_1 at these times and if S_2 were to perform Σ'_2 at these times, then outcome not-e would occur (at t_n).

We might wish to add clauses to the analysis to ensure that S_1 would get his preferred outcome if S_2 were neutral on the issue, but this refinement may be neglected. A far more important refinement concerns the elaboration of the analysis to cover partitions of three or more outcomes.[18] But this complication will also have to be omitted here.

As in the case of collective action, selections of sequences of acts by actors with opposing interests are typically interdependent. If S_1 and S_2 realize that they have conflicting preferences, each will be guided in his choice of action by whatever information he has about the acts his opponent has performed or plans to perform in the future. As before, informational resources are crucial in determining the acts one would select, and therefore important in determining one's relative power.

In our door example we imagined that both Jones and I rely on our own strength alone. In characteristic situations in the political sphere, however, relative power depends on other assets, including positions of influence over other persons that stem from authority, kinship, personal magnetism, or other relationships. In seeking to achieve one's ends in opposition to others, one frequently performs acts designed to call forth aid from other persons. These acts might be orders, commands, or simple requests for help. To illustrate the importance of this, let us revise the door example to include a brawny and faithful companion of mine who is always willing and able to assist me. In this amended case it is no longer true that Jones would get his preferred outcome if his preference were in opposition to mine. If I wanted the door to be closed, for example, I would perform basic acts by which I would ask my friend for help, and then I would perform acts of pushing at the door which, in unison with my friend's pushing, would ensure that the door be closed even if Jones tries to keep it open. Thus, given my brawny and faithful companion, I would get whichever outcome I would prefer on the door issue, no matter how Jones might feel about it.

Is it true, however, that I have more power than Jones w.r.t. *E*? There may be a strong temptation to deny this. It might well be argued that it is only the power of the *two* of us, my companion and me, that exceeds the power of Jones. This view can be defended by pointing out that if we are considering *hypothetical* desires, and *hypothetical* sequences of acts, we should also consider hypothetical desires and acts by the companion. If we do this, we shall quickly see that I do not have the ability, given *any* desires and acts by my companion, to beat Jones at whatever he tries to do. I could be said to have this ability only on the assumption that the companion's desires and acts are wholly contingent on mine. But why should this contingency or dependency be assumed: Admittedly, I introduced the example by saying that the companion is willing to do my bidding, and it would violate this stipulation to hypothesize that I ask him for help but that he does not desire (on the whole) to do what I ask him to do. But why should such a hypothesis not be permitted? In talking about power we are already in the business of making counterfactual assumptions about various people's desires and acts. Why not make counterfactual assumptions about the companion's desires and acts as well? The problem, in short, is this: When making comparisons of power between individuals (or, indeed, in making non-comparative judgements of power), what should be regarded as fixed and what should be regarded as a candidate for counterfactualization?

The answer I propose is that it all depends on what sorts of power comparisons we wish to make. If we wish to compare Jones and myself, then our desires and acts are subject to counterfactualization, while the desires and acts of everyone else are to be taken as contingent on ours – at least, if there is anything in the actual world that makes their desires and acts contingent on ours. In other words, in comparing the power of Jones and myself, the *initial* changes we make in constructing different possible worlds concern the desires of Jones and myself; the only other changes that are made are ones nomologically required by these initial changes. On the other hand, if we wish to compare the power of Jones, myself, and my companion, then we would make *initial* counterfactualizations involving my companion's desires as well. Because of these different counterfactuals, of course, different assessments of power are going to be made. There is nothing inconsistent or paradoxical about this, however; it merely reflects the fact that whenever judgements about power are made, certain things are subjected to counterfactualization and others held fixed. A judgement about a person's power that makes certain counterfactualizations cannot be expected to be identical with a judgement that makes different (initial) counterfactualizations. Within certain limits, however, a number of different counterfactual assumptions may legitimately be made.[19]

To illustrate these points consider a departmental secretary who is given substantial responsibility and initiative by the chairman. If we ask about the secretary's power w.r.t. a variety of issues (e.g. assignment of offices, teaching hours, classrooms, etc.) it is not so clear what should be said. On the one hand we may hold fixed, or constant, the chairman's propensity to go along with the secretary's decisions; in other words, we regard the chairman's trust as one of the secretary's *resources*. If so, we would attribute considerable power to the secretary. On the other hand, we may also compare the secretary's power with that of the chairman; we might ask what would happen if the secretary wanted one outcome and the chairman preferred a contrary one. Normally the chairman would win in such cases (let us suppose), and hence the secretary's power is less than the chairman's.

I think we can see from this that a clear, overall picture of someone's power (w.r.t. a given issue) demands a consideration of more than his *individual* power (as defined in section I); it also requires attention to his power *relative* to other persons (and groups of persons). This is a point that is implicit in Weber's and Mills' characterizations of power as the ability to get one's way *despite* (possible) *resistance*. That individual power by itself does not give us the whole story is evident in the following example. Suppose that S^* has a rain-making machine, and this gives him power w.r.t. the noon-time weather (since, in the natural course of events, it would not rain at noon). Suppose, in addition, that if S were humbly to beg and plead with S^* to make rain for him (S), then S^* would accede to S's wishes. If so, then according to our analysis of 'individual power', S has individual power w.r.t. the noon-time weather. But clearly, if S's only way of affecting the weather is by throwing himself on S^*'s mercy, we would not be inclined to credit S with much power w.r.t. the weather. This can be explained in terms of our theory by appeal to a comparison of power between S and S^*. It is obvious that S^*'s power w.r.t. the weather exceeds that of S. And this must be taken seriously in one's overall appraisal of S's power w.r.t. the weather.

An important problem arises here, however. Suppose that S is able to influence S^* to use his rain-making machine, not by *pleading* with S^*, but by *threatening* him with dire consequences should he (S^*) refuse to employ the machine to make rain. Here we would say that S has quite a lot of power w.r.t. the weather, more, at any rate, than in the previous example. This difference, however, cannot be captured by our account of comparative power, at least not by the account as it stands now. For even in this case our account of comparative power would have us say that S^* has more power than S w.r.t. the weather. This is because *if S^* wanted non-rain on the whole* – despite S's threat – then non-rain would occur.[20] What this shows is that our analysis of comparative power must be supplemented or refined in some further way. As our discussion intimates, the needed refinement concerns the element of *cost*. The difference between pleading and threatening is that the latter imposes (prospective) *costs* on S^* which the former does not (at least not such heavy costs). By making use of the notion of cost, we can hope to develop an account of comparative power that will handle the difference we have detected.

<h3 style="text-align:center">IV   COST AND DEGREES OF POWER</h3>

The necessity of incorporating the element of cost into our theory was acknowledged early in the paper but postponed until now. Heretofore we have assumed that the only factor motivating the choice of a person's action is his desire or aversion for outcomes of issue E. As noted earlier, though, this assumption is unrealistic. The performance of a sequence of acts often leads to undesired consequences; at a minimum, it typically involves the expenditure of valuable resources or assets. The performance of a sequence of acts, then, involves some *cost*. Now although a person may want outcome e, and although he may believe that the performance of sequence Σ is the only way for him to get e, he may decide not to perform Σ if the expected cost of performing it exceeds the benefit he would get from e. A directly related point we have neglected is the fact that a person can want an outcome to a greater or lesser degree. We have assumed until now that a person either wants e, wants not-e, or is neutral between them; we have not worried about the strength (actual or hypothetical) of a desire. Once the element of cost is introduced, however, strengths of desire and aversion must be included as well, for the choice of courses of action will depend on whether or not the value of an outcome *exceeds* the (expected) cost of obtaining it.

Introduction of the element of cost has immediate bearing on power. As we have seen, the expected cost of a sequence of action may dissuade a person from performing that sequence even if he wants the outcome to which (he believes) it will lead. It follows, therefore, that the cost of a sequence is a determining factor of whether or not a person *would* get a certain outcome *if* he wanted it (to such-and-such a degree). Hence, it is a determining factor of his power w.r.t. an issue.

The importance of cost in the analysis of power was first stressed by John C. Harsanyi.[21] He illustrates the idea as follows.

It is misleading to say that two political candidates have the same power over two comparable constituencies if one needs much more electioneering effort and expenditure to achieve a given majority, even if in the end both achieve the same majorities; or that one can achieve favorable treatment by city officials only at the price of large donations to party funds, while the other can get the same favorable treatment just for the asking.

Harsanyi stresses how inaccurate an analysis of power can be if it disregards the costs to an agent.

For instance, suppose that an army commander becomes a prisoner of enemy troops, who try to force him at gun point to give a radio order to his army units to withdraw from a certain area. He may well have the power to give a contrary order, both in the sense of having the physical ability to do so and in the sense of there being a very good chance of his order being actually obeyed by his army units – but he can use this power only at the cost of his life . . . [I]t would clearly be very misleading in this situation to call him a powerful individual in the same sense as before his capture.

To generalize this point, we can say that if it is extremely costly for an agent to obtain certain outcomes of an issue – e.g. if it would require the sacrifice of his life, health or fortune – then he cannot be said to have much power w.r.t. that issue. The amount of power an agent has w.r.t. an issue is thus inversely proportional to the cost of obtaining outcomes of that issue.

The element of cost, then, enters into the analysis of power at the level of individual power. But it is even more important when we turn to comparisons of power, that is, when we consider what would happen in situations of conflict. When two persons have opposing preferences concerning an issue, one of them (or both) frequently tries to get his preferred outcome by the use of threats or sanctions designed to *deter* his opponent from performing certain acts. The intended effect of a threat is not to make the opponent literally *unable* to perform a certain sequence of basic acts; rather it is to make that sequence more *costly* for him to perform. To the extent that the ability to deter people by successful threats is an essential ingredient in the possession of power, it is vital that we incorporate the element of cost into our theory. How, exactly, may this element be incorporated?

The first problem is how to construe the notion of cost and how to measure it. The most promising approach, I think, is suggested by the economist's notion of opportunity cost. To say that the achievement of outcome *e* would be costly for *S* is to say that the activity by which *S* might obtain *e* would have consequences that are less desirable, or have lower utility, than an alternative course of action open to *S*. If obtaining outcome *e* would require an expenditure of money, then the cost of obtaining *e* is a function of the utility that would have accrued to *S* from using the money in some alternative way. If *e* can only be achieved at the cost of imprisonment, then the cost of obtaining *e* is a function of the difference in utility between going to prison and remaining a free man. It is evident that in determing the cost of an activity we must refer to the agent's desires, or utility assignments, for various outcomes. In this context, though, we consider the *actual* desires of the agent, not hypothetical desires. True, we continue to regard desires vis-à-vis the outcomes of the issue in question (*e* and not-*e*) as subject to counterfactualization. But other desires are held constant (at least so far as this is compatible with whatever counterfactualization is made).[22] Assume that a Senator can obtain passage of a certain bill only if he engages in activity that would cost him his reelection. If he is in fact highly averse to losing the election, then the cost would be very high, and we shall say that his power w.r.t. the passage of the bill is correspondingly reduced. But if he in fact cares very little about reelection, then his cost is not so great, and he has more power w.r.t. the passage of the bill.

Problems of cost become complicated when we turn to comparisons of power, and hence to (potential) conflict situations. The complications here are twofold. First, both agents, S_1 and S_2, may be in a position to threaten his opponent with certain penalties, thereby imposing costs on the opponent. Secondly, however, the activity of posing these threats, or of making them credible, may be costly to the threatener himself. In assessing the relative power of S_1 and S_2, therefore, all of the following must be combined: (1) the costs that S_1 can impose on possible courses of action by S_2, (2) the costs *to* S_1 of imposing these costs on S_2, (3) the costs that S_2 can impose on possible courses of action by S_1, and (4) the costs *to* S_2 of imposing these costs on S_1.[23]

To combine these elements and incorporate them into our theory of power, let us make use of matrices resembling those of game theory. In constructing such matrices the following assumptions will be adopted. (1) Issue E is partitioned, as usual, into two outcomes, e and not-e. (2) Two agents, Row and Column, have various sequences of basic acts open to them. For simplicity we depict only three sequences of acts for each agent. (3) It is assumed that inter-personal assignments of utility can be made. (4) A three-by-three matrix, like matrix 1, gives information on three subjects. First, it says what outcome would occur if Row and Column were to choose certain sequence of acts. This outcome is listed in the center of each box of the matrix. Matrix 1 says, for example, that if Row were to choose r_2 and Column were to choose c_3, then outcome e would occur. Secondly, the entry in the lower left-hand corner of each box indicates the cost to Row of the corresponding pair of sequences of acts. Thirdly, the entry in the upper right-hand corner of each box indicates the cost to Column of that pair of courses of action. (5) To ascertain the cost of a pair of activities to a given agent, say Row, we proceed as follows. We begin by *ignoring* all utilities assigned by Row to the outcomes of E. We next consider the (expected) consequences *apart* from e and not-e themselves, of the various alternative sequences of acts open to Row. These consequences might include the expenditure of a certain amount of money and energy, or it might include the commitment of a certain item of patronage, or it might include the undergoing of certain penalties or sanctions.[24] We then select, among all the alternatives open to Row, the sequence(s) of acts that would yield Row the highest utility. This sequence of acts has *zero* (opportunity) cost, and hence the numeral zero is inserted as the entry for Row in each box corresponding to that sequence of action.[25] To determine the cost entry for Row in all other boxes of the matrix, we compare the utility that would accrue to him from each combination of courses of action by Row and Column with the (zero) utility of his best alternative. This *difference* in utility is the cost to Row of that combination of activities, and it is inserted in his corner as a negative quantity. (6) Finally, it is assumed that each agent knows what the outcomes and costs would be (both to himself and to his opponent) of all possible combinations of sequences of acts.

To illustrate this procedure, consider matrix 1. Looking first at the entries in the center of the boxes, it is clear that Row has a sequence of acts available to him – *viz.*, r_2 – that would ensure the occurrence of e, and he has a course of action available to him – viz., r_3 – that would ensure not-e. It is clear, however, that both r_2 and r_3 would be very costly for Row to perform. Setting aside the potential benefit of outcome e or outcome not-e, the best sequence of acts open to Row – that is, the sequence that would yield the greatest utility (or the least disutility) – is r_1. In comparison with r_1, sequences r_2 and r_3 are very unattractive. But r_1 would neither ensure outcomes e nor ensure outcome not-e. Hence although there *are* sequences of acts available to Row that would ensure either of the two outcomes, these sequences of acts are very costly, and it is not clear that Row would perform either of these sequences even if he wanted the outcome it could ensure.

Assuming that Row is a 'rational' agent, what sequence of acts will be perform? That depends on whether he prefers e or prefers not-e, and it depends on how much, or how strongly, he prefers one to the other. It also depends, of course, on what Column is likely to do, which in turn depends on Column's preference as between e and not-e. Since we are interested primarily in comparisons of power, let us suppose that Row and Column have *opposing* preferences. This supposition can be satisfied in two ways: (a) Row prefers e while Column prefers not-e, and (b) Row prefers not-e whereas Column prefers e. Next, some assumption must be made concerning the *degrees* of preference. Let us assume, in each case that the degree of preference for *both* agents is the same, viz. 100 utils. We have, then, two (hypothetical) cases on which to focus: (A) Row prefers e to not-e by 100 utils while Column prefers not-e to e by 100 utils, and (B) Row prefers not-e to e by 100 utils while Column prefers e to not-e by 100 utils. What would happen in each case?

Only a little reflection is needed to see that, in each situation, Row and Column would perform sequences of acts that lead to *Column*'s getting his preferred outcome. In each case Row's degree of preference for a given outcome (whether e or not-e) would not suffice to motivate him to perform either r_2 or r_3. The cost of ensuring either outcome would outweigh the benefit from that outcome. Hence, Row would opt for r_1, thereby leaving it up to Column's choice of action to determine whether e or not-e occurs. Now in case (A), where we imagine Column to prefer not-e, he

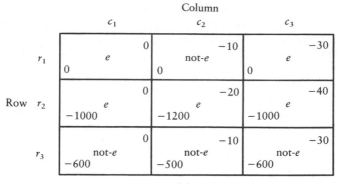

Matrix 1

would select sequence c_2. Admittedly, sequence c_2 is more costly, by 10 utils, than sequence c_1. But Column is assumed to prefer not-e to e by 100 utils, and so he would be better off, all things considered, to perform c_2. By selecting c_2, given that Row selects r_1, Column gets his preferred outcome (not-e). By similar reasoning (indeed, even more obviously), Column would get his preferred outcome in case (B); for in this case Row would perform r_1 and Column would perform c_1, a combination that would result in outcome e. Thus, in both hypothetical cases, Column would get his preferred outcome; and this is true despite the fact that Row has 'winning' strategies available to him, and knows that he has these strategies, for both e and not-e.

Let us step back now and take a new look at where our analysis leaves us. According to our initial conception, the idea of power was understood in terms of functional dependencies between the desires of an agent and the outcomes of an issue. We have stressed, however, that the outcomes of an issue are a function, not of desires *simpliciter*, but of *degrees* of desire. If Row's preference for e over not-e were not of the magnitude 100, but rather of the magnitude 2000, he would perform a different sequence of acts, and the outcome of the issue would be different. Now in the first three sections of the paper, we have talked about desiring e or not-e (or of being neutral between them). But the introduction of degrees of desire can help us add further refinements to our theory of power; specifically, it enables us to work toward *an* account of *degrees* of *power*.[26]

How are degrees of power related to functional dependencies between degrees of desire and outcomes of an issue? The answer is straightforward: *The extent of a person's power w.r.t. an issue is (ceteris paribus) inversely related to the degree of desire required for him to obtain a preferred outcome.* This answer is directly tied to considerations of cost. If obtaining a preferred outcome is very costly for an agent, then it will require a higher degree of desire to motivate him to get that outcome. (Cf. the captured commander.) And the greater the cost of getting an outcome, the less is a man's power w.r.t. that issue.

There is a clear, intuitive idea here that we seek to capture. If a person is in a position vis-à-vis an issue such that even the slightest concern, the merest whim, would suffice for him to get his preferred outcome, then he has great power w.r.t. that issue. But if a man is in a position such that only very great concern would make it worth the trouble, effort, or expenditure of resources to obtain his preferred outcome, then he does not have so much power w.r.t. the issue. If a mere whim on the part of a well-placed corporation executive would suffice to get an appropriate piece of legislation enacted, then he has great power w.r.t. that issue. I might be able to get a similar piece of legislation enacted, but only if I wanted it badly enough to go to a great deal of trouble and effort. This implies that my power w.r.t. this kind of issue is much smaller than the executive's. Similarly, if the executive and I are on opposing sides of some issue, and if it is true that a moderate desire on his part for his most preferred outcome and a large desire on my part for my most preferred outcome would result in a victory for him, then his power exceeds mine. If we apply this idea in the case of matrix 1, it is not at all clear that Row's power exceeds Column's.

It is a consequence of the current suggestion that sometimes a man who has less power w.r.t. an issue will get his preferred outcome over one who has more power on that issue. This can happen when the degree of preference of the less powerful man far exceeds the degree of preference of the more powerful one. Suppose, for example, that Row prefers outcome *e* to not-*e* by 2000 utils, while Column prefers not-*e* to *e* by only 100 utils. (Actually, it doesn't matter here what the strength of Column's preference is.) Then Row will choose r_2 and will get his preferred outcome. This does not conclusively falsify the suggestion that Column has more power on the issue than Row. There is no reason to suppose that a more powerful person on a given issue will always get his way over a less powerful one. On the contrary, it seems reasonable to define relative power in such a way that a powerful but relatively uncaring man may lose out to a less powerful but strongly motivated fellow. What a definition of relative power must ensure is that a man who is powerful w.r.t. a given issue will get his way if the issue is one of considerable importance to him, at least if he is contending against someone whose concern for the issue is comparatively small.

The foregoing discussion suggests that we may conceive of a two-person power relationship as a function which maps pairs of degrees of desire (of the two agents) onto outcomes of the issue in question. This may be illustrated with the aid of simple graphs. Let X and Y be two agents and let e and not-e be two outcomes of an issue. X's preference w.r.t. these outcomes is measured along the X-axis of a coordinate system. A positive number along the X-axis represents a degree of preference by X for e over not-e, and a negative number represents a degree to which X prefers not-e over e. The zero-point signifies indifference between e and not-e. Similarly, Y's preference as between e and not-e is measured along the Y-axis. A point in the coordinate system will then represent a pair of degrees of preference (or desire) by X and Y. The point (+100, −200), for example, represents a preference of 100 utils for e over not-e on the part of X and a preference of 200 utils for not-e over e on the part of Y. Now suppose that the power position of X and Y is such that if X were to want e to degree 100 and Y were to want not-e to degree 200 then e would occur. We shall represent this fact by darkening, or filling in, the point (+100, −200). (Of course we cannot literally darken *points*, but appropriate areas can be darkened.) If, on the other hand, such a combination of desires by X and Y would result in not-e, then the point (+100, −200) will be marked by cross-hatching. (Again, it is only areas that can be so marked.) Using these conventions, we can proceed to represent various possible relationships of power of X and Y w.r.t. issue E. Indeed, we can give information concerning both their *collective* power on the issue, and their *relative* power.

Consider graph 1. Looking at the northeast and southwest quadrants, we see that X and Y have the highest degree of *collective* power w.r.t. the issue (at least vis-à-vis this partition). For if X and Y both prefer e to not-e then e will occur − no matter how small their degree of preference, and if they both prefer not-e to e then not-e will occur − again no matter how small their degree of preference. Looking at the northwest and southeast quadrants, we see what would happen if X and Y had opposing preferences. The graph tells us that, in case of opposing preference, the agent with the stronger preference gets his way. If Y's preference for e over not-e is greater than X's preference for not-e over e, then e will occur; whereas not-e will occur if the converse holds. Similarly, if Y's preference for not-e over e exceeds X's for e over not-e, then not-e

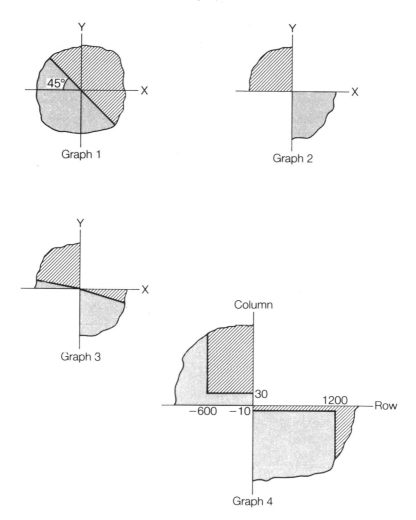

will occur; and *e* will occur if the converse holds. Here we may conclude that *X*'s power and *Y*'s power w.r.t. *E* are equal.

Since our primary interest is in comparisons of power, let us restrict our attention to northwest and southeast quadrants. Graphs 2 and 3 depict power-relationships where it is natural to say that *Y* has more power than *X*. Graph 2 says that *Y* gets his way no matter how small his preference and no matter how large *X*'s opposing preference. In other words, graph 2 says that Y is able to ensure either e or not-e at no cost whatever. (This would be true if the courses of action that would ensure e and not-e, respectively, had equal intrinsic attractiveness for Y and were each more attractive, apart from their effect on issue E, than any alternative course of action.) Graph 3 again implies, I believe, that Y has more power than X, but here his excess of power is not as great. According to this graph there is a wide range of cases in which Y would get his preferred outcome with a smaller degree of preference than X, but there are no cases in which X would get his preferred outcome with a smaller degree of preference than Y. Other cases might also be mentioned in which one agent fairly clearly has more power than another. But I shall not pursue this further in this paper. There will be many cases, of course, in which overall comparisons of power are difficult to make. One such case is that of matrix 1, which is depicted in graphical form in graph 4. Here the pattern of power is complicated, and it is not perfectly evident what conclusion should be drawn. No doubt the judgement we would intuitively make partly depends on the order of magnitude that the numbers in question convey. In any case, we should not expect our theory to yield precise judgements of power comparisons in all cases. Quite obviously, our pre-analytic judgements about power are not so precise to begin with, and we should heed Aristotle's advice not to expect (or impose) more precision than the subject-matter allows. What our theory does provide, however, is a framework for expressing in a systematic way the crucial factors that enter into an appraisal of the relative degree of power of two agents w.r.t. an issue.

Before leaving the topic of power and cost, I wish to mention a difficulty confronting our theory that I do not know how to handle. Our use of the notion of opportunity cost has one disadvantage. By measuring cost, and hence power, in terms of the best alternative course of action open to the agent, one makes the degree of cost depend upon actions open to the agent that may have no connection at all with issue E. Suppose, for example, that you can obtain outcome e with an expenditure of \$100. I come along and offer to sell you for \$100 an extremely valuable painting that you would love to own. According to our theory, it would follow that I have reduced your power w.r.t. issue E. If we assume, at any rate, that you only have \$100 to spend (or less than \$200), buying the painting and spending \$100 to get outcome e will be mutually exclusive courses of action. Hence, when I present you with this new opportunity, I thereby increase the cost to you of obtaining outcome *e*. This consequence of our theory is somewhat counter-intuitive (though not entirely counterintuitive, I think), but I do not know how to deal with it without abandoning our theory completely. It seems clear, however, that the notion of cost must play a central role in any adequate theory of power. The approach we have sketched here seems very promising, and it should not lightly be abandoned.

V   OVERALL POWER AND POWER 'OVER' PEOPLE

The foregoing analysis has focused on the power that an agent or group of agents have w.r.t. a single issue. But the concern of most discussions of power in the political arena is not the power of individuals or groups vis-à-vis selected *single* issues, but rather the *overall* power of individuals or groups. We do not merely want to say that Melvin Laird or Nelson Rockefeller has more power than I do w.r.t. this or that particular issue; we want to say that each of these men has more power than I do *on the whole*. On what basis, however, are such judgements to be made? Is it that Rockefeller has power (or a higher degree of power) w.r.t. a larger *number* of issues than I do? How are we supposed to *count* the number of issues w.r.t. which each of us has power? Issues, it would seem, can be divided up in any way one chooses, and hence both Rockefeller and I could be said to have power w.r.t. indefinitely many issues. A better answer to our question would appeal not to the number of issues over which we have power, but to their *importance*. I may have power w.r.t. what I eat for dinner tonight, what grades my students get, what sentences are written on my blackboard, etc. But Rockefeller has power w.r.t. 'really important' issues. But how is the 'importance' of an issue to be measured? One element that should go into the determination of 'importance' (for present purposes) is the number of people that would be affected by the issue. The fact that I have more power than Rockefeller does w.r.t. what will be written on my blackboard doesn't count for much in assessing my overall power as compared with Rockefeller's. On the other hand, the fact that Rockefeller has more power than I do w.r.t. the issues of taxation and expenditure of the State of New York is a very important reason for saying that he has more overall power. One thing that helps account for this is that taxation and expenditure policies of the State of New York affect a very large number of people.

But what do we mean when we say that an issue '*affects*' a person? And can one issue 'affect' a man *more* or *less* than another issue? The answer to the first question, I think, is suggested by looking at the second. I am inclined to say that one issue affects a person more than another issue if the outcomes of the first issue would make a larger difference to his *welfare* than the outcomes of the second. An issue whose outcomes would make no difference whatever to his welfare does not affect him at all. In determining a man's overall power, therefore, we must look not only at the number of persons that would be affected by the issues w.r.t. which he has power, but also at *how much* difference in welfare the outcomes of the issue would cause. This principle accords nicely with our intuitions about the 'important' issues of the day. The issue of war or peace, the issue of inflation and unemployment, the issue of pollution and measures for combating it, the issue of poverty and racism, are some of the major issues of contemporary American life. They all have in common the two features we have mentioned: first, they all affect the welfare of a large number of people, and secondly, the outcomes of these issues make a very large difference in the welfare of these people. It is not surprising, therefore, that individuals or groups who have power w.r.t. these issues, and especially w.r.t. a large number of these issues, are regarded as having a great deal of overall power.

In determining a man's overall power, we shall not simply be interested in the *single* issues w.r.t. which he has power; we shall also be extremely interested in the question of his power w.r.t. *conjunctions* of issues. Suppose there are two independent issues, E and E^*, each partitioned into three outcomes. Issue E has outcomes e_1, e_2 and e_3, and issue E^* has outcomes e_1^*, e_2^* and e_3^*. Further suppose that Smith is in a position to ensure any of the outcomes of E through a payment of $100 and is in a position to ensure any of the outcomes of E^* through a payment of $100. Then if Smith has exactly $100, he has (individual) power w.r.t. *each* of these issues. Now suppose, however, that we consider the *conjunctive* issue E & E^*. This issue has nine possible outcomes: e_1 & e_1^*, e_1 & e_2^*, . . . , e_3 & e_2^*, e_3 & e_3^*. It does not follow from our original supposition that Smith has (individual) power w.r.t. this conjucntive issue. For if he only has $100 he will not be in a position to ensure any of the nine indicated outcomes. If we suppose that Smith has $200, however, it will follow that he not only has power w.r.t. each of the outcomes, E and E^*, but that he also has power w.r.t. the conjunctive issue, E & E^*. Obviously, in determining the economic and political power of men and groups, attention to conjunctions of issues is of crucial importance. If a man has power w.r.t. a conjunction of many issues, each of which significantly affects the welfare of many people, then he is a very powerful man.

In the foregoing paragraphs the notion of welfare has been taken for granted, and we shall continue to do this in the remainder of the paper. For illustrative purposes let us associate a man's welfare with the satisfaction or non-satisfaction of his desires. (It is not clear that welfare should be identified with satisfaction of desires – rather than, say, with the satisfaction of needs or interests – but this is close enough for the moment.) Suppose that the degree of desire (or utility) assigned by Jones to the possible outcomes of E are as follows($(e_1)+100$, $(e_2)+70$, $(e_3)+20$, $(e_4)-40$, and $(e_5)-100$. Further suppose that Jones has no power at all w.r.t. issue E, but that Smith has enough power to ensure any one of the outcomes e_2, e_3, and e_4 (though not e_1 or e_5). We can then say that Smith has the power to make a fairly substantial difference in Jones's welfare – in particular, a difference of 110 utils (the difference between the utility of the best outcome for Jones that Smith can ensure and the utility of the worst outcome that Smith can ensure). Now if Smith had the power to ensure any of the five outcomes of E, and not just the middle three, then Smith's power over Jones would be even greater. Of course, our assessment of Smith's power over Jones is partly a function of the *degree* of power Smith has w.r.t. these outcomes. If it would be quite costly for Smith to secure any of these outcomes, then his power over Jones is less than it would be if the cost to Smith were small. Thus, in determining an agent's overall power, there are several factors to be considered: (1) the issues w.r.t. which the agent has *some* power, (2) the conjunctions of these issues w.r.t. which he has power, (3) the degree of power (in terms of cost) he has w.r.t. these issues, (4) the number of people affected by these issues, and (5) the amounts of the differences in these people's welfare that depend on the outcomes of these issues.

During most of our discussion we have concentrated on the notion of having power 'with respect to' an 'issue'. The term 'power', however, frequently occurs in sentences of the form 'X has power over Y', where 'Y' designates a person or group of people. We still owe an account, therefore, of having power *over* a *person*. Our remarks in the previous paragraph suggest such an account. Smith has power *over Jones*, we might say, if and only if Smith has power w.r.t. issues that affect Jones – i.e. that make a difference to Jones's welfare.

In addition to the support already given to this approach, the welfare account fits neatly with the relation between power and dependence that is often cited by sociologists.[27] If agent X controls certain objects or events which Y desires, or on which he sets a value, then Y is 'dependent' on X for the satisfaction of his desires or interests. Intuitively, this looks like a case in which X has power 'over' Y. This intuition is captured by the welfare approach we have sketched; for if Y is dependent on X for the satisfaction of his desires or interests, then X has power w.r.t. issues that affect the welfare of Y.

The suggested account of having power *over* people is in accord with a number of treatments of power in the literature. But many other writers take a somewhat different approach. Writers such as R. H. Tawney, Robert Dahl, J. C. Harsanyi, and Herbet Simon conceive of power over people as the ability to affect the *behavior* of those people.[28] Tawney, for example, defines 'power' as 'the capacity of an individual, or group of individuals, to modify the conduct of other individuals or groups in the manner which he desires . . .' (*Equality*, p. 230). Similarly, Robert Dahl says: '*A* has power over *B* to the extent that he can get *B* to do something that *B* would not otherwise *do*' (*Equality*, pp. 202–3).

Now as a complementary approach to the welfare account, the behavior approach is certainly welcome. But if it is intended to replace the welfare approach, I think it is unsatisfactory. Considered as a replacement, the behavior approach has three problems. First, it is difficult to see how it can throw much light on the determination of the *degrees* of power that person X has over person Y. The main possibility here would be to concentrate on the *number* of acts of Y w.r.t. which X has power.[29] But principles for counting acts or items of behavior are very controversial. On the theory I favor, most cases of changing the behavior of an individual would involve changes in *indefinitely many* acts. Moreover, on any approach to act-individuation one should be able to make temporal divisions any way one pleases, so it will be impossible to decide when one, two or three acts have been affected. The welfare approach, by contrast, holds greater promise for the measurement of degrees of power.

A second problem for the behavior approach is that behavior control is not clearly a sufficient condition for the exercise of power. Suppose that you are about to sit in a chair. I politely ask you to sit in the next chair instead, and since it is equally comfortable, you oblige. Here I have affected your behavior: I have induced you to do something you would not otherwise have done. But have I exercised *power over* you? This is doubtful. The reason it is doubtful, I think, can be explained by the welfare approach. First of all, there is no difference for your welfare between sitting in the one chair or sitting in the other. Secondly, since my method of inducing the change in behavior did not depend on threats or deprivation of opportunities, there is nothing in the case to suggest that I have any means of (importantly) affecting your welfare. A similar case is that of a sky-writer, whose tracks cause many people to perform acts they would not otherwise perform, viz., look up at the sky. There is little temptation to say that the sky-writer has exercised power over these people. Although he causes a change in behavior, this change is unaccompanied by any (or very much) change in welfare.

A third problem for the behavior approach is the existence of cases where behavior control fails but where there is inclination to talk of the exercise of power. Suppose I threaten to beat you up unless you do act A. You refuse to comply and so I beat you up. Here I have failed to control your behavior, but isn't my beating you up itself an exercise of power?[30] I am inclined to think that it is. My having power w.r.t. your getting beaten up is a form of power over you, even when unaccompanied by power w.r.t. your doing A. Again, this case is easily accounted for by the welfare approach, since my having power w.r.t. the issue of your getting beaten up is clearly having power w.r.t. an issue that importantly affects your welfare.

It goes without saying, of course, that power w.r.t. behavior and power w.r.t. welfare are in general closely interdependent. (This point is stressed by many authors, including Harsanyi and Thibaut and Kelley to mention just a few.) If X has power w.r.t. issues that affect Y's welfare, and if he knows how they would affect Y's welfare, then he is in a position to make threats or offers to Y in order to affect his behavior.[31] Moreover, certain ways of affecting behavior characteristically result in behavior that is less valuable to the agent affected. If X deters Y by threat from performing an act, or if X prevents Y from performing an act he otherwise would have performed, then there is typically a loss in utility for Y. Even though Y averts the threatened sanction or penalty by complying with X's desires, the substitute course of action is normally less valuable for Y than the act he would have performed had X not intervened. For these reasons, then, there is a close connection between power w.r.t. the *behavior* of Y and power w.r.t. issues affecting the *welfare* of Y.

Nevertheless, it must be admitted that there are cases of power 'over' people that involve only power w.r.t. their behavior, not power w.r.t. their welfare. The most obvious cases of this sort are cases of what Max Weber calls 'imperative control' or 'imperative coordination' (*Herrschaft*). When the commands of an authority in a corporate group are accepted by the group as 'legitimate', there is a tendency to obey the commands without the need for coercion (or reward). In many such cases, moreover, compliance with these commands has no effect (or very little effect) on the welfare of the compliers. For very often the behavior called for by these imperatives is more-or-less routine behavior of functionaries which is quite inconsequential as far as they themselves are concerned. Needless to say, the possession of imperative control is normally an extremely valuable resource to have in controlling the welfare of people. That is, it normally *enables* its possessor to have significant degrees of power w.r.t. issues that affect people's welfare. The point, however, is that we can abstract from this power w.r.t. welfare and still be left with something important that would ordinarily be called power '*over*' people. Thus, it is important to retain the notion of behavior control as a distinct category of power 'over' people, despite its large overlap with the category of welfare control.

A third category of power 'over' people is also called for, though again the overlap with the other categories will be substantial. The third category is power to *persuade*, or more generally, power w.r.t. various psychological states of others, especially *desires*, *beliefs* and *attitudes*. To the extent that a 'charismatic' leader has power w.r.t. the attitudes of his followers, and to the extent that the controller of communication media has power w.r.t. the desires and beliefs of the public, such men have power 'over' others. To be sure, power of this sort is closely connected with power w.r.t. behavior and power w.r.t. welfare. The difference between true and false belief, for example, will frequently make a difference to one's ability or inability to satisfy one's interests. Nevertheless, there are many cases in which the connection between desires and beliefs, on the one hand, and behavior and welfare, on the other, is at best very indirect and complicated. Many beliefs are never acted upon, and changes in desire are hard to relate to changes in welfare. For these reasons, then, it is worth including the third category as a distinct category of power 'over' others.

A further reason for emphasizing the third category must also be mentioned. Our analysis of power w.r.t. an issue, it should be recalled, makes an essential appeal both to hypothetical desires of an agent and to his actual desires (which determine the *cost* of an activity). It is obvious, therefore, that X's having power w.r.t. Y's desires can have an important bearing on Y's power w.r.t. an issue. In fact, this point raises an important question about our analysis of power w.r.t. issues. According to our analysis, we are interested in whether an outcome of an issue would occur *if* agent Y wanted that outcome. But suppose agent X is in a position to ensure that Y will *not* want this outcome. What does this imply about Y's power w.r.t. that issue? This question must be taken up in a more fully developed theory of power, but this is not the occasion for such a development.[32]

NOTES

1 A few of the most prominent works in the field are the following: Robert A. Dahl, 'The concept of power', *Behavioral Science*, 2 (1957); J. R. P. French, Jr., 'A formal theory of social power', *Psychological Review*, 63 (1956); H. Goldhamer and E. Shils, 'Types of power and status', *American Journal of Sociology*, 45 (1939); J. C. Harsanyi, 'Measurement of social power, opportunity costs, and the theory of two-person bargaining games', *Behavioral Science*, 7 (1962); H. D. Lasswell and A. Kaplan, *Power and Society* (Yale University Press, New Haven, 1950); J. G. March, 'An introduction to the theory and measurement of influence', *American Political Science Review*, 49 (1955); Bertrand Russell, *Power: A New Social Analysis* (W. W. Norton, New York, 1938); L. S. Shapley and M. Shubik, 'A method for evaluating the distribution of power in a committee system', *American Political Science Review*, 48 (1954). For a critical review of relevant literature and some reservations about the utility of the power concept for empirical research, see J. G. March, 'The power of power', in D. Easton (ed.), *Varieties of Political Theory* (Prentice-Hall, Englewood Cliffs, N.J., 1966).

2 See Robert Dahl, 'The concept of power', *Behavioral Science*, 2 (1957), pp. 212–13. Actually, Dahl's chameleon just decides to *vote* with the predicted outcome, but I assume that his *desires* change to favor it as well.

3 For further details on the notion of a basic act-type, see my book *A Theory of Human Action* (Prentice-Hall, 1970), chapter III, section 4 (and also chapter VII, section 1). In this paper I am ignoring certain complications, such as the existence of 'standard conditions'. I shall also asume, for the most part, that all persons have the same basic act repertoire, though in one of my examples (in section III) I shall drop this assumption.

4 In ordinary language we frequently use the term 'power' without having a particular dated issue in mind. If John has a rain-making machine, for example, we might say that he has power over 'the weather', without specifying the time in question. This loose talk about power can be understood in terms of power w.r.t. dated issues. To say that John has power w.r.t. the weather (in general), is to say that there are dated issues involving the weather w.r.t. which John has power. Having a rain-making machine gives John power over the weather 'in general' because there are particular times at which it would not rain in the normal course of events, and w.r.t. rain *at these times* John has power. To say that John has power over the weather, in this sense, does

not imply that John has power w.r.t. *every* dated issue involving the weather. If it is going to rain at time *t* no matter what John does (and if, in addition, he cannot control how hard it rains), then John has no power w.r.t. the issue of whether or not it rains *at t*. Assuming that he has no rain-prevention equipment, at any rate, he is impotent w.r.t. the issue of whether or not it rains *at t*.

5 Actually, (I') needs still further refinement. First, it is not enough to require that *S* would perform the relevant acts; he must perform these acts *in order to* achieve the given outcome (or at least *in the belief* that his performance of them would not prevent the occurrence of that outcome). Secondly, the analysis still remains open to counter-examples of the sort that beset (I). Suppose that *S* is not paralyzed and he falsely believes that whenever he snaps his fingers this causes rain clouds to disperse. It is true of *S*, then, that if he wanted non-rain he would snap his fingers (moreover, he would snap them in order to obtain non-rain). Further suppose, as in the earlier example, that S^* has the ability to detect *S*'s desires by ESP, and he has resolved to make the weather conform with *S*'s desire. Now although *S*'s snapping his fingers would not be causally relevant to the occurrence of non-rain, there is a sequence of basic acts such that if *S* wanted non-rain he would perform these acts, and if he performed these acts non-rain would occur. Thus, *S* satisfies (I') w.r.t. the issue of rain or non-rain. But it is doubtful that we would credit *S* with power w.r.t. this issue.

What goes wrong here is that *S* is mistaken about the contribution that his finger-snapping would make to the occurrence of non-rain. He erroneously believes that this act would directly cause the dispersal of the clouds, and he is completely ignorant of the role of S^*. To circumvent such problems we need a provision requiring that the agent's *conception* of the relevance of his action to the outcome must correspond to the relevance his action *would* indeed have. I do not know how to formulate such a provision in adequate detail (similar problems are encountered in the analysis of intentional action and in the analysis of knowing), but I shall suggest a vague formulation for the present.

Each of the conjuncts of (I') should be amended as follows:
'There is a sequence of basic act-types such that

a   if *S* wanted *e* [not-*e*], then, at appropriate times between t_1 and t_n, he would perform these acts, either (i) in order to achieve outcome *e* [not-*e*], or (ii) in the belief that they would not preclude the occurrence of *e* [not-*e*] and

b   if *S* performed these acts at these appropriate times, then they would contribute to the occurrence of *e* [not-*e*] in the way *S* would expect them to contribute, and *e* [not-*e*] would occur (at t_n).'

(Notice that my reformulation of clause (b) does not imply that *S*'s action would *cause* the outcome. This is because I want to allow, for one of the outcomes, that it would occur in the 'normal' course of events. This is all right as long as *S realizes*, for the appropriate outcome, that his action would merely 'allow' this outcome to occur, rather than *cause* it to occur.)

The indicated reformulation should be regarded as my 'official' analysis of individual power. I omit it from the text because I want to use (I′) as a model for later analyses; to use the more refined analysis, I fear, would obscure the more important structural features of the theory.

6 Cf. W. V. Quine, *Word and Object* (The Technology Press, Cambridge, Mass., 1960), pp. 222–6.

7 Perhaps we should draw a distinction here between an 'epistemic' sense of 'power' and a 'non-epistemic' sense of 'power'. The epistemic sense is captured by (I′) as it stands, whereas the non-epistemic sense can be obtained from (I′) by deleting clauses (1)(a) and (2)(a). This distinction would parallel the distinction between the epistemic and non-epistemic senses of 'ability' that I draw in *A Theory of Human Action*, p. 203. For our purposes, however, the epistemic sense of 'power' seems much more important than the non-epistemic sense.

8 Robert Stalnaker, 'A theory of conditionals', in Nicholas Rescher (ed.), *Studies in Logical Theory*, American Philosophical Quarterly Monograph Series (Basil Blackwell, Oxford, 1968).

9 The difficulties here are well known. Cf. Nelson Goodman, *Fact, Fiction and Forecast* (Harvard University Press, Cambridge, Mass., 1955).

10 It is necessary to rule out partitions with 'gimmicky' outcomes. For example, we do not want to partition the weather issue into the three outcomes: (a) it does not rain, (b) it rains with my right hand raised, (c) it rains with my right hand not raised. Unfortunately, I do not know how to formulate a general condition to rule out such a 'gimmicky' partition.

11 Actually, a further condition – condition (d) – must be added. To see the necessity for this, suppose that a man will be chosen from a list of ten candidates, and let E be the issue of who will be chosen. Suppose we consider two partitions of the issue, P and $P′$. P is the partition whose outcomes are (i) a Democrat is chosen and (ii) a Republican is chosen. $P′$ is the partition whose outcomes are (i′) an Eastsider is chosen and (ii′) a Westsider is chosen. (Both of these pairs are exhaustive and mutually exclusive.) Further suppose that in W_1 S could ensure either of the outcomes of P but not of $P′$, whereas in W_2 S could ensure either of the outcomes of $P′$ but not of P. Then it follows from (a), (b) and (c) that S has more power w.r.t. E in W_1 than in W_2 *and also* that he has more power w.r.t. E in W_2 than in W_1. To avoid this difficulty, the following condition may be added:

  d There is no other partition $P′$ of E, whose outcomes constitute set E^{**}, for which there are subsets E''' and E'''' such that E'''' contains at least two members, E''' is a proper subset of E'''', in W_1 E''' is the largest subset of E^{**} any of whose members S can ensure, and in $W_2 E'''$ is the largest subset of E^{**} any of whose members S can ensure.

12 *New York Magazine*, vol. IV, no. 1 (4 January 1971), p. 25.

13 *The Theory of Social and Economic Organization* (Oxford University Press, New York, 1947), p. 152. Italics are mine.

14 *The Power Elite* (Oxford University Press, New York, 1959), p. 9. Italics are mine.

15 Cf. Thomas Schelling, *The Strategy of Conflict* (Harvard University Press, Cambridge, Mass., 1960), and David K. Lewis, *Convention* (Harvard University Press, Cambridge, Mass., 1969), chapter 1.

16 Although Smith does not have individual power w.r.t. the issue of whether or not Brown is alive at noon, he does have individual power w.r.t. the (distinct) issue of whether or not *he* (Smith) *kills* Brown. Thus, even apart from our distributive principle, we have a way of accounting for the intuition that Smith has *some* power here.

17 In the game whose matrix is shown below, Column and Row make one move each, simultaneously, with no information about the move of his opponent. We can say here that for any move by Column there is a move available to Row which would 'win' for Row; but similarly, for any move by Row there is a move available to Column which would 'win' for Column.

	c_1	c_2
r_1	$+100$	-100
r_2	-100	$+100$

18 In typical political situations it will be necessary to partition an issue into numerous possible outcomes, e.g. the different possible compromises that might be reached on a piece of legislation, or the different wage increases that might be given to a union. Suppose there is a partition of E into 10 outcomes, and suppose that if S_1 and S_2 had diametrically opposite rank orderings then the outcome which is fourth on S_1's list (and seventh on S_2's list) would occur. Does it follow that S_1 has more power than S_2 w.r.t. E? This is not evident (even neglecting other partitions). Further complications arise if S_1 and S_2 have different but not diametrically opposite rank orderings.

19 Reflection on these kinds of cases suggests that statements expressing comparisons of power might be parsed, not in terms of a two-place relation 'x has more power than y', but rather in terms of a three- (or more) place relation such as 'x has more power than y given z as a resource'. This sort of treatment would make explicit which person(s) are being treated as resources. It would also have the virtue of forestalling certain problems of transitivity that might otherwise arise.

20 I assume that the machine can only be operated by S^*; thus, S can only

affect the weather *through* S*, not by operating the machine himself.

21 'Measurement of social power, opportunity, costs, and the theory of two-person bargaining games', *Behavioral Science*, 7 (1962), pp. 67–80.

22 This point raises difficult problems. If we counterfactualize *S*'s desires vis-à-vis *E*, it may seem plausible to counterfactualize a variety of other desires of his as well. It would not be plausible to consider the (counterfactual) hypothesis that Nixon wants a Democrat to be elected in 1972 without supposing other significant changes in his set of desires. The difficulty here is to decide which changes to make. There is no unique set of changes one is forced to make; numerous counterfactualizations are equally admissible. This is undoubtedly one of the reasons why judgements about power in ordinary life are so ambiguous and difficult to agree about: it is possible to counterfactualize in many different ways, yet these different alternatives are not normally made explicit. For the sake of simplicity we shall assume in the remainder of the text that *no* additional changes are made in the agent's desires beyond the changes in his desire vis-à-vis *E*.

23 Strictly speaking, it is not the *actual* costs to be undergone by a person that are relevant to his power; rather it is his *expected* costs. To avoid any further complications, however, let us assume that both S_1 and S_2 have perfect information about the consequences of their activities, so that expected and actual costs are the same.

24 A question here arises whether to include the (expected) effects of *e* and of not-*e* in determining the cost of an activity or whether to include these under the utility assigned to *e* and not-*e* themselves (hence omitting them from the determination of cost). This is a tricky question, since the degree to which a given outcome of *E* is desired commonly depends upon expected consequences of that outcome. What I propose is the following. If *C* is expected to result from outcome *e*, then if *C* would constitute one of the agent's *reasons* for wanting *e*, then it is included under the value of *e* (*not* in the category of *cost*). If *C* would be an *unwelcome* consequence of *e* (e.g. going to jail), then it is included in the category of cost.

25 For convenience we assume, in this case, that the utility accruing to Row from this course of action is always the same, no matter which sequence of acts is chosen by Column.

26 The introduction of many-outcome partitions also provides a tool for distinguishing degrees of power; but the new approach, making use of degrees of desire, is a more powerful one, I believe.

27 Cf. J. W. Thibaut and H. H. Kelley, *The Social Psychology of Groups* (Wiley and Sons, New York, 1959), chapter 7 and R. M. Emerson, 'Power-dependence relations', *American Sociological Review*, 27 (1962).

28 R. H. Tawney, *Equality* (Harcourt, Brace, New York, 1931); Robert Dahl, 'The concept of power'; J. C. Harsanyi, 'Measurement of social power, opportunity costs, and the theory of two-person bargaining

games'; Herbert Simon, 'Notes on the observation and measurement of political power', *Journal of Politics*, **15** (1953).

29 Another possibility, stressed by Dahl and his followers, concerns the amount of change X can make in the *probability* that Y will perform certain acts. This suggestion rests on a problematic appeal to the (objective) probability of an individual event, however, and I do not think it is ultimately satisfactory.

30 Here too Dahl might appeal to a change in the *probability* of an action; he might say that by threatening you, I at least increase the probability that you will do A. But this may simply be false (assuming we can make sense of such statements). If you are extremely averse to doing act A, then there may be no change at all in the probability that you will do A. (The probability that you would do A may have been zero before the threat and zero after it.)

31 For certain purposes one must carefully distinguish between offers and threats. Cf. Robert Nozick, 'Coercion', in S. Morgenbesser, P. Suppes and M. White (eds), *Philosophy, Science and Method* (St Martin's Press, New York, 1969). But these differences go beyond the purview of this paper.

32 I am indebted to the Philosophy Department of Harvard University for a George Santayana Fellowship which supported my work on this paper. Ancestors of the paper were read at the University of Michigan, Harvard University, the University of Pennsylvania, and the Society for Ethical and Legal Philosophy. I have received helpful comments from so many people that it is difficult to acknowledge my debts to them in a short space. Special thanks are owed Holly S. Goldman, who read many versions of the paper and made numerous constructive suggestions.

9

Domination and Freedom

GEORG SIMMEL

I   DOMINATION, A FORM OF INTERACTION

Nobody, in general, wishes that his influence completely determine the other individual. He rather wants this influence, this determination of the other, to act back upon *him*. Even the abstract will-to-dominate, therefore, is a case of interaction. This will draws its satisfaction from the fact that the acting or suffering of the other, his positive or negative condition, offers itself to the dominator as the product of *his* will. The significance of this solipsistic exercise of domination (so to speak) consists, for the superordinate himself, exclusively in the consciousness of his efficacy. Sociologically speaking, it is only a rudimentary form. By virtue of it alone, sociation occurs as little as it does between a sculptor and his statue, although the statue, too, acts back on the artist through his consciousness of his own creative power. The practical function of this desire for domination, even in this sublimated form, is not so much the exploitation of the other as the mere consciousness of this possibility. For the rest, it does not represent the extreme case of egoistic inconsiderateness. Certainly, the desire for domination is designed to break the *internal* resistance of the subjugated (whereas egoism usually aims only at the victory over his *external* resistance). But still, even the desire for domination has some interest in the other person, who constitutes a value for it. Only when egoism does not even amount to a desire for domination; only when the other is absolutely indifferent and a mere means for purposes which lie beyond him, is the last shadow of any sociating process removed.

The definition of later Roman jurists shows, in a relative way, that the elimination of *all* independent significance of one of the two interacting parties annuls the very notion of society. This definition was to the effect that the *societas leonina*[1] must not be conceived of as a social contract. A comparable statement has been made regarding the lowest-paid workers in modern giant enterprises which preclude all effective competition among rivaling entrepreneurs for the services of these laborers. It has been said that the difference in the strategic positions of workers and employers is so overwhelming that the work contract ceases to be a 'contract' in the ordinary sense of the word, because the former are unconditionally at the mercy of the latter. It thus appears that the moral maxim never to use a man as a mere means is actually the formula of every sociation. Where the significance of the one party sinks so low that its effect no longer enters the relationship with the other, there is as little ground for speaking of sociation as there is in the case of the carpenter and his bench.

Within a relationship of subordination, the exclusion of all spontaneity whatever is actually rarer than is suggested by such widely used popular expressions as 'coercion', 'having no choice', 'absolute necessity', etc. Even in the most oppressive and cruel cases of subordination, there is still a considerable measure of personal freedom. We merely do not become aware of it, because its manifestation would entail sacrifices which we usually never think of taking upon ourselves. Actually, the 'absolute' coercion which even the most cruel tyrant imposes upon us is always distinctly relative. Its condition is our desire to escape from the threatened punishment or from other consequences of our disobedience. More precise analysis shows that the super-subordination relationship destroys the subordinate's freedom only in the case of direct physical violation. In every other case, this relationship only demands a price for the realization of freedom – a price, to be sure, which we are not willing to pay. It can narrow down more and more the sphere of external conditions under which freedom is clearly realized, but, except for physical force, never to the point of the complete disappearance of freedom. The moral side of this analysis does not concern us here, but only its sociological aspect. This aspect consists in the fact that interaction, that is, action which is mutually determined, action which stems exclusively from personal origins, prevails even where it often is not noted. It exists even in those cases of superordination and subordination – and therefore makes even those cases *societal* forms – where according to popular notions the 'coercion' by one party deprives the other of every spontaneity, and thus of every real 'effect', or contribution to the process of interaction.

II AUTHORITY AND PRESTIGE

Relationships of superordination and subordination play an immense role in social life. It is therefore of the utmost importance for its analysis to clarify the spontaneity and co-efficiency of the subordinate subject and thus to correct their widespread minimization by superficial notions about them. For instance, what is called 'authority' presupposes, in a much higher degree than is usually recognized, a freedom on the part of the person subjected to authority. Even where authority seems to 'crush' him, it is based not *only* on coercion or compulsion to yield to it.

The peculiar structure of 'authority' is significant for social life in the most varied ways; it shows itself in beginnings as well as in exaggerations, in acute as well as in lasting forms. It seems to come about in two different ways. A person of superior significance or strength may acquire, in his more immediate or remote milieu, an overwhelming weight of his opinions, a faith, or a confidence which have the character of objectivity. He thus enjoys a prerogative and an axiomatic trustworthiness in his decisions which excel, at least by a fraction, the value of mere subjective personality, which is always variable, relative, and subject to criticism. By acting 'authoritatively', the quantity of his significance is transformed into a new quality; it assumes for his environment the physical state – metaphorically speaking – of objectivity.

But the same result, authority, may be attained in the opposite direction. A super-individual power – state, church, school, family or military organizations – clothes a person with a reputation, a dignity, a power of ultimate decision, which would never flow from his individuality. It is the nature of an authoritative person to make decisions with a certainty and automatic recognition which logically pertain only to impersonal, objective axioms and deductions. In the case under discussion, authority descends upon a person from above, as it were, whereas in the case treated before, it arises from the qualities of the person himself, through a *generatio aequivoca*.[2] But evidently, at this point of transition and change-over [from the personal to the authoritative situation], the more or less voluntary faith of the party subjected to authority comes into play. This transformation of the value of personality into a super-personal value gives the personality something which is beyond its demonstrable and rational share, however slight this addition may be. The believer in authority himself achieves the transformation. He (the subordinate element) participates in a sociological event which requires his spontaneous cooperation. As a matter of fact, the very feeling of the 'oppressiveness' of authority suggests that the autonomy of the subordinate party is actually presupposed and never wholly eliminated.

Another nuance of superiority, which is designated as 'prestige', must be distinguished from 'authority'. Prestige lacks the element of super-subjective significance; it lacks the identity of the personality with an objective power or norm. Leadership by means of prestige is determined entirely by the strength of the individual. This individual force always remains conscious of itself. Moreover, whereas the average type of leadership always shows a certain mixture of personal and superadded-objective factors, prestige leadership stems from pure personality, even as authority stems from the objectivity of norms and forces. Superiority through prestige consists in the ability to 'push' individuals and masses and to make unconditional followers of them. Authority does not have this ability to the same extent. The higher, cooler, and normative character of authority is more apt to leave room for criticism, even on the part of its followers. In spite of this, however, prestige strikes us as the more voluntary homage to the superior person. Actually, perhaps, the recognition of authority implies a more profound freedom of the subject than does the enchantment that emanates from the prestige of a prince, a priest, a military or spiritual leader. But the matter is different in regard to the *feeling* on the part of those led. In the face of authority, we are often defenseless, whereas the élan with which we follow a given prestige always contains a consciousness of spontaneity. Here, precisely because devotion is only to the wholly personal, this devotion seems to flow only from the ground of personality with its inalienable freedom. Certainly, man is mistaken innumerable times regarding the measure of freedom which he must invest in a certain action. One reason for this is the vagueness and uncertainty of the explicit conception by means of which we account for this inner process. But in whatever way we interpret freedom, we can say that some measure of it, even though it may not be the measure we suppose, is present wherever there is the feeling and the conviction of freedom.[3]

III   LEADER AND LED

The seemingly wholly passive element is in reality even more active in relationships such as obtain between a speaker and his audience or between a teacher and his class. Speaker and teacher appear to be nothing but leaders; nothing but, momentarily, superordinate. Yet whoever finds himself in such or a similar situation feels the determining and controlling re-action on the part of what seems to be a purely receptive and guided mass. This applies not only to situations where the two parties confront one another physically. All leaders are also led; in innumerable cases, the master is the slave of his slaves. Said one of the greatest German party leaders referring to his followers: 'I am their leader, therefore I must follow them'.

In the grossest fashion, this is shown by the journalist. The journalist gives content and direction to the opinions of a mute multitude. But he is nevertheless forced to listen, combine, and guess what the tendencies of this multitude are, what it desires to hear and to have confirmed, and whither it wants to be led. While apparently it is only the public which is exposed to *his* suggestions, actually he is as much under the sway of the *public's* suggestion. Thus, a highly complex interaction (whose two, mutually spontaneous forces, to be sure, appear under very different forms) is hidden here beneath the semblance of the pure superiority of the one element and a purely passive being-led of the other.

The content and significance of certain personal relations consist in the fact that the exclusive function of one of the two elements is service for the other. But the perfect measure of this devotion of the first element often depends on the condition that the other element surrenders to the first, even though on a different level of the relationship. Thus, Bismarck remarked concerning his relation to William I:

> A certain measure of devotion is determined by law; a greater measure, by political conviction; beyond this, a personal feeling of *reciprocity* is required. – My devotion had its principal ground in my loyalty to royalist convictions. But in the special form in which this royalism existed, it is after all possible only under the impact of a certain reciprocity – the reciprocity between master and servant.

The most characteristic case of this type is shown, perhaps, by hypnotic suggestion. An outstanding hypnotist pointed out that in every hypnosis the hypnotized has an effect upon the hypnotist; and that, although this effect cannot be easily determined, the result of the hypnosis could not be reached without it. Thus here, too, appearance shows an absolute influence, on the one side, and an absolute being-influenced, on the other; but it conceals an interaction, an exchange of influences, which transforms the pure one-sidedness of superordination and subordination into a *sociological* form.

IV   INTERACTION IN THE IDEA OF 'LAW'

I shall cite some cases of superordination and subordination in the field of law. It is easy to reveal the interaction which actually exists in what seems a purely unilateral situation. If the absolute despot accompanies his orders by the threat of punishment or the promise of reward, this implies that he himself wishes to be bound by the decrees he issues. The subordinate is expected to have the right to request something of him; and by establishing the punishment, no matter how horrible, the despot commits himself not to impose a more severe one. Whether or not afterward he actually abides by the punishment established or the reward promised is a different question: the *significance* of the relation is that, although the superordinate wholly determines the subordinate, the subordinate nevertheless is assured of a claim on which he can insist or which he can waive. Thus even this extreme form of the relationship still contains some sort of spontaneity on his part.

The motive of interaction within an apparently one-sided and passive subordination appears in a peculiar modification in a medieval theory of the state. According to this theory, the state came into existence because men mutually obligated one another to submit to a common chief. Thus, the ruler – including, apparently, the unconditional ruler – is appointed on the basis of a mutual contract among his subjects. Whereas contemporaneous theories of domination saw its reciprocal character in the contract between ruler and ruled, the theory under discussion located this mutual nature of domination in its very basis, the people: the obligation to the prince is conceived to be the mere articulation, expression, or technique of a reciprocal relation among the individuals of whom his people is composed. In Hobbes, in fact, the ruler has no means of breaking the contract with his subjects because he has not made one; and the corollary to this is that the subject, even if he rebels against his ruler, does not thereby break a contract concluded with *him*, but only the contract he has entered with all other members of the society, to the effect of letting themselves be governed by this ruler.

It is the *absence* of this reciprocity which accounts for the observation that the tyranny of a group over its own members is worse than that of a prince over his subjects. The group – and by no means the political group alone – conceives of its members, not as confronting it, but as being included by it as its own links. This often results in a peculiar inconsiderateness toward the members, which is very different from a ruler's personal cruelty. Wherever there is, formally, confrontation (even if, contentually, it comes *close* to submission), there is interaction; and, in principle, interaction always contains some limitation of *each* party to the process (although there may be individual exceptions to this rule). Where superordination shows an extreme inconsiderateness, as in the case of the group that simply *disposes* of its members, there no longer is any confrontation with its form of interaction, which involves spontaneity, and hence limitation, of both superordinate and subordinate elements.

This is very clearly expressed in the original conception of Roman law. In its purity, the term 'law' implies a submission which does not involve any spontaneity or counter-effect on the part of the person subordinate to the law. And the fact that the subordinate has actually cooperated in making it – and more, that *he* has given himself the law which binds him – is irrelevant. For in doing so, he has merely decomposed himself into the subject and object of lawmaking; and the law which the subject applies to the object does not change its significance only by the fact that both subject and object are accidentally lodged in the same physical person. Nevertheless, in their conception of law, the Romans directly allude to the idea of interaction. For originally, '*lex*' means 'contract', even though in the sense that the conditions of the contract are fixed by its proponent, and the other party can merely accept or reject it in its totality. In the beginning, the *lex publica populi romani* implied that the king proposed this legislation, and the people were its acceptors. Hence the very concept which most of all seems to exclude interaction is, nevertheless, designed to refer to it by its linguistic expression. In a certain sense this is revealed in the prerogative of the Roman king that he alone was allowed to speak to the people. Such a prerogative, to be sure, expressed the jealously guarded exclusiveness of his rulership, even as in ancient Greece the right of everybody to speak to the people indicated complete democracy. Nevertheless, this prerogative implies that the significance of speaking to the people, and, hence, of the people themselves, was recognized. Although the people merely *received* this one-sided action, they were nonetheless a *contractor* (whose party to the contract, of course, was only a single person, the king).

The purpose of these preliminary remarks was to show the properly sociological, social-formative character of superordination and subordination even where it appears as if a social relationship were replaced by a purely mechanical one – where, that is, the position of the subordinate seems to be that of a means or an object for the superordinate, without any spontaneity. It has been possible, at least in many cases, to show the sociologically decisive *reciprocal effectiveness*, which was concealed under the one-sided character of influence and being-influenced.

NOTES

1 'Sociation with a lion', that is, a partnership in which all the advantage is on one side. [Trans.].
2 'Equivocal birth' or 'spontaneous generation' [Trans.].
3 Here – and analogously in many other cases – the point is not to define the concept of prestige but only to ascertain the existence of a certain variety of human interactions, quite irrespective of their designation. The presentation, however, often begins appropriately with the concept which linguistic usage makes relatively most suitable for the discovery of the relationship, because it suggests it. This sounds like a merely definitory procedure. Actually, however, the attempt is never to find the content of a concept, but to describe, rather, an actual content, which only occasionally has the chance of being covered, more or less, by an already existing concept.

10
Power and Organization

JOHN KENNETH GALBRAITH

THE ANATOMY OF POWER: AN OVERVIEW

The subject [is] not . . . remote, philosophical, or esoteric.

Adolf A. Berle, Jr, *Power*

1

Few words are used so frequently with so little seeming need to reflect on their meaning as power, and so it has been for all the ages of man. In association with kingship and glory it was included in the ultimate scriptural accolade to the Supreme Being; millions still offer it every day. Bertrand Russell was led to the thought that power, along with glory, remains the highest aspiration and the greatest reward of humankind.[1]

Not many get through a conversation without a reference to power. Presidents or prime ministers are said to have it or to lack it in the requisite amount. Other politicians are thought to be gaining in power or losing it. Corporations and trade unions are said to be powerful, and multinational corporations dangerously so. Newspaper publishers, the heads of the broadcasting networks, and the more articulate, uninhibited, intelligent, or notorious of their editors, columnists, and commentators are the powers that be. The Reverend Billy Sunday is remembered as a powerful voice; the Reverend Billy Graham is now so described. So is the Reverend Jerry Falwell; indeed, such has been his seeming power as a moral leader that he has been thought by some to be giving morality a bad name.

J.K. Galbraith, *The Anatomy of Power*, London: Hamish Hamilton, 1984, chapter 1 'The Anatomy of Power: An Overview', pp. 1–13, and chapter 14 'The Age of Organization', pp. 131–43, copyright © 1983 by John Kenneth Galbraith, is reprinted by permission of Houghton and Mifflin Company and Hamish Hamilton Ltd.

The references continue. The United States is a large and otherwise important country; so is the Soviet Union. But it is their power that evokes the common notice; they are the great powers, or the superpowers. Britain, once also a great power, is no longer powerful. All know that in recent times the United States has been losing some of its industrial power to Germany and Japan. None of these and the myriad other references to power is ever thought to require explanation. However diversely the word is used, the reader or listener is assumed to know what is meant.

And doubtless most do – to a point. Max Weber, the German sociologist and political scientist (1864–1920), while deeply fascinated by the complexity of the subject, contented himself with a definition close to everyday understanding: power is 'the possibility of imposing one's will upon the behavior of other persons'.[2] This, almost certainly, is the common perception; someone or some group is imposing its will and purpose or purposes on others, including on those who are reluctant or adverse. The greater the capacity so to impose such will and achieve the related purpose, the greater the power. It is because power has such a commonsense meaning that it is used so often with so little seeming need for definition.

But little more about power is so simple. Unmentioned in nearly all references to it is the highly interesting question as to how the will is imposed, how the acquiescence of others is achieved. Is it the threat of physical punishment, the promise of pecuniary reward, the exercise of persuasion, or some other, deeper force that causes the person or persons subject to the exercise of power to abandon their own preferences and to accept those of others? In any meaningful reference to power, this should be known. And one should also know the sources of power – what it is that differentiates those who exercise it from those who are subject to the authority of others. By what license do some have the right, whether in large matters or small, to rule? And what causes others to be ruled? It is these questions – how power is enforced, what accords access to the methods of enforcement – that this book [*The Anatomy of Power*] addresses.

2

The instruments by which power is exercised and the sources of the right to such exercise are interrelated in complex fashion. Some use of power depends on its being concealed – on their submission not being evident to those who render it. And in modern industrial society both the instruments for subordinating some people to the will of others and the sources of this ability are subject to rapid change. Much of what is believed about the exercise of power, deriving as it does from what was true in the past, is obsolete or obsolescent in the present.

Nonetheless, as Adolf Berle observed, the subject is not a remote or esoteric thing. No one should venture into it with the feeling that it is a mystery that only the privileged can penetrate. There is a form of scholarship that seeks not to extend knowledge but to exclude the unknowing. One should not surrender to it and certainly not on a subject of such great practical importance as this. All conclusions on power can be tested against generally acceptable historical evidence and most of them against everyday observation and uncomplicated common sense. It will help, however, to have the basic facts of power in mind at the outset and thus to proceed with a clear view of its essential character – its anatomy.

3

Power yields strongly, in a secular way, to the rule of three. There are three instruments for wielding or enforcing it. And there are three institutions or traits that accord the right to its use.

It is a measure of how slightly the subject of power has been analyzed that the three reasonably obvious instruments of its exercise do not have generally accepted names. These must be provided: I shall speak of condign, compensatory, and conditioned power.

Condign power wins submission by the ability to impose an alternative to the preferences of the individual or group that is sufficiently unpleasant or painful so that these preferences are abandoned. There is an overtone of punishment in the term, and this conveys the appropriate impression.[3] It was the undoubted preference of the galley slave to avoid his toil, but his prospective discomfort from the lash for any malingering at the oars was sufficiently unpleasant to ensure the requisite, if also painful, effort. At a less formidable level, the individual refrains from speaking his or her mind and accepts the view of another because the expected rebuke is otherwise too harsh.

Condign power wins submission by inflicting or threatening appropriately adverse consequences. Compensatory power, in contrast, wins submission by the offer of affirmative reward – by the giving of something of value to the individual so submitting. In an earlier stage of economic development, as still in elementary rural economies, the compensation took varied forms – including payments in kind and the right to work a plot of land or to share in the product of the landlord's fields. And as personal or public rebuke is a form of condign power, so praise is a form of compensatory power. However, in the modern economy, the most important expression of compensatory power is, of course, pecuniary reward – the payment of money for services rendered, which is to say for submission to the economic or personal purposes of others. On occasion, where reference to pecuniary payment conveys a more exact meaning, this term will be used.

It is a common feature of both condign and compensatory power that the individual submitting is aware of his or her submission – in the one case compelled and in the other for reward. Conditioned power, in contrast, is exercised by changing belief. Persuasion, education, or the social commitment to what seems natural, proper, or right causes the individual to submit to the will of another or of others. The submission reflects the preferred course; the fact of submission is not recognized. Conditioned power, more than condign or compensatory power, is central, as we shall see, to the functioning of the modern economy and polity, and in capitalist and socialist countries alike.

4

Behind these three instruments for the exercise of power lie the three sources of power – the attributes or institutions that differentiate those who wield power from those who submit to it. These three sources are personality, property (which, of course, includes disposable income), and organization.

Personality – leadership in the common reference – is the quality of physique, mind, speech, moral certainty, or other personal trait that gives access to one or more of the instruments of power. In primitive societies this access was through physical strength to condign power; it is a source of power still retained in some households or youthful communities by the larger, more muscular male. However, personality in modern times has its primary association with conditioned power – with the ability to persuade or create belief.

Property or wealth accords an aspect of authority, a certainty of purpose, and this can invite conditioned submission. But its principal association, quite obviously, is with compensatory power. Property – income – provides the wherewithal to purchase submission.

Organization, the most important source of power in modern societies, has its foremost relationship with conditioned power. It is taken for granted that when an exercise of power is sought or needed, organization is required. From the organization, then, come the requisite persuasion and the resulting submission to the purposes of the organization. But organization, as in the case of the state, also has access to condign power – to diverse forms of punishment. And organized groups have greater or lesser access to compensatory power through the property of which they are possessed.

This brings up a final point. As there is a primary but not exclusive association between each of the three instruments by which power is exercised and one of the sources, so there are also numerous combinations of the sources of power and the related instruments. Personality, property, and organization are combined in various strengths. From this comes a varying combination of instruments for the enforcement of power. The isolation or disentangling of the sources and instruments in any particular exercise of power, the assessment of their relative importance, and the consideration of the changes in relative importance over time are the task of this book.

In earliest Christian days, power originated with the compelling personality of the Savior. Almost immediately an organization, the Apostles, came into being, and in time the Church as an organization became the most influential and durable in all the world. Not the least of its sources of power was its property and the income thus disposed. From the combination of personality (those of the Heavenly Presence and a long line of religious leaders), the property, and, above all, the unique organization came the conditioned belief, the benefices or compensation, and the threat of condign punishment either in this world or the next that, in the aggregate, constituted the religious power. Such is the complex of factors incorporated in and, in great measure, concealed by that term. Political power, economic power, corporate power, military power, and other such references similarly and deeply conceal an equally diverse interrelationship. When they are mentioned, their inner nature is not pursued.[4] My present concern is with what is so often kept hidden.

5

As with much concerning power, the purposes for which it is sought are widely sensed but more rarely articulated. Individuals and groups seek power to advance their own interests, including, notably, their own pecuniary interest. And to extend to others their personal, religious, or social values. And to win support for their economic or other social perception of the public good. The business-man buys the submission of his workers to serve his economic purposes – to make money. The religious leader persuades his congregation or his radio or television audience because he thinks his beliefs should be theirs. The politician seeks the support, which is to say the submission, of voters so that he may remain in office. Preferring clean to dirty air, the conservationist seeks to enforce respect for his preference on those who make automobiles or own factories. The latter seek submission to their own desire for lower costs and less regulation. Conservatives seek submission to their view of the economic and social order and the associated action; liberals or socialists seek similar submission to theirs. In all cases organization – the coming together of those with similar interests, values, or perceptions – is integral to the winning of such submis-sion, to the pursuit of power.

Everyday language comments regularly on the reasons for which power is being pursued. If it is narrowly confined to the interest of an individual or group, one says it is being sought for selfish ends; if it reflects the interest or perception of a much larger number of people, those involved are thought inspired leaders or statemen.

It is also recognized that the purposes for which power is being sought will often be extensively and thoughtfully hidden by artful misstatement. The politician who seeks office on behalf of the pecuniary interests of affluent supporters will be especially eloquent in describing himself as a public benefactor, even a diligent and devoted friend of the poor. The adequately educated businessman no longer employs workers to enhance his profit; his deeper pur-pose is to provide employment, advance community well-being, and ensure the success of the free enterprise system. The more fervent evangelist is overtly concerned with the salvation of sinners, bringing the unrighteous to grace; anciently he has been known to have his eye on the collection plate. A deeply ingrained and exceed-ingly valuable cynicism is the appropriate and frequent response to all avowals of the purposes of power; it is expressed in the omnipre-sent question, 'What is he really after?'

Much less appreciated is the extent to which the purpose of power is the exercise of power itself.[5] In all societies, from the most primitive to the ostensibly most civilized, the exercise of power is profoundly enjoyed. Elaborate rituals of obeisance – admiring multitudes, applauded speeches, precedence at dinners and banquets, a place in the motorcade, access to the corporate jet, the military salute – celebrate the possession of power. These rituals are greatly rewarding; so are the pleas and intercessions of those who seek to influence others in the exercise of power; and so, of course, are the acts of exercise – the instructions to subordinates, the military commands, the conveying of court decisions, the statement at the end of the meeting, when the person in charge says, 'Well, this is what we'll do.' A sense of self-actuated worth derives from both the context and the exercise of power. On no other aspect of human existence is vanity so much at risk; in William Hazlitt's words, 'The love of power is the love of ourselves.' It follows that power is pursued not only for the service it renders to personal interests, values, or social perceptions but also for its own sake, for the emotional and material rewards inherent in its possession and exercise.

However, that power is thus wanted for its own sake cannot, as a matter of basic decency, be too flagrantly conceded. It is accepted that an individual can seek power to impose his moral values on others, or to further a vision of social virtue, or to make money. And, as noted, it is permissible to disguise one purpose with another – self-enrichment can be hidden behind great community service, sordid political intent behind a passionate avowal of devotion to the public good. But it is not permissible to seek power merely for the very great enjoyment that it accords.[6]

Yet while the pursuit of power for the sake of power cannot be admitted, the reality is, as ever, part of the public consciousness. Politicians are frequently described as 'power-hungry'; the obvious implication is that they seek power to satisfy an appetite. Corporations take over other corporations not in pursuit of profits but in pursuit of the power that goes with the direction of a yet larger enterprise. This, too, is recognized. American politicians – senators, congressmen, cabinet officers, and Presidents – regularly sacrifice wealth, leisure, and much else to the rigors of public office. That the nonspecific exercise of power and the access to its rituals are part of the reason is fairly evident. Perhaps only from those so rewarded are the pleasures of power for its own sake extensively concealed.

6

A reference to power is rarely neutral; there are few words that produce such admiring or, in the frequent case, indignant response. A politician can be seen by some as a powerful and thus effective leader; seen by others, he is dangerously ruthless. Bureaucratic power is bad, but public servants with power to render effective public service are very good. Corporate power is dangerous; so, however, is a weakly administered enterprise. Unions in their exercise of power indispensably defend the rights of the workers; otherwise perceived, they are deeply in conflict with the liberty of their members and the well-being of employers and the public at large.

Much obviously depends on the point of view – on the differential responses arising from whose submission is being sought, whose ox is being gored. The politician who wins a tax reform of which one approves has engaged in a wise exercise of power; to those who must pay, it is or can be arbitrary, even unconscionable. The admiration for the exercise of power that wins a new airport is not shared by the people whose property abuts the landing strip.

The response to power is also, in substantial measure, a legacy of its past. Until nearly within living memory, black workers in the United States and white serfs in Imperial Russia were impelled to the will of the overseer, owner, or landlord by application of the whip. Power meant condign power of a particularly painful and sanguinary sort. The world has also had thousands of years of harsh experience with condign enforcement by military organization, an experience that is not yet at an end. It is this history and more that has given power its chilling name.

Further, much exercise of power depends on a social conditioning that seeks to conceal it. The young are taught that in a democracy all power resides in the people. And that in a free enterprise system all authority rests with the sovereign consumer operating through the impersonal mechanism of the market. Thus is hidden the public power of organization – of the Pentagon, the weapons firms, and other corporations and lobbyists. Similarly concealed by the mystique of the market and consumer sovereignty is the power of corporations to set or influence prices and costs, to suborn or subdue politicians, and to manipulate consumer response. But eventually it becomes apparent that organizations *do* influence government, bend it and therewith the people to their need and will. And that corporations are not subordinate to the market; instead the market that is supposed to regulate them is, in some measure, an instrument in their hands for setting their prices and incomes. All this being in conflict with social conditioning, it evokes indignation. Power thus concealed by social conditioning and then revealed seems deeply illegitimate.

Yet power, *per se*, is not a proper subject for indignation. The exercise of power, the submission of some to the will of others, is inevitable in modern society; nothing whatever is accomplished without it. It is a subject to be approached with a skeptical mind but not with one that has a fixation of evil. Power can be socially malign; it is also socially essential.[7] Judgement thereon must be rendered, but no general judgement applying to all power can possibly serve.

THE AGE OF ORGANIZATION

1

The social conditioning of high capitalism was broad and deep. So was the countering response it engendered. And both continue influential to this day. The market remains to many the solvent of industrial power; the modern corporation is still thought to be led as by an invisible hand to what is socially the best. The Marxist ideas are still a specter of evil – or hope. And herein lies one of the problems of social conditioning as an instrument of power: it is accepted as the reality by those who employ it, but then, as underlying circumstances change, the conditioning does not. Since it is considered *the* reality, it conceals the new reality. So it is in the most recent great movement in the dynamics of power – the rise of organization as a source of power and the concurrent lessening in the comparative roles of personality and property. The older vision of the economic order is still avowed, and for it policy is still prescribed. Meanwhile a new order has arrived and has the modern relevance. Over this the older social conditioning spreads a deep disguise.

The rise of organization in modern times is, for those who are willing to see it, clearly visible. Its influence is felt in the economy, in the polity, and in the special and somber case of the military power; it manifests itself in a hundred forms of citizen and (as it is called) special-interest effort to win the submission of others, either directly or by way of the state. The management-controlled corporation, the trade union, the modern bureaucratic state, groups of farmers and oil producers working in close alliance with governments, trade associations, and lobbies – all are manifestations of the age of organization. All attest to a relative decline in the importance of both personality and, though in lesser measure, property as sources of power. And all signify a hugely increased reliance on social conditioning as an instrument for the enforcement of power. Property, as earlier observed, has much of its remaining importance as a source of power not in the submission it purchases directly but in the special conditioning by way of the media – television commercials, radio commercials, newspaper advertising, and the artistry of advertising agencies and public relations firms – for which it can pay.

2

The shift in the sources of power in the modern business enterprise is of the most striking clarity. The dominant personalities of high capitalism have disappeared. During the last century and into the present one, the names of the great entrepreneurs were synonymous with the American industrial scene. And the case was the same, if less dramatically so, in the other industrial countries. Now, outside the particular industry and not always therein, no one knows the name of the head of General Motors, Ford, Exxon, Du Pont, or the other large corporations. The powerful personality has been replaced by the management team; the entrepreneur has yielded to the faceless organization man. Thus the decline of personality as a source of power.

The role of property has similarly declined. In the age of high capitalism none could doubt the power originating in the ownership of capital. It was this property that accorded the right to run the business, and it was this that gave access to influence in legislatures, over Presidents and prime ministers, and with the public at large. Property as a source of industrial power is not negligible now – as ever in these matters there are no perfect cases – but it has, nonetheless, suffered a major relative decline. The thousand largest industrial enterprises in the United States, all vast organizations, currently contribute about two thirds of all private production of goods and services, and the concentration of economic activity has followed a similar course in the other industrial countries. In few of these corporations and in none of the biggest does ownership by the individual stockholder give access to authority within the firm. This has long been so; it is fifty years since the pioneering scholars Adolf A. Berle, Jr, and Gardiner C. Means concluded that in the majority of the largest two hundred corporations in the United States control had passed to the management, which is to say the managers elected the board of directors, which then, in an incestuous way, selected the management that had selected them.[8] The continuing transfer of power from owners to managers – from property to organization – has been a pervasively characteristic feature of industrial development ever since.

Two factors contributed to the decline of property in relation to management. With the passage of time, ownership holdings in the enterprise were dispersed by inheritance, including, inevitably, to some heirs eminently disqualified by disposition or intelligence to exercise the power that property conferred. And, at the same time, the industrial tasks became increasingly complex. Corporate size, sophisticated technology, and the need for specialized management and marketing skills united to exclude from decision-making those whose principal qualification was the ownership of the property. Power passed beyond the intellectual reach of the nonparticipant and thus beyond his or her capacity to intervene effectively. And increasingly within the enterprise, decisions emerged not from the single competence of any one individual but from the several contributions of specialists meeting in committee or close daily association.[9]

The decline of property in relation to organization as a source of power has not been accepted easily. A certain legitimacy is still thought to be attached to property. Its importance is affirmed by quasi-religious observances; the young are still told that *ultimate* power in the modern corporation rests with the stockholder. 'When, for example, John purchased a new issue of stock from the Keim Corporation last year . . . [it gave] him a voice in the decision of "his" firm's management when he meets with other stockholders at annual meetings'.[10] University faculties and students labor under the belief that, by the exercise of its vote in stockholders' meetings, their institution can substantially affect corporate decisions. At such yearly meetings a repetitively devout obeisance is accorded to property ownership; the obligatory reference, as indicated by the Department of Commerce pamphlet quoted above, is to 'your company'. No important management decisions are ever altered by any of these observances.[11]

3

With the shift in the sources of power from personality and property to organization went a marked diminution in the relative effectiveness of compensatory power and, as might be expected, a very great increase in the exercise of conditioned power. This was evident, among other places, in the relationship of the industrial firm to the union, of which earlier mention has been made. The trade union, as a countervailing exercise of power in the purchase of labor, had emerged before the age of organization. We have seen that it met with a far more adamant opposition from the early entrepreneurs – in the United States from Henry Clay Frick, Henry

Ford, and Sewell Avery[12] – than from the organization men. The property-owning industrialist was frequently interested in power for its own sake, in subduing the workers as an act of personal will and purpose; a vice president in charge of labor relations, on the other hand, is measured in part by his ability to keep the peace. And – a not insignificant point – he is not defending his own personal property from the aggressions of the workers. The age of organization[13] has thus brought a major easing of the compensatory power once exercised over the labor force.

When it came to the exercise of the same kind of power over consumers or customers, the change with the rise of organization was rather more subtle and, in some respects, contradictory in practical effect. Here, as with the employment of workers, power consists at its greatest in getting the most submission for the least cost. Much can be had for little if the buyer's need is great and if alternatives are not available; the consumer is exploited, as is the worker in the parallel case of submission. The classic example of such exercise of power is the monopoly of some essential or much-desired product for which there is no clear substitute; there being no alternative seller, the need and power are large. Competition enters as the remedy; hence its reputation as the basic solvent of power.

Organization and associated industrial development have had a marked, even profound, effect on both competition and monopoly. A major purpose of the great industrial enterprise, the labor union, the farm organization, the organization of petroleum-exporting states, or the professional or trade association, is to restrain or eliminate price competition – to ensure, so far as may be possible, that there is no alternative at a lower price. In the case of modern industrial enterprises, this does not require formal communication; it is sufficient that there be a common understanding that price competition, if allowed to get out of hand, will be at cost to the power of all. Even the classical tradition in economics has come generally to concede the commitment to such implicit restraint – to what is called oligopoly pricing. Thus a primary purpose of organization has been to escape the power-limiting tendencies, otherwise called the discipline, of the market, and this has been widely successful.

But opposing influences have also been at work. The affluence associated with modern industrial development has greatly diminished the pressure of any given consumer need; the expansion in the number and variety of products and services has directly increased the alternatives available to the consumer. The choice among consumer products is infinitely greater than in the last century and therewith the sources of enjoyment and ostentation. Consequently, monopoly has ceased to be the ogre that it was in the earlier days of compensatory power. Those who might be subject to its force have the possibility now of buying something else or not buying at all. A little-noticed but highly significant result is that monopoly as a social ill has ceased, in recent times, to be an important subject of agitation in the industrial lands.

The consequence of this development has been a major shift from compensatory to conditioned power. One answer to the excessive availability of alternatives is to persuade people that they are not *real* alternatives – to cultivate the belief that the product or service in question has qualities that are unique. From this comes the massive modern commitment to commercial advertising. Advertising is not, as some would suggest, a new and vital form of market competition. Rather, it seeks through conditioned power to retain some of the authority over the buyer that was earlier associated with compensatory power.

The change here is evident in the symmetrical response of consumers to the power of sellers of goods and services. When they were subject to compensatory power – to the power that required of them much for little – they established cooperatives or buying associations to exercise a compensatory power of their own in return. These groups sought to buy more for less, developed alternative sources of supply, or appealed to the government to regulate prices or otherwise dissolve the market power of the seller. The price of the product, the index of relative compensatory power, was the central concern. This is so no longer. The preoccupation of the modern consumer is now all but exclusively with the advertising of the product, with countering the exercise of conditioned power in order to learn what is true or what is deemed to be true. This is also manifest in the actions of government agencies on behalf of the consumer. Prices are best an afterthought; central to all concern is the validity of advertising claims, what passes for truth in advertising. This is the modern purpose of the consumer movement; it is the predictable response to the passage from the exercise of compensatory power to the exercise of conditioned power.

4

When the modern industrial enterprise seeks support for its purposes from the state, conditioned power is again the instrument that it invokes or that is ultimately involved. The forthright purchase of legislators and other public officials is not unknown; however, it is now regarded as offending the finer ethical sense, and, to a considerable extent, it has also been suppressed by law. The major exercise of power by the corporation over the legislator or public official is by cultivating belief in its needs or purposes either directly or in the constituency to which he is beholden. What is called a powerful lobby is one skilled in such direct conditioning or one that can appeal effectively to sizable responsive groups and associations and through them to their political representatives.[14] No one can suppose that pecuniary resources – property – are unimportant in this connection. However, they have their importance not in direct compensatory action but, as earlier noted, in the larger social conditioning they can buy, including that which may be used on behalf of a pliable or supportive legislator or against one who is adversely inclined.

The exercise of conditioned power in the modern state – the persuasion of legislators, public officials, or their constituencies – is no slight thing. It assails the eyes and ears and is a subject of major political comment and concern. However, it is probably not as efficient as the direct purchase, or compensatory power, that was commonplace in the era of high capitalism. Also, as we have already seen, compensatory power had its inescapable nexus with property, and property, in turn, was possessed in largest amount by the industrial capitalists. Conditioned power also requires pecuniary resources to pay for the diverse forms of persuasion – television, radio, and newspaper advertising, speeches, personal blandishment – on which it relies. But even granting this need, it is more generally available than the compensatory power it replaces. Resources can be found; money can be raised. In some measure, if often very slight, conditioned power is available to all who can form an organization.

5

Not only is conditioned power more widely available in the age of organization, but that available to the modern large corporation is, in some respects at least, weaker than the conditioned power associated with the pre-eminence of capital or property in the last century.

As massive organization manifested in the great industrial enterprise has become the basic fact of modern industrial life, the social conditioning on which its power extensively depends has not, as already noted, kept pace. Instead, it has remained basically unchanged from the age of classical capitalism. Power is still held to be dissolved by the market and by competition. And it is assumed that power, whatever its intention, is always guided to socially desirable ends by the miracle of the market and the competitive struggle therein. In consequence, the social conditioning of the last century is perpetuated in circumstances of increasing implausibility in the world of great organizations.

The continuing use of the earlier conditioning is vividly evident in economic instruction. The real world is one of great interacting organizations – corporations, unions, and the state. The interaction between union wage claims and corporate prices has become the principal modern cause of inflation. But a textbook that took as its point of departure the reality of such interaction would not be acceptable for college or university use, and, significantly, it would not lend itself to the geometrical and other mathematical refinements that are compatible with the assumption of market competition and without which the teaching of economics is not considered wholly reputable.

The social conditioning that is sustained by this instruction does have a certain effect. Hundreds of thousands of otherwise intelligent young people have their thoughts guided innocuously away from the exercise of industrial power. We have seen that power is served in many ways and that no service is more useful than the cultivation of the belief that it does not exist. 'To recognize that micro-economics must now deal with a world of pervasive oligopoly . . . would threaten some basic ideological defences of the *laissez-faire* system.'[15]

But social conditioning, however deep and pervasive, cannot collide too obviously with reality. The presence and power of the modern great corporations – Exxon, General Motors, Shell, Philips – are hidden only with increasing difficulty behind the market façade. In consequence, a reference to neoclassical economics, the conditioning medium of instruction, has come to have a vaguely pejorative sound; something no longer quite real is implied. Once economic instruction is perceived not as the reality but as the guidance away from the reality, its conditioning value is, not surprisingly, impaired.

The conflict with reality becomes greater when the classical social conditioning passes out of the field of education into everyday executive expression and the public relations and advertising effort of the large industrial firm. Then qualifications disappear; the power-dissolving role of the market becomes an absolute; Exxon is held to be indistinguishable from the corner grocery or the village pharmacy in its exercise of power. As a consequence, the persuasive effect is confined to the unduly susceptible, those capable of believing anything today, who, accordingly, will believe something else tomorrow. For yet others an important effect of the social conditioning of corporate propaganda, as significantly it is often called, is to cultivate disbelief. There must be some misuse of power when those who so obviously possess it are so at pains to deny having it. In the industrial countries it is now a minor mark of sophistication that one does not believe what one reads or hears in the public-interest advertising of the great corporation. The conditioned and compensatory power of the modern business enterprise remains considerable, but it cannot be supposed that it rivals the forthright compensatory power of the great capitalist firm in the age of high capitalism.

There is a further indication of this decline in the relation of the modern corporation to the state. In the last century, when the state was an ally, an adversary relationship between government and business would have been unthinkable. Now government and business are widely regarded as mutual enemies. The social conditioning of the modern corporate enterprise is extensively concerned with the intrusive, limiting, and otherwise malign tendencies of the state. (Only in the area of military power is there full harmony between government and its dependent corporate enterprises.) In important measure, the reason lies in the shift from compensatory to conditioned power. Compensatory power was the clear monopoly of the business firm. The legislators and public officials it purchased were not likely to show hostility to their paymasters. Conditioned power allows many more interests access to the state; some of these are hostile to the business power and thus contribute to the adversary relationship, seeming or real, between corporate enterprise and modern government.

But the state also has changed; in contrast with its role in the last century, it is much less the instrument of those who seek its power, much more a power in its own right. Organization and conditioned power are again the operative forces. The modern state encompasses a large organization – bureaucracy – which, in turn, has made the state extensively the instrument of its own purposes.

NOTES

1 'Of the infinite desires of man, the chief are the desires for power and glory', *Power: A New Social Analysis* (W. W. Norton, New York, 1938), p. 11.

2 Max Weber on *Law in Economy and Society* (Harvard University Press, Cambridge, Mass., 1954), p. 323. See Reinhard Bendix. *Max Weber: An Intellectual Portrait* (Doubleday, Garden City, New York, 1960), pp. 294–300. Elsewhere Weber said of power that it is the ability of one or more persons to 'realize their own will in a communal act against the will of others who are participating in the same act'.

3 I have taken some liberties in the selection and use of this term. According to strict dictionary usage, *condign* has an adjectival relationship to *punishment*. A condign punishment is, broadly speaking, an appropriate or fitting one. Were one scrupulously pedantic, the reference here and throughout would be to *condign punishment*. I omit the latter word with the thought, first articulated by Lewis Carroll, that one can have a word mean what one chooses it to mean – 'neither more nor less'. A tempting alternative would have been 'coercive' power as used by Dennis H. Wrong in *Power: Its Forms, Bases and Uses* (Harper Colophon Books, New York, 1980). His discussion of coercive authority (pp. 41–4) parallels in a general way my use of *condign power*. However, it less specifically implies the instrument to which the individual (or group) surrenders, that which brings the submission.

4 As others have held, 'Perhaps no subject in the entire range of the social sciences is more important, and at the same time so seriously neglected, as the role of power in economic life', Melville J. Ulmer, 'Economic power and vested interests', in *Power in Economics,* edited by K. W. Rothschild (Penguin Books, Harmondsworth, 1971), p. 245.

5 'The healthy individual who gains power loves it', Dr Harvey Rich (a Washington, DC, psychoanalyst, quoted in the *New York Times*, 9 November 1982). Bertrand de Jouvenel puts the matter more vividly: 'The leader of any group of men . . . feels thereby an almost physical enlargement of himself. . . . Command is a mountain top. The air breathed there is different, and the perspectives seen there are different, from those of the valley of obedience.' (*On Power: Its Nature and the History of Its Growth* (Viking Press, New York, 1949), p. 116.)

6 John F. Kennedy, a man of some candor in public expression, nearly did so. 'I run for President', he said, 'because that is where the action is.' By *action* he was close to meaning power.

7 'Power has two aspects . . . It is a social necessity . . . It is also a social menace', De Jouvenel, *On Power*, p. 283.

8 *The Modern Corporation and Private Property* (Macmillan, New York, 1933). The shift in power was further affirmed by the studies of R. A. Gordon, among them *Business Leadership in the Large Corporation* (Bookings Institution, Washington, DC, 1945), and in the more general writings of James Burnham. See *The Managerial Revolution* (John Day, New York, 1941). The bureaucratization of modern economic enterprise was strongly emphasized by Joseph A. Schumpeter – 'it is an inevitable complement to modern economic development' – in *Capitalism, Socialism, and Democracy*, 2nd edn (Harper and Brothers, New York, 1947), p. 206. It is obvious that the shift from property to

organization as the prime source of power in the industrial enterprise is not a discovery of recent date. For a comprehensive contemporary treatment of this subject see Edward S. Herman, *Corporate Control, Corporate Power*, A Twentieth Century Fund Study (Cambridge University Press, Cambridge, 1981).

9　These are matters with which I have dealt in *The New Industrial State*, 3rd edn (Houghton Mifflin, Boston, 1978). C. Wright Mills made the point some 25 years ago: 'Decision-making ... at the top [of the corporation] is slowly being replaced by the worried-over efforts of committees, who judge ideas tossed before them, usually from below the top levels' (*The Power Elite* (Oxford University Press, New York, 1956), p. 134.)

10　From 'Do You Know Your Economic ABC's? Profits in the American Economy', an instructional pamphlet on economics (Washington, DC: United States Department of Commerce, 1965), pp. 17–18.

11　'[S]tockholders, though still politely called "owners", are passive. They have the right to receive only. The condition of their being is that they do not interfere in management. Neither in law nor, as a rule, in fact do they have that capacity.' Adolf A. Berle, Jr., *Power Without Property: A New Development in American Political Economy* (Harcourt, Brace, New York, 1959), p. 74.

12　Of Carnegie become United States Steel, the Ford Motor Company, and Montgomery Ward, respectively.

13　Along, of course, with the effect of higher wages, unemployment compensation, and Social Security, all of which have widened the gap between condign and compensatory power and lowered the level of compulsion associated with the latter.

14　Thus in the United States the power for their own purposes of war veterans, people living on Social Security, and members of the National Rifle Association.

15　Thomas Balogh, *The Irrelevance of Conventional Economics* (Weidenfeld and Nicolson, London, 1982), p. 60.

11
Disciplinary Power and Subjection

MICHEL FOUCAULT

The course of study that I have been following until now – roughly since 1970/71 – has been concerned with the *how* of power. I have tried, that is, to relate its mechanisms to two points of reference, two limits: on the one hand, to the rules of right that provide a formal delimitation of power; on the other, to the effects of truth that this power produces and transmits, and which in their turn reproduce this power. Hence we have a triangle: power, right, truth.

Schematically, we can formulate the traditional question of political philosophy in the following terms: how is the discourse of truth, or quite simply, philosophy as that discourse which *par excellence* is concerned with truth, able to fix limits to the rights of power? That is the traditional question. The one I would prefer to pose is rather different. Compared to the traditional, noble and philosophic question it is much more down to earth and concrete. My problem is rather this: what rules of right are implemented by the relations of power in the production of discourses of truth? Or alternatively, what type of power is susceptible of producing discourses of truth that in a society such as ours are endowed with such potent effects? What I mean is this: in a society such as ours, but basically in any society, there are manifold relations of power which permeate, characterize and constitute the social body, and these relations of power cannot themselves be established, consolidated nor implemented without the production, accumulation, circulation and functioning of a discourse. There can be no possible exercise of power without a certain economy of discourses of truth which operates through and on the basis of this association. We are subjected to the production of truth through power and we cannot exercise power except through the production of truth. This is the case for every society, but I believe that in ours the relationship between power, right and truth is organized in a highly specific fashion. If I were to characterize, not its mechanism itself, but its intensity and constancy, I would say that we are forced to produce the truth of power that our society demands, of which it has need, in order to function: we *must* speak the truth; we are constrained or condemned to confess or to discover the truth. Power never ceases its interrogation, its inquisition, its registration of truth: it institutionalizes, professionalizes and rewards its pursuit. In the last analysis, we must produce truth as we must produce wealth, indeed we must produce truth in order to produce wealth in the first place. In another way, we are also subjected to truth in the sense in which it is truth that makes the laws, that produces the true discourse which, at least partially, decides, transmits and itself extends upon the effects of power. In the end, we are judged, condemned, classified, determined in our undertakings, destined to a certain mode of living or dying, as a function of the true discourses which are the bearers of the specific effects of power.

So, it is the rules of right, the mechanisms of power, the effects of truth or if you like, the rules of power and the powers of true discourses, that can be said more or less to have formed the general terrain of my concern, even if, as I know full well, I have traversed it only partially and in a very zig-zag fashion. I should like to speak briefly about this course of research, about what I have considered as being its guiding principle and about the methodological imperatives and precautions which I have sought to adopt. As regards the general principle involved in a study of the relations between right and power, it seems to me that in Western societies since medieval times it has been royal power that has provided the essential focus around which legal thought has been elaborated. It is a response to the demands of royal power, for its profit and to serve as its instrument or justification, that the juridical edifice of our own society has been developed. Right in the West is the King's right. Naturally everyone is familiar with the famous, celebrated, repeatedly emphasized role of the jurists in the organization of royal power. We must not forget that the re-vitalization of Roman Law in the twelfth century was the major event around which, and on whose basis, the juridical edifice which had collapsed after the fall of the Roman Empire was reconstructed. This resurrection of Roman Law had in effect a technical and constitutive role to play in the establishment of the authoritarian, administrative, and, in the final analysis, absolute power of the monarchy. And when this legal edifice escapes in later centuries from the control of the monarch, when, more accurately, it is turned against that control, it is always the limits of this sovereign power that are put in question, its prerogatives that are challenged. In other words, I believe that the King remains the central personage in the whole legal edifice of the West. When it comes to the general organization of the legal system in the West, it is essentially with the King, his rights, his power and its eventual limitations, that one is dealing. Whether the jurists were the King's henchmen or his adversaries, it is of royal power that we are speaking in every case when we speak of these grandiose edifices of legal thought and knowledge.

There are two ways in which we do so speak. Either we do so in order to show the nature of the juridical armoury that invested royal power, to reveal the monarch as the effective embodiment of sovereignty, to demonstrate that his power, for all that it was absolute, was exactly that which befitted his fundamental right. Or, by contrast, we do so in order to show the necessity of imposing limits upon this sovereign power, of submitting it to certain rules of right, within whose confines it had to be exercised in order for it to remain legitimate. The essential role of the theory of right, from medieval times onwards, was to fix the legitimacy of power; that is the major problem around which the whole theory of right and sovereignty is organized.

When we say that sovereignty is the central problem of right in Western societies, what we mean basically is that the essential function of the discourse and techniques of right has been to efface the domination intrinsic to power in order to present the latter at the level of appearance under two different aspects: on the one hand, as the legitimate rights of sovereignty, and on the other, as the legal obligation to obey it. The system of right is centred entirely upon the King, and it is therefore designed to eliminate the fact of domination and its consequences.

My general project over the past few years has been, in essence, to reverse the mode of analysis followed by the entire discourse of right from the time of the Middle Ages. My aim, therefore, was to invert it, to give due weight, that is, to the fact of domination, to expose both its latent nature and its brutality. I then wanted to show not only how right is, in a general way, the instrument of this domination – which scarcely needs saying – but also to show the extent to which, and the forms in which, right (not simply the laws but the whole complex of apparatuses, institutions and regulations responsible for their application) transmits and puts in motion relations that are not relations of sovereignty, but of domination.

Moreover, in speaking of domination I do not have in mind that solid and global kind of domination that one person exercises over others, or one group over another, but the manifold forms of domination that can be exercised within society. Not the domination of the King in his central position, therefore, but that of his subjects in their mutual relations: not the uniform edifice of sovereignty, but the multiple forms of subjugation that have a place and function within the social organism.

The system of right, the domain of the law, are permanent agents of these relations of domination, these polymorphous techniques of subjugation. Right should be viewed, I believe, not in terms of a legitimacy to be established, but in terms of the methods of subjugation that it instigates.

The problem for me is how to avoid this question, central to the theme of right, regarding sovereignty and the obedience of individual subjects in order that I may substitute the problem of domination and subjugation for that of sovereignty and obedience. Given that this was to be the general line of my analysis, there were a certain number of methodological precautions that seemed requisite to its pursuit. In the very first place, it seemed important to accept that the analysis in question should not concern itself with the regulated and legitimate forms of power in their central locations, with the general mechanisms through which they operate, and the continual effects of these. On the contrary, it should be concerned with power at its extremities, in its ultimate destinations, with those points where it becomes capillary, that is, in its more regional and local forms and institutions. Its paramount concern, in fact, should be with the point where power surmounts the rules of right which organize and delimit it and extends itself beyond them, invests itself in institutions, becomes embodied in techniques, and equips itself with instruments and eventually even violent means of material intervention. To give an example: rather than try to discover where and how the right of punishment is founded on sovereignty, how it is presented in the theory of monarchical right or in that of democratic right, I have tried to see in what ways punishment and the power of punishment are effectively embodied in a certain number of local, regional, material institutions, which are concerned with torture or imprisonment, and to place these in the climate – at once institutional and physical, regulated and violent – of the effective apparatuses of punishment. In other words, one should try to locate power at the extreme points of its exercise, where it is always less legal in character.

A second methodological precaution urged that the analysis

should not concern itself with power at the level of conscious intention or decision; that it should not attempt to consider power from its internal point of view and that it should refrain from posing the labyrinthine and unanswerable question: 'Who then has power and what has he in mind? What is the aim of someone who possesses power?' Instead, it is a case of studying power at the point where its intention, if it has one, is completely invested in its real and effective practices. What is needed is a study of power in its external visage, at the point where it is in direct and immediate relationship with that which we can provisionally call its object, its target, its field of application, there — that is to say — where it installs itself and produces its real effects.

Let us not, therefore, ask why certain people want to dominate, what they seek, what is their overall strategy. Let us ask, instead, how things work at the level of on-going subjugation, at the level of those continuous and uninterrupted processes which subject our bodies, govern our gestures, dictate our behaviours, etc. In other words, rather than ask ourselves how the sovereign appears to us in his lofty isolation, we should try to discover how it is that subjects are gradually, progressively, really and materially constituted through a multiplicity of organisms, forces, energies, materials, desires, thoughts, etc. We should try to grasp subjection in its material instance as a constitution of subjects. This would be the exact opposite of Hobbes' project in *Leviathan*, and of that, I believe, of all jurists for whom the problem is the distillation of a single will — or rather, the constitution of a unitary, singular body animated by the spirit of sovereignty — from the particular wills of a multiplicity of individuals. Think of the scheme of Leviathan: insofar as he is a fabricated man, Leviathan is no other than the amalgamation of a certain number of separate individualities, who find themselves reunited by the complex of elements that go to compose the State; but at the heart of the State, or rather, at its head, there exists something which constitutes it as such, and this is sovereignty, which Hobbes says is precisely the spirit of Leviathan. Well, rather than worry about the problem of the central spirit, I believe that we must attempt to study the myriad of bodies which are constituted as peripheral *subjects* as a result of the effects of power.

A third methodological precaution relates to the fact that power is not to be taken to be a phenomenon of one individual's consolidated and homogeneous domination over others, or that of one group or class over others. What, by contrast, should always be kept in mind is that power, if we do not take too distant a view of it, is not that which makes the difference between those who exclusively possess and retain it, and those who do not have it and submit to it. Power must be analysed as something which circulates, or rather as something which only functions in the form of a chain. It is never localized here or there, never in anybody's hands, never appropriated as a commodity or piece of wealth. Power is employed and exercised through a net-like organization. And not only do individuals circulate between its threads; they are always in the position of simultaneously undergoing and exercising this power. They are not only its inert or consenting target; they are always also the elements of its articulation. In other words, individuals are the vehicles of power, not its points of application.

The individual is not to be conceived as a sort of elementary nucleus, a primitive atom, a multiple and inert material on which power comes to fasten or against which it happens to strike, and in so doing subdues or crushes individuals. In fact, it is already one of the prime effects of power that certain bodies, certain gestures, certain discourses, certain desires, come to be identified and constituted as individuals. The individual, that is, is not the *vis-à-vis* of power; it is, I believe, one of its prime effects. The individual is an effect of power, and at the same time, or precisely to the extent to which it is that effect, it is the element of its articulation. The individual which power has constituted is at the same time its vehicle.

There is a fourth methodological precaution that follows from this: when I say that power establishes a network through which it freely circulates, this is true only up to a certain point. In much the same fashion we could say that therefore we all have a fascism in our heads, or, more profoundly, that we all have a power in our bodies. But I do not believe that one should conclude from that that power is the best distributed thing in the world, although in some sense that is indeed so. We are not dealing with a sort of democratic or anarchic distribution of power through bodies. That is to say, it seems to me – and this then would be the fourth methodological precaution – that the important thing is not to attempt some kind of deduction of power starting from its centre and aimed at the discovery of the extent to which it permeates into the base, of the degree to which it reproduces itself down to and including the most molecular elements of society. One must rather conduct an *ascending* analysis of power, starting, that is, from its infinitesimal mechanisms, which each have their own history, their own trajectory, their own techniques and tactics, and then see how these mechanisms of power have been – and continue to be – invested, colonized, utilized, involuted, transformed, displaced, extended, etc., by ever more general mechanisms and by forms of global domination. It is not that this global domination extends itself right to the base in a plurality of repercussions: I believe that the manner in which the phenomena, the techniques and the procedures of power enter into play at the most basic levels must be analysed, that the way in which these procedures are displaced, extended and altered must certainly be demonstrated; but above all what must be shown is the manner in which they are invested and annexed by more global phenomena and the subtle fashion in which more general powers or economic interests are able to engage with these technologies that are at once both relatively autonomous of power and act as its infinitesimal elements. In order to make this clearer, one might cite the example of madness. The descending type of analysis, the one of which I believe one ought to be wary, will say that the bourgeoisie has, since the sixteenth or seventeenth century, been the dominant class; from this premise, it will then set out to deduce the internment of the insane. One can always make this deduction, it is always easily done and that is precisely what I would hold against it. It is in fact a simple matter to show that since lunatics are precisely those persons who are useless to industrial production, one is obliged to dispense with them. One could argue similarly in regard to infantile sexuality – and several thinkers, including Wilhelm Reich have indeed sought to do so up to a certain point. Given the domination of the bourgeois class, how can one understand the repression of infantile sexuality? Well, very simply – given that the human body had become essentially a force of production from the time of the seventeenth and eighteenth century, all the forms of its expenditure which did not lend themselves to the constitution of the productive forces – and were therefore exposed as redundant – were banned, excluded and repressed. These kinds of deduction are always possible. They are simultaneously correct and false. Above all they are too glib, because one can always do exactly the opposite and show, precisely by appeal to the principle of the dominance of the bourgeois class, that the forms of control of infantile sexuality could in no way have been predicted. On the contrary, it is equally plausible to suggest that what was needed was sexual training, the encouragement of a sexual precociousness, given that what was fundamentally at stake was the constitution of a labour force whose optimal state, as we well know, at least at the beginning of the nineteenth century, was to be infinite: the greater the labour force, the better able would the system of capitalist production have been to fulfil and improve its functions.

I believe that anything can be deduced from the general pheno-menon of the domination of the bourgeois class. What needs to be done is something quite different. One needs to investigate histori-cally, and beginning from the lowest level, how mechanisms of power have been able to function. In regard to the confinement of the insane, for example, or the repression and interdiction of sexuality, we need to see the manner in which, at the effective level of the family, of the immediate environment, of the cells and most basic units of society, these phenomena of repression or exclusion possessed their instruments and their logic, in response to a certain number of needs. We need to identify the agents responsible for them, their real agents (those which constituted the immediate social *entourage*, the family, parents, doctors etc.), and not be content to lump them under the formula of a generalized bourgeoi-sie. We need to see how these mechanisms of power, at a given moment, in a precise conjuncture and by means of a certain number of transformations, have begun to become economically advan-tageous and politically useful. I think that in this way one could easily manage to demonstrate that what the bourgeoisie needed, or that in which its system discovered its real interests, was not the exclusion of the mad or the surveillance and prohibition of infantile masturbation (for, to repeat, such a system can perfectly well tolerate quite opposite practices), but rather, the techniques and procedures themselves of such an exclusion. It is the mechanisms of that exclusion that are necessary, the apparatuses of surveillance, the medicalization of sexuality, of madness, of delinquency, all the micro-mechanisms of power, that came, from a certain moment in time, to represent the interests of the bourgeoisie. Or even better, we could say that to the extent to which this view of the bourgeoisie and of its interests appears to lack content, at least in regard to the problems with which we are here concerned, it reflects the fact that it was not the bourgeoisie itself which thought that madness had to be excluded or infantile sexuality repressed. What in fact happened instead was that the mechanisms of the exclusion of madness, and of the surveillance of infantile sexuality, began from a particular point in time, and for reasons which need to be studied, to reveal their political usefulness and to lend themselves to economic profit, and that as a natural consequence, all of a sudden, they came to be colonized and maintained by global mechanisms and the entire State system. It is only if we grasp these techniques of power and demonstrate the economic advantages or political utility that derives from them in a given context for specific reasons, that we can understand how these mechanisms come to be effectively incor-porated into the social whole.

To put this somewhat differently: the bourgeoisie has never had any use for the insane; but the procedures it has employed to exclude them have revealed and realized – from the nineteenth century onwards, and again on the basis of certain transformations – a political advantage, on occasion even a certain economic utility, which have consolidated the system and contributed to its overall functioning. The bourgeoisie is interested in power, not in madness, in the system of control of infantile sexuality, not in that phenomenon itself. The bourgeoisie could not care less about delinquents, about their punishment and rehabilitation, which economically have little importance, but it is concerned about the complex of mechanisms with which delinquency is controlled, pursued, punished and reformed etc.

As for our fifth methodological precaution: it is quite possible that the major mechanisms of power have been accompanied by ideological productions. There has, for example, probably been an ideology of education, an ideology of the monarchy, an ideology of parliamentary democracy, etc.; but basically I do not believe that what has taken place can be said to be ideological. It is both much more and much less than ideology. It is the production of effective instruments for the formation and accumulation of knowledge – methods of observation, techniques of registration, procedures for investigation and research, apparatuses of control. All this means that power, when it is exercised through these subtle mechanisms, cannot but evolve, organize and put into circulation a knowledge, or rather apparatuses of knowledge, which are not ideological constructs.

By way of summarizing these five methodological precautions, I would say that we should direct our researches on the nature of power not towards the juridical edifice of sovereignty, the State apparatuses and the ideologies which accompany them, but towards domination and the material operators of power, towards forms of subjection and the inflections and utilizations of their localized systems, and towards strategic apparatuses. We must eschew the model of Leviathan in the study of power. We must escape from the limited field of juridical sovereignty and State institutions, and instead base our analysis of power on the study of the techniques and tactics of domination.

This, in its general outline, is the methodological course that I believe must be followed, and which I have tried to pursue in the various researches that we have conducted over recent years on psychiatric power, on infantile sexuality, on political systems, etc. Now as one explores these fields of investigation, observing the methodological precautions I have mentioned, I believe that what then comes into view is a solid body of historical fact, which will ultimately bring us into confrontation with the problems of which I want to speak this year.

This solid, historical body of fact is the juridical–political theory of sovereignty of which I spoke a moment ago, a theory which has had four roles to play. In the first place, it has been used to refer to a mechanism of power that was effective under the feudal monarchy. In the second place, it has served as instrument and even as justification for the construction of the large-scale administrative monarchies. Again, from the time of the sixteenth century and more than ever from the seventeenth century onwards, but already at the time of the wars of religion, the theory of sovereignty has been a weapon which has circulated from one camp to another, which has been utilized in one sense or another, either to limit or else to re-inforce royal power: we find it among Catholic monarchists and Protestant anti-monarchists, among Protestant and more-or-less liberal monarchists, but also among Catholic partisans of regicide or dynastic transformation. It functions both in the hands of aristocrats and in the hands of parliamentarians. It is found among the representatives of royal power and among the last feudatories. In short, it was the major instrument of political and theoretical struggle around systems of power of the sixteenth and seventeenth centuries. Finally, in the eighteenth century, it is again this same theory of sovereignty, re-activated through the doctrine of Roman Law, that we find in its essentials in Rousseau and his contemporaries, but now with a fourth role to play: now it is concerned with the construction, in opposition to the administrative, authoritarian and absolutist monarchies, of an alternative model, that of parliamentary democracy. And it is still this role that it plays at the moment of the Revolution.

Well, it seems to me that if we investigate these four roles there is a definite conclusion to be drawn: as long as a feudal type of society survived, the problems to which the theory of sovereignty was addressed were in effect confined to the general mechanisms of power, to the way in which its forms of existence at the higher level of society influenced its exercise at the lowest levels. In other words, the relationship of sovereignty, whether interpreted in a wider or a narrower sense, encompasses the totality of the social body. In effect, the mode in which power was exercised could be defined in its essentials in terms of the relationship sovereign–subject. But in the seventeenth and eighteenth centuries we have the production of an important phenomenon, the emergence, or rather the invention, of a new mechanism of power possessed of highly specific procedural techniques, completely novel instruments, quite different apparatuses, and which is also, I believe, absolutely incompatible with the relations of sovereignty.

This new mechanism of power is more dependent upon bodies and what they do than upon the Earth and its products. It is a mechanism of power which permits time and labour, rather than wealth and commodities, to be extracted from bodies. It is a type of power which is constantly exercised by means of surveillance rather than in a discontinuous manner by means of a system of levies or obligations distributed over time. It presupposes a tightly knit grid of material coercions rather than the physical existence of a sovereign. It is ultimately dependent upon the principle, which introduces a genuinely new economy of power, that one must be able simultaneously both to increase the subjected forces and to improve the force and efficacy of that which subjects them.

This type of power is in every aspect the antithesis of that mechanism of power which the theory of sovereignty described or sought to transcribe. The latter is linked to a form of power that is exercised over the Earth and its products, much more than over human bodies and their operations. The theory of sovereignty is something which refers to the displacement and appropriation on the part of power, not of time and labour, but of goods and wealth. It allows discontinuous obligations distributed over time to be given legal expression but it does not allow for the codification of a continuous surveillance. It enables power to be founded in the physical existence of the sovereign, but not in continuous and permanent systems of surveillance. The theory of sovereignty permits the foundation of an absolute power in the absolute expenditure of power. It does not allow for a calculation of power in terms of the minimum expenditure for the maximum return.

This new type of power, which can no longer be formulated in terms of sovereignty, is, I believe, one of the great inventions of bourgeois society. It has been a fundamental instrument in the constitution of industrial capitalism and of the type of society that is its accompaniment. This non-sovereign power, which lies outside the form of sovereignty, is disciplinary power. Impossible to describe in the terminology of the theory of sovereignty from which it differs so radically, this disciplinary power ought by rights to have led to the disappearance of the grand juridical edifice created by that theory. But in reality, the theory of sovereignty has continued not only to exist as an ideology of right, but also to provide the organizing principle of the legal codes which Europe acquired in the nineteenth century, beginning with the Napoleonic Code.

Why has the theory of sovereignty persisted in this fashion as an ideology and an organizing principle of these major legal codes? For two reasons, I believe. On the one hand, it has been, in the eighteenth and again in the nineteenth century, a permanent instrument of criticism of the monarchy and of all the obstacles that can thwart the development of disciplinary society. But at the same time, the theory of sovereignty, and the organization of a legal code centred upon it, have allowed a system of right to be superimposed upon the mechanisms of discipline in such a way as to conceal its actual procedures, the element of domination inherent in its techniques, and to guarantee to everyone, by virtue of the sovereignty of the State, the exercise of his proper sovereign rights. The juridical systems — and this applies both to their codification and to their theorization — have enabled sovereignty to be democratized through the constitution of a public right articulated upon collective sovereignty, while at the same time this democratization of sovereignty was fundamentally determined by and grounded in mechanisms of disciplinary coercion.

To put this in more rigorous terms, one might say that once it became necessary for disciplinary constraints to be exercised through mechanisms of domination and yet at the same time for their effective exercise of power to be disguised, a theory of sovereignty was required to make an appearance at the level of the legal apparatus, and to re-emerge in its codes. Modern society, then, from the nineteenth century up to our own day, has been characterized on the one hand, by a legislation, a discourse, an organization based on public right, whose principle of articulation is the social body and the delegative status of each citizen; and, on the other hand, by a closely linked grid of disciplinary coercions whose purpose is in fact to assure the cohesion of this same social body. Though a theory of right is a necessary companion to this grid, it cannot in any event provide the terms of its endorsement. Hence these two limits, a right of sovereignty and a mechanism of discipline, which define, I believe, the arena in which power is exercised. But these two limits are so heterogeneous that they cannot possibly be reduced to each other. The powers of modern society are exercised through, on the basis of, and by virtue of, this very heterogeneity between a public right of sovereignty and a polymorphous disciplinary mechanism. This is not to suggest that there is on the one hand an explicit and scholarly system of right which is that of sovereignty, and, on the other hand, obscure and unspoken disciplines which carry out their shadowy operations in the depths, and thus constitute the bedrock of the great mechanism of power. In reality, the disciplines have their own discourse. They engender, for the reasons of which we spoke earlier, apparatuses of knowledge (*savoir*) and a multiplicity of new domains of understanding. They are extraordinarily inventive participants in the order of these knowledge-producing apparatuses. Disciplines are the bearers of a discourse, but this cannot be the discourse of right. The discourse of discipline has nothing in common with that of law, rule, or sovereign will. The disciplines may well be the carriers of a discourse that speaks of a rule, but this is not the juridical rule deriving from sovereignty, but a natural rule, a norm. The code they come to define is not that of law but that of normalization. Their reference is to a theoretical horizon which of necessity has nothing in common with the edifice of right. It is human science which constitutes their domain, and clinical knowledge their jurisprudence.

In short, what I have wanted to demonstrate in the course of the last few years is not the manner in which at the advance front of the exact sciences the uncertain, recalcitrant, confused dominion of human behaviour has little by little been annexed to science: it is not through some advancement in the rationality of the exact sciences that the human sciences are gradually constituted. I believe that the process which has really rendered the discourse of the human sciences possible is the juxtaposition, the encounter between two lines of approach, two mechanisms, two absolutely heterogeneous types of discourse: on the one hand there is the re-organization of right that invests sovereignty, and on the other, the mechanics of the coercive forces whose exercise takes a disciplinary form. And I believe that in our own times power is exercised simultaneously through this right and these techniques and that these techniques and these discourses, to which the disciplines give rise invade the area of right so that the procedures of normalization come to be ever more constantly engaged in the colonization of those of law. I believe that all this can explain the global functioning of what I would call a *society of normalization*. I mean, more precisely, that disciplinary normalizations come into ever greater conflict with the juridical systems of sovereignty: their incompatibility with each other is ever more acutely felt and apparent; some kind of arbitrating discourse is made ever more necessary, a type of power and of knowledge that the sanctity of science would render neutral. It is precisely in the extension of medicine that we see, in some sense, not so much the linking as the perpetual exchange or encounter of mechanisms of discipline with the principle of right. The developments of medicine, the general medicalization of behaviours, conducts, discourses, desires, etc., take place at the point of intersection between the two heterogeneous levels of discipline and sovereignty. For this reason, against these usurpations by the disciplinary mechanisms, against this ascent of a power that is tied to scientific knowledge, we find that there is no solid recourse available to us today, such being our situation, except that which lies precisely in the return to a theory of right organized around sovereignty and articulated upon its ancient principle. When today one wants to object in some way to the disciplines and all the effects of power and knowledge that are linked to them, what is it that one does, concretely, in real life, what do the Magistrates Union[1] or other similar institutions do, if not precisely appeal to this canon of right, this famous, formal right, that is said to be bourgeois, and which in reality is the right of sovereignty? But I believe that we find ourselves here in a kind of blind alley: it is not through recourse to sovereignty against discipline that the effects of disciplinary power can be limited, because sovereignty and disciplinary mechanisms are two absolutely integral constitutents of the general mechanism of power in our society.

If one wants to look for a non-disciplinary form of power, or rather, to struggle against disciplines and disciplinary power, it is not towards the ancient right of sovereignty that one should turn, but towards the possibility of a new form of right, one which must indeed be anti-disciplinarian, but at the same time liberated from the principle of sovereignty. It is at this point that we once more come up against the notion of repression, whose use in this context I believe to be doubly unfortunate. On the one hand, it contains an obscure reference to a certain theory of sovereignty, the sovereignty of the sovereign rights of the individual, and on the other hand, its usage introduces a system of psychological reference points borrowed from the human sciences, that is to say, from discourses and practices that belong to the disciplinary realm. I believe that the notion of repression remains a juridical–disciplinary notion whatever the critical use one would make of it. To this extent the critical application of the notion of repression is found to be vitiated and nullified from the outset by the two-fold juridical and disciplinary reference it contains to sovereignty on the one hand and to normalization on the other.

NOTES

1 This Union, established after 1968, has adopted a radical line on civil rights, the law and the prisons.

12
Power and Privilege

GERHARD LENSKI

FORCE AND ITS TRANSFORMATION

Of the two principles which govern the distributive process, need and power, the first is relatively simple and poses few problems of great importance or difficulty. Unhappily, the same cannot be said of the second. Of all the concepts used by sociologists, few are the source of more confusion and misunderstanding than power. Hence it is necessary to spell out in some detail the nature of this concept and how it functions in the distributive process.

As a starting point, it may be well to return briefly to one of the postulates introduced in the last chapter [of *Power and Privilege*]. There it was assumed that survival is the chief goal of the great majority of men. If this is so, then it follows that *the ability to take life is the most effective form of power*. In other words, more men will respond more readily to the threat of the use of *force* than to any other. In effect, it constitutes the final court of appeals in human affairs; there is no appeal from force in a given situation except the exercise of superior force. Hence force stands in the same relationship to other forms of power as trumps to the other suits in the game of bridge, and those who can exercise the greatest force are like those who control trumps.

This fact has been recognized by countless observers of the human scene in every age. As Pascal put it, 'Not being able to make that which is just strong, man has made that which is strong just.' Cicero made the same point when he said, 'Laws are dumb in the midst of arms', and Hobbes asserted that 'Covenants without the sword are but words, and of no strength to secure a man at all.'

This principle is also recognized by the leaders of nations, the practical men of affairs. Every sovereign state restricts, and where

Reprinted with permission of the author from Gerhard Lenski, *Power and Privilege: A Theory of Social Stratification*, New York: McGraw Hill, 1966, pp. 50–80.

possible prohibits, the independent exercise of force by its subjects. States may be tolerant of many things, but never of the growth of independent military organizations within their territories. The reason is obvious: any government which cannot suppress each and every forceful challenge to its authority is overthrown. Force is the foundation of sovereignty.

On this point there is no dispute between conservatives and radicals. Their arguments are concerned only with the ends served by the state's use of force. Conservatives insist that might is employed only as the handmaiden of right, to restrain and rebuke those who put self-interest above the common good, while radicals maintain that the state employs might to suppress right, in defense of selfish interests.

If force is the foundation of political sovereignty, it is also the foundation of the distributive system in every society where there is a surplus to be divided. Where coercive power is weak, challenges inevitably occur, and the system is eventually destroyed and replaced by another based more firmly on force. Men struggling over control of the surplus of a society will not accept defeat so long as there is a higher court of appeals to which they may take their case with some likelihood of success and profit to themselves.

The principle involved here is essentially the same as the principle of escalation with which modern military men are so concerned. Small wars based on small weapons inevitably grow into more deadly wars utilizing more deadly weapons if, by advancing the level of conflict, one of the parties anticipates turning defeat into victory. Similarly, in the case of conflicts within societies, the parties involved are always motivated to take the issue to the final court of appeals so long as there is the likelihood of benefiting by it. While men will not resort to armed revolution for trivial gains, when control over the entire surplus of a society is involved, the prospect is more enticing. The attractiveness varies directly with the weakness of the current regime.

Nevertheless, as Edmund Burke, the famed English conservative, recognized, 'The use of force alone is but temporary. It may subdue for a moment; but it does not remove the necessity of subduing again; and a nation is not governed, which is perpetually to be conquered.' Though force is the most effective instrument for seizing power in a society, and though it always remains the foundation of any system of inequality, it is not the most effective instrument for retaining and exploiting a position of power and deriving the maximum benefits from it. Therefore, regardless of the objectives of a new regime, once organized opposition has been destroyed it is to its advantage to make increasing use of other techniques and instruments of control, and to allow force to recede into the background to be used only when other techniques fail.

If the new elite has materialistic goals and is concerned solely with self-aggrandizement, it soon discovers that the rule of might is both inefficient and costly. So long as it relies on force, much of the profit is consumed by the costs of coercion. If the population obeys only out of fear of physical violence, a large portion of the time, energy, and wealth of the elite are invariably consumed in the effort to keep it under control and separate the producers from the product of their labors. Even worse, honor, which normally ranks high in the scale of human values, is denied to those who rule by force alone.[1]

If materialistic elites have strong motives for shifting from the rule of might to the rule of right, ideologically motivated elites have even stronger. If the visions and ideals which led them to undertake the terrible risks and hardships of revolution are ever to be fulfilled, the voluntary cooperation of the population is essential, and this cannot be obtained by force. Force is, at best, the means to an end. That end, the establishment of a new social order, can never be fully attained until most members of society freely accept it as their own. The purpose of the revolution is to destroy the old elite and their institutions, which prevent the fulfillment of this dream. Once they are destroyed, an ideological elite strives to rule by persuasion. Thus *those who seize power by force find it advantageous to legitimize their rule once effective organized opposition is eliminated.* Force can no longer continue to play the role it did. It can no longer function as the private resource of a special segment of the population. Rather it must be transformed into a public resource used in the defense of law and order.

This may seem to be the equivalent of saying that those who have at great risk to themselves displaced the old elite must now give up all they have won. Actually, however, this is not at all necessary since, with a limited exercise of intelligence, force can be transformed into authority, and might into right.

There are various means by which this transformation can be effected. To begin with, by virtue of its coercive power, a new elite is in a good position to rewrite the law of the land as it sees fit. This affords them a unique opportunity, since by its very nature law is identified with justice and the rule of right. Since legal statutes are stated in general and impersonal terms, they appear to support abstract principles of justice rather than the special interests of particular men or classes of men. The fact that laws exist prior to the events to which they are applied suggests an objective impartiality which also contributes to their acceptance. Yet laws can always be written in such a way that they favor some particular segment of society. Anatole France saw this clearly when he wrote, 'The law in its majestic equality forbids the rich as well as the poor to sleep under bridges, to beg in the street, and to steal bread.' Edwin Sutherland provided detailed documentation of the presence of such bias, as have a host of others.[2] In short, laws may be written in such a way that they protect the interests of the elite while being couched in very general, universalistic terms.

Often a new elite finds that it does not even need to change the laws to accomplish its ends. Typically the old laws were written to serve the interests of the holders of certain key offices, and once these offices have been seized, the new elite can use them as resources to build their fortunes or attain other goals.

Institutions which shape public opinion serve as a second instrument for legitimizing the position of new elites. Through the use of a combination of inducements and threats, educational and religious institutions, together with the mass media and other molders of public opinion, can usually be transformed into instruments of propaganda for the new regime. A determined and intelligent elite working through them can usually surround itself with an aura of legitimacy within a few months or years.

The concept of 'propaganda', or the manipulation of consensus, is an integral element in the synthetic theory of stratification. A recognition of this phenomenon and the special role it plays in the distributive process enables us to avoid the impasse which has driven Dahrendorf and others to despair of ever reconciling the conservative and radical traditions. Consensus and coercion are more closely related than those who preach the Janus-headed character of society would have us believe. *Coercive power can often be used to create a new consensus.*

There is probably no better example of this than the Soviet Union. Here a small minority seized control of the machinery of state in 1917 and used the coercive powers of the state to transform the educational system of the nation and the mass media into one gigantic instrument of propaganda. Within a single generation the vast majority of Russians were converted to a sincere and genuine support of most of the basic elements of the Communist Party's program.[3]

In the short run, propaganda may be used to support a great variety of programs and policies adopted by an elite. In the long run, however, its basic aim is the dissemination of an ideology which provides a moral justification for the regime's exercise of power. Gaetano Mosca put it this way:

> Ruling classes do not justify their power exclusively by *de facto* possession of it, but try to find a moral and legal basis for it, representing it as the logical and necessary consequence of doctrines and beliefs that are generally recognized and accepted.[4]

Most of the theories of political sovereignty debated by philosophers have been intellectualized versions of some popular ideology. This can be seen in the now discredited belief in the divine right of kings. In our own day, the belief in popular sovereignty serves the same justifying function. A basic element in our current American ideology is the thesis expressed by Lincoln that ours is a 'government of the people, by the people, for the people'. Another basic element is incorporated in Francis Scott Key's oft-sung phrase, 'the land of the free'. It is difficult to exaggerate the contribution of these beliefs to the political stability of our present political system and of the distributive system based on it.

Finally, the transformation of the rule of might into the rule of right is greatly facilitated by the pressures of daily life, which severely limit the political activities of the vast majority of mankind. Though the majority may become politically active in a significant way for a brief time in a revolutionary era, the necessity of securing a livelihood quickly drives most from the political arena. For better or worse, few men have the financial resources which enable them to set aside their usual economic activities for long. As a result, the affairs of state in any civilized society, and in many that are not, are directed by a small minority. The majority are largely apolitical. Even in popular democracies the vast majority do no more than cast a ballot at infrequent intervals. The formulation of public policy and the various other tasks required by the system are left in the hands of a tiny minority. This greatly facilitates the task of a new regime as it seeks to make the transition from the rule of might to the rule of right.

THE RULE OF RIGHT

On first consideration it may seem that the rule of right is merely the rule of might in a new guise, and therefore no real change can be expected in the distributive process. Such a view is as unwarranted as that which denies the role might continues to play in support of vested interests, even under the rule of right. The fact is that, as the basis of power is shifted from might to right, certain subtle but important changes occur which have far-reaching consequences.

To begin with, if the powers of the regime are to be accepted as rightful and legitimate they must be exercised in some degree, at least, in accord with the conceptions of justice and morality held by the majority — conceptions which spring from their self-interest and partisan group interests. Thus, even though the laws promulgated by a new elite may be heavily slanted to favor themselves, there are limits beyond which this cannot be carried if they wish to gain the benefits of the rule of right.

Second, after the shift to the rule of law, the interests of any single member of the elite can no longer safely be equated with the interests of the elite as a whole. For example, if a member of the new elite enters into a contractual arrangement with some member of the nonelite, and this turns out badly for him, it is to his interest to ignore the law and break the contract. However, this is not to the interest of the other members of the elite since most contractual arrangements work to their benefit. Therefore, it is to their interest to enforce the law in support of the claims of the nonelite to preserve respect for the law with all the benefits this provides them.

Vilfredo Pareto, the great Italian scholar who has contributed so much to our understanding of these problems, has pointed out a third change associated with the shift from the rule of might to the rule of right. As he observed, those who have won power by force will, under the rule of right, gradually be replaced by a new kind of person and in time these persons will form a new kind of elite. To describe the nature of this change, Pareto wrote of the passing of governmental power from 'the lions' to 'the foxes'.[5] The lions are skilled in the use of force, the foxes in the use of cunning. In other words the shift from the rule of might means that new skills become essential, and therefore there is a high probability that many of the elite will be displaced because they lack these skills. This displacement is greatly facilitated by the fact that the interests of the elite as a class are no longer identical with the interests of each individual member, which means that individually they become vulnerable. Even those who hang on are forced to change, so that in time the nature of the elite as a class is substantially altered, provided it is not destroyed first by a new leonine revolution or coup. Though this change means increased reliance on intelligence and less on force, as Pareto's choice of the term 'fox' and his emphasis on 'cunning' indicate, the shift to the rule of right is not the beginning of the millennium when lambs can lie down safely with lions – or foxes. Nor is it the end of the era in which self-interest and partisan group interests dominate human action.

As Pareto's analysis suggests, the rule of the foxes means not merely the rise and fall of individuals, but also changes in the power position of whole classes. Specifically, it means some decline in the position of the military and a corresponding rise by the commercial class and the class of professional politicians, both of which are traditionally skilled in the use of cunning. To a lesser degree, it means some improvement in the status of most of the nonmanual classes engaged in peaceful, civilian pursuits.

Fourth, and finally, the transition from the rule of might to the rule of right usually means greater decentralization of power. Under the rule of might, all power tends to be concentrated in the hands of an inner circle of the dominant elite and their agents. Independent centers of power are viewed as a threat and hence are destroyed or taken over. Under the rule of right, however, this is not the case. So long as they remain subject to the law, diverse centers of power can develop and compete side by side. This development is not inevitable, but it can, and probably will, happen once the elite no longer has to fear for the survival of the new regime. As many observers have noted, the degree of unity within a group tends to be a function of the degree to which the members perceive their existence as threatened by others.

In view of these changes, it becomes clear that shifts from the rule of might to the rule of right and vice versa constitute one of the more important sources of variation within societal types defined in technological terms. In other words, even among societies at the same level of technological development, we must expect differences along the lines indicated above, reflecting differences in their position on the might-right continuum.

THE VARIETIES OF INSTITUTIONALIZED POWER

As the foregoing makes clear, *with the shift from the rule of might to the rule of right, power continues to be the determinant of privilege, but the forms of power change.* Force is replaced by institutionalized forms of power as the most useful resource in the struggle between individuals and groups for prestige and privilege, though force still remains in the picture as the ultimate guarantee of these more genteel forms.

Institutionalized power differs from force in a number of ways which deserve note. To begin with, it is a socially acceptable form of power, which means that those who exercise it are less likely to be challenged and more likely to obtain popular support than are those who use force. Second, institutionalized power tends to be much more impersonal. Individuals claim the benefits of institutionalized power not because of their personal qualities or accomplishments, which might easily be challenged, but simply because they occupy a certain role or office or own a certain piece of property. To be sure, it is often assumed that those who enjoy the benefits of institutionalized power are entitled to them by virtue of superior accomplishments or personal qualities, but this is not the crucial issue and the beneficiary does not have to demonstrate these things. It is enough just to be the occupant of the role or office or the owner of the property. Institutionalized power insures that the benefits flow automatically to such persons without regard to their personal qualities or accomplishments. This is, of course, the chief reason why those who gain power by force strive to convert force into institutionalized power.

Institutionalized power takes many forms, but it always involves the possession of certain enforceable rights which increase one's capacity to carry out one's own will even in the face of opposition. It would be impossible to identify and discuss all these many forms here, but it is important to identify some of the more basic and show their varied nature.[6]

One of the basic distinctions within the category of institutionalized power is that between *authority* and *influence*. Authority is the enforceable right to command others. Influence, by contrast, is much more subtle. It is the ability to manipulate the social situation of others, or their perception of it, by the exercise of one's resources and rights, thereby increasing the pressures on others to act in accordance with one's own wishes.[7] Though these two forms of institutionalized power are quite distinct on the analytical level, they are often hopelessly intertwined on the empirical.

Institutionalized power varies not only in the mode of its action but also in terms of the foundations on which it rests. Here one can speak of a distinction between *the power of position* and *the power of property*. The power of position means *the power which rightfully belongs to the incumbent of any social role or organizational office possessing authority or influence*. This can be seen in the case of officers of state who enjoy great authority and influence so long as they continue to occupy their post, but who lose it when they are replaced. While this is one of the more impressive examples of the power of position, the same basic phenomenon can be seen in the case of the incumbents of a host of lesser roles. One must include under this heading not merely positions in political organizations, but also those in economic, religious, educational, and military organizations, together with age and sex roles, roles in kin groups, roles in racial and ethnic groups, and every other kind of role or office with authority or influence.

A second foundation on which institutionalized power commonly rests is the *private ownership of property*. Though property and position have often been closely linked, the connection is neither necessary nor inevitable. The ownership of property is frequently dissociated from occupancy of a particular office or role. Since property is, by definition, something in short supply and hence of value, the owner of property controls a resource which can be used to influence the actions of others. The more he owns, the greater is his capacity to influence, and thus the greater his power. In some instances, as in the ownership of slaves or of a political office which has been purchased, the power of property can take the form of authority. It also takes the form of authority to the extent that the owner is entitled to proscribe certain actions by others – that is, order them not to do certain things, such as trespass on his land.

Before concluding this brief introduction to institutionalized power, it may be well to take note of Simmel's observation that where the rule of law or right prevails, there is always a two-way flow of influence (and sometimes, one might add, of authority as well) between the more powerful and the less powerful.[8] This point is easily forgotten, since the very concept 'power' suggests a one-directional flow. To say that there is a two-way flow does not mean that the flow is equally strong in both directions, but it does mean that one should not ignore the secondary flow or the factors responsible for it and the consequences of it.[9]

NOTES

1 For a good discussion of the limitations of rule by force, see Robert Dahl and Charles Lindblom, *Politics, Economics, and Welfare* (Harper & Row, New York, 1953), pp. 107–9. See also Karl A. Wittfogel, *Oriental Despotism: A Comparative Study of Total Power* (Yale University Press, New Haven, Conn., 1957), chapter 4.

2 Edwin Sutherland, *White Collar Crime* (Holt, New York, 1949). For a very different kind of documentation of the partiality of laws, see Philip Stern, *The Great Treasury Raid* (Random House, New York, 1964) or any of the many excellent books on political lobbying by vested interests and the benefits derived therefrom.

3 For documentation of this sweeping generalization, see Alex Inkeles

and Raymond Bauer, *The Soviet Citizen* (Harvard University Press, Cambridge, Mass., 1959). On the basis of interviews with hundreds of displaced persons from the Soviet Union immediately after World War II, these writers concluded that there was only limited questioning of the wisdom of state socialism, centralized planning, and the other major elements of Soviet domestic policy. The chief criticisms were directed at the means employed by the Party in achieving its ends – especially the use of terror. This same conclusion has been reached by most other experts on the Soviet Union.

4 Gaetano Mosca, *The Ruling Class*, translated by Hannah Kahn (McGraw-Hill, New York, 1939), p. 70.

5 See Vilfredo Pareto, *The Mind and Society*, translated by A. Bongiorno and Arthur Livingstone and edited by Livingstone (Harcourt, Brace & World, New York, 1935), vol. III, especially paragraphs 2170–2278.

6 There have been numerous attempts to classify the various forms of power, but none have been completely successful. For three of the better efforts, see Herbert Goldhamer and Edward Shils, 'Types of power and status', *American Journal of Sociology*, 45 (1939), pp. 171–82; Harold Lasswell and Abraham Kaplan, *Power and Society: A Framework for Political Inquiry* (Yale University Press, New Haven, Conn., 1950), chapter 5; and Robert Bierstedt, 'An analysis of social power', *American Sociological Review*, 15 (1950), pp. 730–8.

7 In many sociological writings the relationship between power and influence is extremely confusing. Sometimes they are treated as synonymous, other times as two distinct phenomena with no area of overlap. Influence should be treated as one special type of power. This approach is consistent both with good English usage and with the insights of some of the abler social theorists. For example, *Webster's Collegiate Dictionary* (5th edn) defines influence as 'the act or the power of producing an effect *without apparent force or direct authority*' (emphasis added).

8 George Simmel, *The Sociology of George Simmel*, edited and translated by Kurt Wolff (The Free Press, New York, 1950), part 3.

9 More recently the same point was made by Robert Dahl and Charles Lindblom in their book *Politics, Economics and Welfare*, part 4, where they point to the existence of four sociopolitical systems, two of which, price systems and polyarchical systems, involve some measure of influence by the less powerful over the more powerful.

13

Macht, Power, *Puissance*: Democratic Prose or Demoniacal Poetry?

RAYMOND ARON

The words 'power' and '*Macht*', in English and German, '*pouvoir*' or '*puissance*' in French, continue to be surrounded by a kind of sacred halo or, it may be preferable to say, imbued with mysterious overtones that have something terrifying about them. The demoniacal character of power (*puissance*), *Die Dämonie der Macht*, is the title of a book that was written after the adventure of the Hitler regime, and suggested by it. Specialists in international relations use the term 'power politics', the equivalent of '*Machtpolitik*', but not without some ambiguity regarding the meaning of this concept, which sometimes designates what is the essence of relations between States, sometimes a doctrine – most frequently condemned – about such relations. Across the Channel, as across the Atlantic, Lord Acton never fails to be quoted: 'Power corrupts, absolute power corrupts absolutely.' Montesquieu before him had written: 'Experience in all ages has proved that every man who possesses power is inclined to abuse it; he goes on exercising it until he comes up against the limits. Who would say so? Virtue itself needs limits.' When C. Wright Mills sought to denounce the minority that rules the United States from the shadows he coined the expression 'power elite', adopting from the tradition of Machiavelli one of these two terms, 'elite', and combining it with the term 'power', execrated by marxists and radicals. For power (*pouvoir*) is an evil in itself; it is doubly so if one adds that it is in the hands of an elite, for, in the American ideological climate, by definition the few will not comprise the best, since power corrupts those that possess it.

Raymond Aron, '*Macht*, power, *puissance*: prose démocratique ou poésie démoniaque?', *European Journal of Sociology*, V, 1 (1964), pp. 27–51, is reprinted with permission of the journal and translated by W. D. Halls.

Let us refuse to listen to these pathetic echoes of the fears and quarrels entertained by thinkers and let us address our questions to the sociologists or political scientists of today. A Dutch sociologist,[1] after reviewing a number of definitions put forward by various authors, arrives at the following formulation: 'power is the possibility, on the part of a person or group, to restrict other persons or groups in the choice of their behaviour, in pursuance of his or its purposes'. And, with the same drift of meaning, C. J. Friedrich writes that power is 'the relationship between men that manifests itself in the behaviour of those who follow (or obey)'. He likewise states: 'When the behaviour of a certain group of men conforms to the wishes of one or several of them, the relation between them shall be called the power of L over A, B, C.'[2]

These definitions are not equivalent, and each presents difficulties. The first one claims to eliminate psychological elements, such as 'consciousness', 'will' and 'motivation'. But the reference to the objectives of the person possessing power, as well as to the restrictions on the choice left to those who undergo it, rules out the possibility of determining the subject–object relationship of power, if we leave out of account what occurs (or what is presumed to occur) in the consciousness of the two parties. Furthermore, this definition is, so to speak, an indirect one: it does not summon to mind the fact that certain people command and others obey, or that some lead and others follow. It does not even suggest that the 'freedom' of those who are the objects of power is suppressed or curtailed. 'The possibility of taking initiative remains completely unimpaired; only the range of choice is restricted.'[3] On the other hand, Friedrich's definition is direct or positive: the power relationship is defined according to usage by the fact that 'certain individuals follow others'. Yet since they do not follow them always or in everything, the difference between the direct or positive definition on the one hand, and on the other, the indirect or negative definition, is not a decisive one.

In the final analysis, modern sociologies of power have all originated in a procedure that might equally well be called formalization or abstraction. Society as we observe it comprises a multiplicity of relationships of command and obedience. The same individual is in turn the one who commands and the one who obeys, not only because of the hierarchy that is peculiar to complex organizations, but also because of the multiplicity of social systems to which each individual belongs. If we therefore resolve to discover a concept that is applicable to all the relationships of command and obedience, both public and private, by right or in fact, in every sphere of collective life, without taking into consideration the means employed by the one who commands and the feelings experienced by the one who obeys – then we shall necessarily end up with an *interpersonal and dissymetrical* relationship, the feature of which will be: 'someone walks or speaks, or takes the initiative, and others follow and listen'. Indeed, in order to empty the relationship of command and obedience even more completely of its real content, one may even say 'that the freedom of choice of some is restricted by the voluntary action of 'an individual or a group'.[4] From that moment onwards power will have ceased to be mysterious, fascinating and demoniacal. How would a society be possible without there being both subjects and objects of power, namely, without the freedom of choice of A, B and C being restricted at every instant by the power of X? Or without A, B and C following the initiative taken by X? In order to create the fiction of a society without 'the power of man over man' F. Hayek is obliged to postulate a radical antithesis between the rule of laws and that of men. He has to acknowledge that most laws leave the individual free to combine means together so as to arrive at ends, whilst the explicit command of one man causes another to be his instrument. Yet why should the demon be exorcised? Purified through a process of scientific abstraction, power (*pouvoir*) no longer spreads either enthusiasm or terror abroad. It has become neutral, pallid, flat. There is no hindrance to it being compared to money, as Talcott Parsons does with alacrity. Power (*pouvoir*) is henceforth the most widely distributed thing in the world. Unequally distributed, for sure: one person possesses much, another little power (*pouvoir*). But Parsons freely admits that it would be untrue to affirm that someone has *no* power (*pouvoir*). The person who possesses only a dime has little money, but despite everything he is not completely devoid of power (*pouvoir*). In the same way, no-one is utterly deprived of power (*pouvoir*) (should one add: under the political system of the United States?), however minute his share in it may be.

Personally, I do not question the legitimacy of the formal conceptualization, which tends to be supra-historical, except on two conditions: one must not fail to recognize the specificity of problems and of historical and social situations; nor must one wrongly assimilate the political order to the economic order, power (*pouvoir*) to money, as if the inequality of the resources or income available to each individual were comparable to the inequality of power (*pouvoir*).

Up to now we have followed usage and employed the term '*pouvoir*' as the equivalent of 'power' and of '*Macht*'. French has two words to translate '*Macht*' and 'power': '*pouvoir*' and '*puissance*'.

Both have the same origin: the Latin verb 'posse' ('to be capable of, to have the strength to'). '*Pouvoir*' is the infinitive of the verb and, according to Littré's definition, 'merely denotes the action', whilst '*puissance*' (the participle) designates 'something lasting and permanent'. One has the *puissance* to do something, and one exercises the *pouvoir* to do it. It is for this reason that we talk of the *puissance* of a machine, and not its *pouvoir*. This distinction would therefore be roughly that between potential and act. It is not unhelpful to recall that in English 'power', depending upon the particular case, is applied to either a 'potential' or an 'act'. Or it designates a potential that is revealed and whose scope is measured by passing to the act itself. In this way can be explained why the kind of sociology that prides itself on being strictly empirical and operational sometimes questions the utility of the term 'power' to the extent that it designates a potential that is never made manifest save through acts (decisions). Originally the duality of 'puissance' and 'pouvoir' was that of 'potential' and 'act', but usage has brought in other shades of meaning. In French it has become common to term '*Pouvoir*' the man, or rather the minority, that decides in the name of the collectivity or takes decisions of a kind that affect the collectivity. In this meaning, which I dare not call vulgar, for the word is used in this sense by many political scientists, *le Pouvoir* is assimilated to the ruling minority in the State. One might even say that *le Pouvoir* is the human incarnation of the State. An author who poses the question to himself as to the reason for the existence and the basis of *le Pouvoir* is in reality asking why all societies, with the exception of some primitive ones, have known a concentration of power – namely, the entrusting to one or several persons of the capacity (which is acknowledged to be legitimate) for making rules for everybody, or for imposing on everybody respect for those rules, or finally for taking decisions that are mandatory, either in fact or in law, on everybody. *One* man declares the collectivity to be at war with another: the other members of the collectivity are subjected to the consequences of that decision to the point where they may risk or sacrifice their lives in combat.

The word '*puissance*' is not used in French in that sense. One talks of 'taking power' ('*prendre le pouvoir*') or 'coming to power' ('*arriver au pouvoir*') (and these expressions are translated into German by using '*Macht*' and into English by using 'power'); we do not use the terms '*arriver à la puissance*' (for coming to power) or '*perdre la puissance*' (for losing it). To accede to or attam power (*puissance*) does not suggest taking possession of the State or of the right to command. On the other hand we speak of a '*grande puissance*' ('Great Power'; '*Großmacht*'), and not of a '*grand pouvoir*', when we mean the main actors on the international stage. It is the opposition between the two expressions '*arriver au pouvoir*' (i.e. to take possession of the State or of the legal right to command) and '*les grandes puissances*'[5] that led me, in *Paix et Guerre entre les nations*, to keep '*puissance*' as the most general concept – the potential for commanding, influencing or constraining that one individual possesses in relation to others – whereas *pouvoir* is only a form of *puissance*: that which characterizes not any kind of exercise of power (*puissance*), but a certain kind of potential and the translation into action of that potential.

From these analyses let us for the moment keep solely the distinction between the participle and the infinitive, the potential and the actual, since the latter is to be found in other languages and is warranted by semantic analysis: that of having the power (*puissance*) to do something and of exercising the power (*pouvoir*) to do so. Whoever possesses a firearm or atomic bombs has the power (*puissance*) to kill a man or millions of men, but he does not necessarily exercise his power (*pouvoir*) to do so. The above example sets us on the track of a further distinction. The power (*puissance*) of a gun or a bomb is entirely physical and although the same word is legitimately used to designate the potential of a machine or a man (or of a group), the power (*puissance*) that sociologists and political scientists study is not *any* kind of power. It is, if I may state it so, the power (*puissance*) of man over man, in other words the capacity of a man to restrict the freedom that another enjoys in his behaviour or to ensure that one or several persons follow or obey him. *As a political concept, power ('puissance') designates a relationship between men. Yet since it simultaneously designates a potential and not an act, it may be stated that power (puissance) is the potential possessed by a man or a group for establishing relationships with other men or other groups that accord with his own desires.*

From now on let us take as the most general concept not the term '*pouvoir*' as sociologists today normally do, but the term '*puissance*'. This word has the double advantage of being able to be employed in most cases where the Germans use '*Macht*' and the Americans or English '*power*'. Furthermore, according to Littré's formulation, in so far as it designates something permanent and lasting, and not only the act or the exercising of it, it has a broader extension than '*pouvoir*'.

Moreover, the vocabulary that is chosen is of little consequence. Above all we must not insinuate a philosophy or an interpretation of reality through the mediation of the terms employed. In this connection what seems to me to be the decisive factor is the stages through which one passes in order to reconstruct society – one that is concrete and global – from the elementary, microscopic relationship of power (*puissance*) I perceive two main paths, which lead to entirely different conceptions.

After 'power' ('*Macht*'), the second fundamental concept of Max Weber is that of '*Herrschaft*', '*domination*', in French. In a social relationship an individual possesses power (*puissance*) as soon as he has a possibility of imposing his will upon another or upon others, even when they resist, whatever may be the reason for this possibility. As for *Herrschaft*, it implies the fact of command (*Befehl*) and the chances that this command will be obeyed by some persons or other. I shall translate '*Herrschaft*' by '*domination*' ('domination' in English), because of the identity of the roots: *Herr*, master, *Dominus*.[6] The concept of domination (or *Herrschaft*) tends, within the vast field of power (*puissance*), to mark off relationships (the behaviour of *A*, *B* and *C* is determined, whether positively or negatively, in certain circumstances and in certain aspects, by the will of *X*), a narrower field in which the one who imposes his will resorts to commanding and expects obedience. The one who is dominating is not *any* powerful (*puissant*) person whatever. The power (*puissance*) relationship must be stabilized for the subject of this relationship to give commands to those who are its objects. That subject must esteem himself assured of his right or capacity to exact and obtain obedience. In this context it would be possible to elaborate a casuistry of relationships of power (*puissance*), depending on whether they occurred by chance or according to rules, whether they were customary or legal, merely a matter of fact or legitimate. We proceed from power (*puissance*), a formalized and abstract concept, to Power (*Pouvoir*) (meaning the 'Powers that be', as against the governed) through the various stages of stabilization, institutionalization, legitimation, concentration and domination.

It is striking – and almost a matter of amusement for the historian of ideas – that Talcott Parsons should have translated '*Herrschaft*' by 'imperative control'. It is wholly as if an American sociologist whose knowledge of the German language is unquestionable, whose striving for objectivity is evident, despite himself could not prevent himself from translating a concept whose sense is perfectly clear by a term that has neither the same meaning nor the same overtones, but which nonetheless chimes better with his mental universe.

From Aristotle to Max Weber, the social relationship of command and obedience has always been known. The notion of 'imperative control', scarcely translatable into French (unless we take the word '*contrôle*' in the sense of the English word 'control' and say, 'authoritarian social control' ('*contrôle social autoritaire*'), dissolves the face-to-face relationship of the one who commands and the one who obeys, in a *system of imposed order* (or imposed discipline). Now, the relationships of domination or of institutionalized power (*pouvoir*) do not constitute the whole system of socially imposed modes of behaviour. Customs, laws, prejudices, beliefs and collective passions are also determinants of the social order. Thus by eliminating the domination of the master over the servant and by replacing it with an *imposed order*, one prepares the elimination of the specifically political relationships about which Western philosophers have speculated.

C. J. Friedrich, who is not a sociologist but a political scientist, was not deceived in this way. He criticizes the translation of '*Herrschaft*' by 'imperative control', which he states 'amount to a gloss and lack clarity'.[7] He suggests using the word 'rule' which he himself defines as 'institutionalized political power' (in the same way the 'ruler' would be the '*Herrscher*'). This translation is clearly preferable to that of Parsons, although '*Herrschaft*', as defined by Max Weber, has a wider meaning than 'institutionalized political power'. Domination presumes a certain level of institutionalization (without which the dominator would not venture to command), but the term 'domination' summons up the direct relationship between master and servant rather than the relationship between the governor and the governed.

Whatever may be the different shades of meaning between '*Herrschaft*', '*domination*' (French) and 'rule', as soon as the concept arises the sociologist, even if his point of departure has been 'power' ('*puissance*') in its widest or vaguest sense, will discover once more the political dimension proper, namely the notion of 'integral power', to use the expression of Th. Geiger, which is the power (*puissance*) of society considered as a whole *over* its members or the concentrated power (*puissance*) of one or several people over the rest, and not the reciprocal relationship of dependence existing between the leaders and members of an organization, party or occupational grouping. On the other hand, as soon as one takes the leap from the elementary relationship of power, whose forms and manifestations are countless in number, to the imposed social order (imperative control) one runs a danger of failing to acknowledge the specificity of the political as such.

Let us indeed represent the totality of society as a system into which individuals and groups are integrated. Each of these individuals or groups strives to ensure for himself or itself a certain power (*puissance*) in the broadest sense of *the capacity to do something* or in the more limited sense of the *capacity to influence the behaviour of others*. No-one wishes to be purely the object of an external power (*puissance*); everyone wishes also to be to a certain extent the subject. Immediately the competition for power appears as the equivalent of the competition for money, and the political domain becomes assimilable to a political market.

This representation is not utterly false: it reflects one aspect of reality, particularly under certain regimes (for example, the American regime). Occupational groupings, political parties and pressure groups appear as rivals, each one seeking to maximize its power ('*puissance*') (the capacity to determine the behaviour or the decisions of others), without a single one appearing to be entirely bereft of that rare good (power), which is never monopolized by anybody, but always shared out, although very unequally, among all.

However, a more detailed analysis is sufficient to allow us to grasp the flaw in the reasoning. The competition for the bases or instruments of power (*puissance*) is comparable to economic competition. The one who seeks to possess the maximum possible amount of capital, or prestige, or number of guns in order to impose his will upon others acts as does *homo economicus*, who aims to maximize his profit or production. But the maximization of the instruments or the means of power (*puissance*) is not the same as that of the maximization of power (*puissance*) itself, for the latter, which is a relationship between men or groups, is not quantifiable in the same way as are things or goods: power (*puissance*) is not absolute but relative. It extends over certain men or certain groups, and not over others; it exercises command over certain kinds of behaviour by the objects of power, but not over others. If so many authors are inclined to mix up the struggle for power (*puissance*) with economic competition, it is firstly because, having identified the struggle for the means (or instruments) of power (*puissance*) with the struggle for power (*puissance*) itself, they have substituted for power (*puissance*) which is a human relationship, some or other determinants of that relationship.

If one compares power (*puissance*) and money, or power (*puissance*) and wealth, the difference in kind is ineluctable. Between the distribution of wealth and the dividing out of power (*puissance*), the analogy is superficial but the distinction a radical one. He who possesses a given amount of money can obtain in exchange a given volume of goods. He can perhaps *buy* the services of certain individuals, but the behaviour of countless other people cannot be bought. Money is the means – one normally effective in modern society – of reaching the natural end of economic activity, namely, that of satisfying one's desires or at least of reducing to a minimum the disparity between desires and resources. But then the economy becomes a differentiated sub-system: money allows one to buy with certainty only those goods brought to the market. It also gives to the one who possesses it in large amounts the capacity to determine in certain respects the behaviour of certain men: there is no degree of proportionality between economic power, defined as the capacity to acquire goods in the market, and political power (*puissance*) defined as the capacity to determine the behaviour of other men.

He who acquires riches inevitably deprives others of them. As the amount of wealth is limited at any moment, it is true in *one* sense (the proposition was true almost without exception in traditional societies) that some are deprived of what the other may amass. In the commercial sphere, both in theory and in reality, this is not so since, in an ideal typical exchange, each party prefers what he receives to what he possessed and gives as equivalent in exchange. But if society is considered as a unity, the goods possessed by the rich automatically diminish what remains available for other members of the collectivity. However, the modern economy, since it is progressive, removes much of its significance from this age-old conception. The volume of goods, limited at any one moment, is nevertheless increasing from one moment to another. If we take into account the dimension of time, it becomes untrue to say that the enrichment of one is automatically compensated for by the impoverishment of one or several others. Growth allows the simultaneous enrichment of all or most members of the collectivity, without necessarily eliminating the element of conflict (*agon*) from the economic world.

The relationship of exchange is, according to the ideal type, an egalitarian one, whereas the relationship of power (*puissance*) is in its essence not symmetrical and unequal. If L causes himself to be followed or obeyed by A, B and C, or if L limits the freedom that A, B and C enjoy to choose their objectives and means, L cannot be the subject of power (*puissance*) without A, B and C being its objects. *A fortiori*, if we advance from power (*puissance*) to domination, on to institutionalized domination, and to legitimized Power (*Pouvoir*), the lack of symmetry is strikingly clear. The normal expression of stabilized power (*puissance*) is that one commands and the other obeys. If one commands, the other obeys. In this sense power (*puissance*) will never be shared out as wealth can be. For the metaphor of a market in which a very large number of competitors vie with one another is substituted that of a hierarchy, of relationships between superiors and inferiors, between masters and servants.

It is true that the power (*puissance*) of L over A, B or C is not total, in the sense that although L prohibits the objects of his power (*puissance*) from undertaking certain actions or dictates to them certain modes of behaviour, it may well be that A, B or C in their turn may remove from L his freedom to make certain choices. The plurality of the domains in which power (*puissance*) is exercised leaves room for reciprocity: it is not that some are pure subjects with others as pure objects. Furthermore, the bases or instruments of power (*puissance*) – wealth, prestige, strength, a position in an hierarchical power (*pouvoir*) structure – are not necessarily in the hands of the same men. The sociology of power (*puissance*) makes an indispensable contribution to political science in so far as it allows one to integrate the study of legitimate Power (*Pouvoir*) into a broader analysis of the manifold structures of power (*puissance*).

Again one should not be misled by the resemblance between the distribution of income and the dispersion of power (*puissance*). The dispersion of power (*puissance*) has several meanings. First of all, it designates what I should prefer to call the differentiation of social sub-systems, from which arises normally the separation of the instruments of power (*puissance*). The same predominant person (ruler, *Herrscher*) is no longer at the same time both king and high priest. He does not possess both weapons and money. The holder of the supreme Power (*Pouvoir*) in the domain of legitimacy, is limited in the exercise of his will by the constitutional rules. Secondly, those 'ruling' in a given sector – the managers of the means of production – clash with those 'ruling' in another sector. The director of General Motors or the United Steel Company must discuss working conditions with the secretaries of trade unions, and incurs the risk of an intervention by the President of the United States if there is a price rise at a time that is judged to be inopportune. Thirdly, within complex organizations, authentic power relationships are not precisely reflected by the formal relationships of authority (let us call 'authority' here the power (*puissance*) possessed by an individual through his position in a social organization, without that organization necessarily being public: the director of a corporation has the right to command, but his authority is political in the broad sense of the word, and not in the narrow sense in which there only belongs to what is political the sub-system which culminates in the legitimate power (*pouvoir*) exercised by one or several persons in the name of everybody and over everybody). The sociology of organizations, of industrial undertakings, of public or private bureaucracies, of unions or parties – such a sociology will investigate how in reality decisions are taken, and up to what point the official distribution of authority and the effective division of power (*puissance*) coincide or diverge (the distinction between them is normally expressed by contrasting *formal* and *informal* power (*puissance*)).

The differentiation of power (*puissance*) is undoubtedly a characteristic of the structure of power (*puissance*) as it is of the social order in its entirety. Differentiation, at the end of the analysis, just like the elementary relationship at the beginning, depoeticizes power (*puissance*). But Power (*Pouvoir*), centralized and legitimate, exercised over everybody by the few in the name of everybody – does this still deserve to be considered with a mixture of anguish and respect if it is the stake in a competition conducted according to the rules and exercised in conformity with written laws and with customs that occasionally restrict what is arbitrary more than do laws? Even more, is not the citizen or the observer of American society himself uncertain of what he ought to fear, being at one time inclined to be afraid of the excess of Power (*Pouvoir*), and at another time fearful of its absence? If no-one can any longer decide in the name of everybody against the few, will not society be doomed to a fatal conservatism during a period of accelerated change?

Should we take seriously C. Wright Mills when he denounces the *power elite*, or the political scientists when they see the United States (or the Western democracies) paralyzed by the dispersion or absence of Power (*Pouvoir*)? And do the theorists of international relations incline us towards a reversion to the comforting prose or to the demoniacal poetry of power (*puissance*)?

H. J. Morgenthau passes for the supreme realist theorist in international relations; better than anybody else he is alleged to have revealed what is at stake as regards power (*puissance*) – the stake that defines the rivalry between nations. The sub-title of his main book, *Politics among Nations*, is: *The struggle for power and peace*. At the beginning of the first chapter in the book Morgenthau writes that 'the concept of political power poses one of the most difficult and controversial problems of political science'. It is a difficulty to which the first pages of the book bear striking witness.

The theory begins with the following proposition:

International politics, like all politics, is a struggle for power. Whatever the ultimate aims of international politics, power is always the immediate aim. Statesmen and people may ultimately seek freedom, security, prosperity, or power itself. They may define their goals in terms of a religious, philosophic, economic, or social ideal. They may hope that this ideal will materialize through its own inner force, through divine intervention, or through the natural development of human affairs. But wherever they strive to realise their goal by means of international politics, they do so by striving for power. The crusaders wanted to free the holy places from domination by the Infidels; Woodrow Wilson wanted to make the world safe for democracy; the National Socialists wanted to open Eastern Europe to German colonization, to dominate Europe and to conquer the world. Since they chose power to achieve these ends, they were actors on the scene of international politics.[8]

In this paragraph, *power* is firstly the *proximate objective* of every actor on the international stage. At the end of the same paragraph *power* has become the chosen means for these same actors to achieve their aims. What therefore is this *power* that is at the same time the *proximate goal* and *universal means* of international politics? It is defined a few lines later as 'man's control over the minds and actions of other men'. As for *political power*, it is the reciprocal relationship of domination between the holders of public authority and between the latter and the people ('mutual relations of control among the holders of public authority and between the latter and the people at large').

Political power (*puissance politique*) as a psychological relationship between those who exercise it and those over whom it is exercised — one may ask how this power could be specific to international relationships. According to these definitions power (*puissance*) in fact is equivalent to the influence or domination of one man over another, a characteristic of every society rather than every form of politics. Moreover, political power (*puissance*), defined by the relationship between the holders of authority and those over whom that authority is exercised, allows even less scope to specify international relationships, since the latter do not possess the duality between the holders of public authority and the people, because each of the actors is the holder, within a given territory, of the 'public authority'.

Morgenthau recognizes that the reference to power (*puissance*) does not allow him to distinguish the specific difference of *international* politics. He does this when he writes a little later: 'the aspiration for power being the distinguishing element of international politics, *as of all politics*,[9] international politics is of necessity power politics'.[10] No-one, it seems to me, will question that international politics is power (*puissance*) politics, if this concept, translated into English, merely means that the international actors, like the national actors, seek to acquire over others either domination or influence, and that this universal aspiration entails struggle and competition. Nobody indeed has denied that every form of politics contains a conflictual dimension, although most authors have also highlighted the complementary dimension of agreement (or, to revert to the concept of Auguste Comte, of consensus). And when Morgenthau adds: 'Would it not be rather surprising if the struggle for power were but an accidental and ephemeral attribute of international politics when it is a permanent and necessary element of all branches of domestic politics?'[11] then we are tempted to reply: indeed, it would most certainly be surprising, but do not those who reject, rightly or wrongly, the expression 'power politics' give it a different meaning? Can power (*puissance*) be at one and the same time the *proximate objective*, the *universal means* and the *constant stake* in international relations without inextricable confusion being introduced into both language and thought?

Political power (*puissance*) as a psychological relationship between those who exercise it and those who undergo it is plainly not the 'universal means' for actors upon the international stage. Power (*puissance*), the relationship between a mind that dominates and another that is subjected to its ascendancy, is a 'universal means' for the effect of one man upon another, and not the means specific to politics, even less so the specific means used in politics between nations. Is power at least the immediate objective of all political activity? Let us recall Japan in the Tokugawa era: its objective was most assuredly not to exercise or be capable of exercising increased influence upon the other actors on the international scene.

In fact H. J. Morgenthau clearly does not ignore the specific differentiating character of politics between nations: 'In international politics in particular, armed strength as a threat or a potentiality is the most important factor making for the political power of a nation.'[12] Later on[13] he lists the conditions necessary for the maintenance of peace within nations, conditions that are not present on the international stage. But everything is stated as if Morgenthau sought to convince his readers that international politics is power politics (*puissance*) by the use of an argument that is diametrically the opposite of the one that thinkers have used for centuries, namely, when he affirms that 'the essence of international politics is identical with its domestic counterpart'.[14] But this identification derives from the notion of *struggle for power*, which is to be found even in the family: 'the conflict between the mother-in-law and the child's spouse is, in its essence, a struggle for power'.

Yet I believe that thinkers in that tradition – and Bergson in *Les deux Sources de la morale et de la religion* continues the tradition – would have admitted, as do Hobbes and Morgenthau, that the *struggle for power* (*puissance*) is universal if one sees it as the expression of an urge rooted in human nature, but they would have maintained that the relationships between members of a community and those between communities considered as unities are distinct *in essence*. The philosophers once used to contrast *civil status* ('*état civil*'), in the legal meaning of that expression, with the *state of nature* ('*état de nature*'). Nations have not alienated their independence or sovereignty in favour of an organ entrusted with the task of stating what the law is, an organ itself provided with the means of force necessary to carry out its verdicts. Lacking a court of law or police, States live in the state of nature, and the time-honoured formula *homo homini lupus* continues to be applicable to the relationships between these cold-blooded monsters.

At the same time it can be explained how the notion of *power politics* (*politique de puissance*) can be interpreted either as the definition of relationships between States or as a doctrine of international politics (as it is or as it should be). To place the emphasis on the specific difference for international relations is to remind ourselves that in the last analysis States are the sole judges of their own highest interests, free to draw the sword when violence, either that of the criminal or the revolutionary, infringes legality within States. It is indeed true – and H. J. Morgenthau is right on this point – that power (*puissance*) is not to be confused with force, and even less with the use of force. Yet the more the theorist of *power politics* obscures the proper object of his study by comparing the struggle between States to the disputes between a mother-in-law and her daughter-in-law, the more the one who hears or reads him desires to strip away the camouflage round the formalized concept in order to understand, beyond 'the relationship existing between consciousnesses', either the struggle whose aim is to maximize the means of power or the struggle by resort to force.

The present situation seems moreover to provide arguments in turn for both the protagonists of the politics of power (*puissance*) and their opponents. Apparently it has never been so true to say that each State or block desires the death of the other. Never has

Hobbes' description of the state of nature between States so faith-
fully reflected reality:

> Yet in all times, Kings, and Persons of soveraigne authority,
> because of their Independency, are in continuall jealousies,
> and in the state and postures of Gladiators, having their
> weapons pointing, and their eyes fixed on one another; that is,
> their Forts, Garrisons and Guns, upon the Frontiers of their
> Kingdomes; and continuall Spyes upon their neighbours,
> which is a posture of War.[15]

Yet at the same time never have States so solemnly pledged themselves not to resort to force. Never have they concluded so many
pacts that are apparently similar to those that the States constitute
within themselves. Finally, never has the disproportion appeared so
striking between the capacity of the Great Powers to impose their
will upon the smaller ones and the disproportion between the
means of force available to both groups. The degree of proportion
is tending to disappear between power (*puissance*) – a relationship
between wills – and force – the instruments of physical constraint.
Each Great Power must tolerate a smaller one that annoys it: the
Soviet Union Albania, and the United States Cuba. Or, if you like,
Albania is the Cuba of the Soviet Union.

In this situation there is nothing that contradicts the essential
nature of the relationship between States as that has manifested
itself over the centuries. Today more than ever the security of a
State, its very existence, depends on its will to exist and the force
that it has at its disposal: when the Soviet Union wished to install
medium-range ballistic missiles on Cuba, and the United States said
no, two wills confronted each other, each armed with terrifying
instruments of destruction, each threatening the other, neither
accepting the verdict of an arbitrator or a tribunal. The relationship
remained essentially what it had been: Hobbes' state of nature,
with ballistic missiles replacing forts and guns.

The relationship between wills or between States should never be
confused with the relationship between the means of force. In the
present age the distinction is made even sharper through a development that is ultimately more logical than paradoxical, because of
the enormity of the means of force available. The symbolic gun-
boats of the nineteenth century cannot be replaced by thermonuclear bombs: the United States has never attempted to constrain
States without atomic arms by the threat to use nuclear weapons.

About 1959–60, at a time when the Soviet Union attempted to make others believe, and when the United States let it be believed, that 'the wind from the East was prevailing over the wind from the West', and that missiles would give the socialist camp military superiority, Mr Kruschev flourished, in vague terms, his weapons of mass destruction. Yet in the end he too came round to the American doctrine: nuclear weapons are reserved for defensive use in diplomacy, and should only be brought into play militarily as a last resort.

From then on the reciprocal neutralization of thermonuclear installations has sanctioned the unchanged nature of the relationships between States – no-one knows what would happen if one State alone possessed such installations. Yet at the same time *this neutralization enlarges out of all proportion the diplomatic field, where relationships of military force do not govern the relationships between the wills of States and do not determine the course of diplomacy or history.* Hegel, speaking of Napoleon, coined the striking phrase: '*Die Ohnmacht des Sieges*'. Perhaps one should evoke '*Die Ohnmacht der Macht*', if by *Macht* is understood the instruments of destruction.

These relationships between States do not nevertheless become similar to social relationships within States. The semi-Parliamentary debates in the United Nations are a new instrument in traditional forms of diplomacy rather than the converting of these forms into the rule of law. What is new is a clearer differentiation in levels. Diplomatic relations between States were more affected by the relative size of military forces in the pre-atomic era, when the use of such forces appeared to be less improbable. Nevertheless States do not give up fighting one another and do not submit their quarrels to rules of non-violence. They stir up or encourage revolts, they send arms to rebels. The so-called socialist States esteem as their allies those that rise up against a capitalist regime; the United States, not without hesitation, chances its luck here and there by playing a game of subversion and counter-subversion (one for which it is ill-equipped because of its political and social system).

Are politics between nations, as they reveal themselves today, terrifying or reassuring, prosaic or demoniacal? Everything seems to occur as if, depending on the moment, opinion tended either towards anguish or towards serenity. One day Lord Russell and Sir Charles Snow are listened to as they allow humanity a few decades at the most – from now to the end of the century – to choose between the thermonuclear apocalypse or the promised land of the world-wide State (or peace on earth to States of ill-will). Such a state of mind is particularly widespread in Great Britain, where pacifism, which was the norm in periods between the wars, feeds at the present time on the horror that nuclear arms inspire. In France the opposite state of mind prevails, made up of two feelings: a kind of refusal to believe in the eventuality of a terrible war, and the consciousness that, in any case, a decision for peace or war does not depend on individuals, and perhaps hardly more so on France or Europe.

For the time being, since the Cuba crisis at the end of 1962, humanity is going through a phase of appeasement. American academics had elaborated a theory of diplomacy and strategy adapted to the atomic age: the common interest between two States who possess nuclear arms is not to plunge into a war to the death, from which by definition only non-belligerents would profit; hence partial solidarity between enemies and partial hostility between allies when the latter – either China or France – refuse to submit to the strategic discipline of their bloc (a discipline where the leader of the bloc seeks to define the terms). Up to the end of 1962 it was wholly as if the Soviet Union refused to subscribe to the theory (or even to understand it) and to enter into the game. On the other hand, since the beginning of 1963 Mr Kruschev is profuse in the assurances, both in words and deeds, of his peaceful intentions, as if he was above all trying to convince the American leaders and the whole of mankind that he had understood and admitted the truth of the American theory: the suspension of nuclear tests (in order to slow down, if not to stop, the armaments race), the red telephone, the fear, openly expressed, that any armed conflict, even a local one, might become general and lead to extremes – in other words the interpretation of the concept of build-up (or of escalation), so as to exclude and not merely to restrict the use of military force. The common action of the two Great Powers against the threat of a large-scale war has become apparent to everybody, to such an extent that it contributes to a break-up within both Eastern and Western blocs.

Assuredly nothing demonstrates that this appeasement is more than a phase as temporary as the previous phase of anguish. For the fundamental facts have not changed. What is new is the destructive power (*puissance*) of the weaponry, in other words the material power (*puissance*) available to those who hold Power (*Pouvoir*). What is not new is the fear that the man holding power (*Pouvoir*) inspires in other men when they think of the consequences that *one* decision taken by him can have. How can this fear be dispelled unless it be by refusing to one single man alone the right and the capacity to take decisions whose consequences would affect millions of men? It is in this way that philosophers and lawyers reasoned when they elaborated the doctrine of the separation of powers. When sociologists take note of the dispersal of power (*puissance*) in society they rejoice at it, so natural to man is the fear of man.

Now, on the international stage it would appear that the concentration of power (*puissance*) is reassuring, and that the very idea of it being dispersed strikes terror. The pacifists join with the leaders of the United States and the Soviet Union in denouncing what they all call 'the proliferation of atomic weapons'. The international system has always been oligarchic, or, if you prefer it, inegalitarian: a few actors, called 'great powers' (*puissances*), have dominated the stage and fixed the unwritten rules of competition. Yet very often the secondary actors were annoyed at their subordinate role and aspired to independence. Why do these secondary actors, who are more numerous than ever before, seem reconciled to a dyarchy?

I perceive two motives: the first is what I called a little earlier *die Ohnmacht der Macht* or *the powerlessness of force*, or even the disproportion between the potential for destruction of thermonuclear devices and political power (*puissance*) (in other words, the two Great Powers cannot succeed in imposing their will by using their military strength in diplomacy). The second is the vague conviction – one that is almost unthinking – that the risk of an accident is less so long as two States alone possess these monstrous instruments. If these two States have forbidden everybody from resorting to the use of regular armies and themselves refrain from using their nuclear weapons except for immobilizing each other, all in all the situation is one of the least possible evil. Power is concentrated, but in a strictly limited field. It continues to give rise to some anguish because no man is fit to dispose of such tools of death. But it is as if, in this case, the temptation to use these weapons were destined to increase with the number of States that might possess them. In this sense the present dyarchy tends to conceal from us the fact that power (*puissance*) is already dispersed to the utmost extent compatible with the essence of relationships between States.[16]

The 'power politics' (*politique de puissance*) or *Machtpolitik* of German writers was a *doctrine* of diplomatic action deduced from the *theory* of international relations. Since these relations were not a prisoner to laws, each actor was responsible for his own destiny and free to draw the sword in the defence of his own highest interests. *Machtpolitik* did not imply imperialism or the will to enlarge the area of sovereignty or to subjugate foreign peoples, but the concept had a nationalist ring about it and originated in a pessimistic philosophy. States at one another's throats in perpetual competition, peaceful and bloodthirsty by turns, survive only through the 'will to power' (*volonté de puissance*) and prosper only by haughtily affirming their independence.

The same concept of *power politics* in English expresses the same theory but teaches an utterly different *doctrine*. The theory highlights the originality of international relations as compared with other social relationships (absence of any court of law and police), but the doctrine that is deduced from it goes, so to speak, in the opposite direction to the German doctrine. The American exponents of the doctrine are opposed to the moralists and lawyers who dream of subjecting the sovereignty of States to laws. They recall the eternal essence of such sovereignties (or when they are theologians, such as Niebuhr, the corruption of human nature) in order to warn thinkers and statesmen against the danger of behaving like beasts whilst wishing to be angels; namely, the danger of making wars incapable of expiation, of concluding a Carthaginian peace on the pretext of punishing States guilty of aggression and of ensuring for all time the safety of democracy. The American exponents of power politics (*puissance*) are moderates, realists, and even pessimists; they recommend a return to the tested practices of diplomacy and condemn any hankering to embark on a crusade. Turning upside down the relationship between values that is proper to national ideology, one of H. J. Morgenthau's disciples, R. E. Osgood, writes that any use of force to pursue any goal save the defence of the national interest should be condemned.

In other words *Machtpolitik* and *power politics* can, depending on circumstances, summon up the romantic grandeur of States at grips with one another for the domination of the world, the subtlety of a Talleyrand or the bourgeois wisdom of diplomats who, for their part, would also say that an unsatisfactory compromise is better than a successful law-suit (a bad agreement is better than a battle won).

If we move from international relations to politics within States, power (*puissance*) becomes both widely spread (who does not possess a little of it?) and indeterminate (at the margin, every time that A determines an act by B, it is an example of the power (*puissance*) of A over B). Employed as a principle of analysis, in the case of American society such a concept inevitably induces the representation of a reality that is relatively in conformity with the democratic ideal. If one studies a complex organization (a great industrial corporation), a political party, a town, an army, Congress or the Presidency of the United States, the difficulty is less one of discovering the limits to the power of those who officially hold Power (*Pouvoir*) than to discover those responsible for the decisions taken. In other words, the theory commonly adopted goes in the direction of what we shall call the dispersal of power. Yet an increasing number of individuals at the same time feel that they lack power (*puissance*) – in other words they feel themselves incapable of influencing the course of events. They are convinced that their fate is determined by forces outside themselves, by obscure forces that no-one can dominate or that are dominated by cynical and obscure minorities. Thus can be explained the violent reaction of C. Wright Mills when he attributes the supreme power to an elite composed of those that control the means of production, generals, and in a subsidiary role, politicians. It is an elite that is concealed by the political game and the tumult of the public forum.

Orthodox sociologists have not taken seriously C. Wright Mills' book, and probably their reaction would not have been different even if the theory of the power elite had rested upon a broader basis of facts and if the conceptualization had been less crude. Not that the sociological theory of the *ruling class* is so greatly contrary to the facts, even in the case of the United States, that a certain credence cannot be given to it. Yet firstly one must again concede to the thesis of the dispersal of power the degree of *evident* truth that it comprises (given the meaning ascribed to the word 'power' (*puissance*).

The sociology of organizations or the sociology of local politics, in their own domains, lead to results that no-one can rightly contest (unless one proceeds with equal minuteness to carry out enquiries whose results would turn out to be the opposite). 'Power' (*puissance*), in the meaning assigned to it, is not a global and undifferentiated potential that someone might possess in all circumstances, vis-à-vis anyone, whatever the sphere in question. If we wish to know: 'Who rules?' in the large corporation, in the municipality, in the factory, in the army or in the State we must rid ourselves of both the metaphysical conception of power (*puissance*) and the juridical conception of Power (*Pouvoir*). When we analyse an organization, it is clearly not sufficient to know what is, on paper, the hierarchy of command in order to know, from this fact alone, what is the distribution of power. The degree of autonomy – namely, the number of decisions that the individual is capable of making – is not necessarily congruent to the level at which each individual is situated in the hierarchy of the organization. Moreover, the personality of the one who fulfils this or that role can strengthen or diminish the power (*puissance*) normally reserved to the one appointed to act the role. In other words, a certain kind of dispersion of power (*puissance*) flows from the very nature of complex organizations. This dispersion could not be brought into question save by refusing to admit the necessary hypothesis for this sort of analysis – namely, *the equivalence of various decisions*.

In the same way, at the municipal level R. Dahl has demonstrated convincingly how affairs were carried on at New Haven, in what respects certain citizens were capable, by taking the initiative, of favouring one project or sabotaging another, in spite of the passiveness or indifference of the majority of the electors. Thus, at least in this small community, he did not uncover the equivalent of a power elite: the same men are not powerful (*puissants*) in all matters; those who hold the various instruments of power (*puissance*) do not constitute a coherent group; they do not, as masters of the town and sure of what their wishes are, spin a web of conspiracy by night behind the façade of democracy. But the decisions to be taken at New Haven are rarely of a kind to overturn individual habits or collective destiny.

Would we have the same kind of representation if we studied under the microscope a town in the American South, where the problems of segregation are acutely posed? Or if we followed the decision-making process in the army, federal diplomacy or Congress? Two facts might cause us to modify these conclusions: the dispersion of power (*puissance*) favours resistance by the privileged just as much as it is a protection against the mythical tyranny of the legislators feared by the Founding Fathers. At a certain level of social organization, what counts is not the number of decisions taken by one or another person, nor the number of cases in which *A* prevails over *B*, or *B* over *C*, or *C* over *A*. What counts is the person who makes the big decisions, those that are irreversible, whose consequences risk being prolonged indefinitely and being experienced by all of the collectivity's members. In the last analysis, the power (*puissance*) of the supreme Power (*Pouvoir*), as Maurras might have said, is absolute – and restricted. It does not extend to all spheres, but in its own domain it belongs to one person alone, and must not be shared. The President of the United States is the Commander-in-Chief: he is the strategist that conducts both war and diplomacy.

Western societies appear to be characterized by the dispersion of power (*puissance*) when they are compared to Soviet societies. The latter inspire terror because of the apparent cumulation of all power (*puissance*) that is concentrated in the minority holding the Power (*Pouvoir*). The same men direct foreign policy and economic planning, interpret the truths of the dogma and determine the distribution of income. Society is absorbed into the State and the State belongs to a more or less cohesive minority. Just as long as this minority itself obeyed the fear spread by a supreme tyrant, power (*puissance*) reached a sort of magnificence that was demoniacal and almost demented. Stalin, 'huddled concealed in his tricks' or walled in with his suspicions, decided that some of the greatest doctors were assassins in white coats, and a chorus of millions of men echoed him, execrating the criminals conjured up by a delirious imagination. We do well to ask ourselves what an honourable citizen can do to further or prevent the construction of dwellings at a moderate rent on council land. But it would be regrettable to forget that the power (*puissance*) we termed demoniacal is conquered by one man alone either because the social organization is necessarily hierarchical, and a decision taken at the summit may send millions of men to their deaths, or because certain individuals touched by grace and born to command have the mysterious gift of sweeping their fellows along with them, awakening both devotion and fear, fascinating both opponents and supporters. When such charismatic personalities succeed in seizing Power (*Pouvoir*) then humanity trembles both in anguish and in hope.

Let us even leave Hitler and Stalin on one side. Let us return to the cautious procedures of analysis. The sociology of decision-making inevitably leaves obscure three aspects of the problem of power (*puissance*):

1 Any complex organization, whether private, or particularly if it is public, entails at one time or another decisions of an historic nature, if we agree to define these according to the following characteristics: they are singular decisions, irreversible, bringing in their wake long-term consequences whose effects all the members of the organization will feel.
2 Such historic decisions are very often taken by one man (or by a *collegium* of a few). However limited its field of application may be, in one sense the Power (*Pouvoir*) remains absolute in the sphere of decisions of an historic nature (diplomacy and strategy).
3 The man of Power (*Pouvoir*) – i.e. one whose capacity to command is stable, institutional and legitimate – has occasionally no

other authority than that which is attached to the function that he fulfils. But authority also designates the quality whereby one personality imposes itself upon others, obtaining their assent, loyalty and obedience not by the threat of punishment but by the supremacy of the will alone. The conjunction of legitimate authority and personal authority is at the origin of great destinies, of those who nourish dreams of glory and memories of horror.

In the absence of such prestigious leaders, decisions of an historic nature are even taken, or seem to be taken, according to democratic procedures, i.e. in a prosaic, foreseeable fashion. When this is so the observer in revolt against his country's regime or diplomacy will not be able to prevent himself from ascribing to a *power elite* a constant influence of which he disapproves. In effect, in the United States the dispersion of power (*puissance*), even at the level of the federal Power (*Pouvoir*) will stifle certain inclinations towards reform without the principles of social order being undermined or the main lines of diplomatic action modified, whoever the holders of the principal roles of Power (*Pouvoir*) may be. But that which C. Wright Mills ascribes to an elite, and at the margin to a conspiracy, could just as well have been attributed to the dispersion of power (*puissance*) and to the democratic nature of the regime.

A society such as the American one remains faithful to its traditional ideologies and passions, to *free enterprise* and *anti-Communism*, to the very extent that nobody possesses an exceptional *authority*. Circumstances such as the crisis of 1963 or the war in 1941 are necessary for the man of Power (*Pouvoir*), legitimate and legal, to become in everybody's eyes the man of destiny, the one who by a yea or a nay, by choosing the landing in Normandy in preference to one in the Balkans, determines for decades the fate of tens of millions of men. In a period of calm, pluralist societies and democratic regimes incline to conservatism and preserve the rights (dubbed privileges by those who dispute them) of various minorities. Is the conservatism the work of a *power elite* or the *dispersion of power*? Has the very question any meaning? In a society where the leading groups are in agreement about the principles of the political regime and the main lines of diplomacy, the rebel believes himself to be the victim of a conspiracy, whereas the empirical sociologist, as honourable citizen, merely observes the complex interplay of interests and ideas. The conspiracy exists only through the resentment felt by the rebel who refuses to see that the normal functioning of the regime is sufficient to guarantee the preservation of what he detests. There would be occasion to cry conspiracy if the broad masses shared in the revolt of the heretic. But the heretic is destined for a solitary life so long as the hour of revolution has not struck. Revolution, like war, provides an opportunity for leaders whose power (*puissance*) is not commensurate with the democratic Power (*Pouvoir*). So long as the Power (*Pouvoir*) remains tightly enmeshed in bonds of tradition and legality, only great events can make it prestigious and poetical. Subject to rules and habits, it is powerless to upset the way of the world because of the very fact that it is dispersed.

One of the Utopias of the twentieth century, which can be sometimes rosily optimistic, sometimes blackly pessimistic, was that of a rational society beyond the confines of history. If this Utopia were already a reality, the sociology of complex organizations and democratic regimes would have exhausted the theme of power (*puissance*) and Power (*Pouvoir*). But this is not the way things are going. The historical period is not yet over and perhaps never will be.

So long as humanity is divided into a multiplicity of sovereign collectivities, one man or a few here and there will determine by means of irreversible decisions the existence of millions of their fellows. This power (*puissance*) of life and death is extended inordinately by thermonuclear weapons. Nor is this all. The more dispersed power (*puissance*) is, the more individuals can experience a feeling that they have no influence over the social order and that the latter has crystallized (it does not matter whether this crystallization is imputed to the dispersion of power or to a conspiracy on the part of the privileged). On the other side of the Iron Curtain, Power (*Pouvoir*) is terrifying because it encompasses the whole collectivity and is reserved to a minority. On our side it is reassuring because its sphere of action is limited and disputed by a host of claimants. But do not the masses still have some nostalgia for a personalized Power (*Pouvoir*), for men of destiny who command and are obeyed because they have a vocation to rule, and not because they have been invested according to some legal procedure?

If one is to believe Hayek, the free society is one where laws and not men rule over men. If this is the definition of liberty, do men always aspire to liberty?

NOTES

1 J. A. A. van Doorn, 'Sociology and the problem of power', *Sociologica Neerlandica*, **1** (1962–3), pp. 3–47.

2 C. J. Friedrich, *Man and his Government* (New York, 1963), p. 161.

3 van Doorn, 'Sociology', p. 13.

4 If this restriction is due to the involuntary action of another person, the latter has no power (*pouvoir*).

5 In French it is not possible to write *politique de pouvoir* to translate *Machtpolitik*, which again suggests that power (*pouvoir*) is not only the act in relationship to the potential, but the potential or the act in part legalized in relationship to the potential or to the act pure and simple.

6 This translation is adopted by one of the best translators of Max Weber, J. Freund. Italian translators have chosen '*potenza*' for '*Macht*' and '*potere*' for '*Herrschaft*'.

The distinction between '*potenza*' and '*potere*' corresponds to that between '*puissance*' and '*pouvoir*', between participle and infinitive. I shall use it in part in the sense that the ruler will be said to have *pouvoir* rather than *puissance* as soon as he exercises his domination (the act in relationship to the potential), and exercises it in conformity with legality or legitimacy.

7 Friedrich, *Man and his Government*, p. 180 note.

8 H. J. Morgenthau, *Politics among Nations* (New York, 1949), p. 13.

9 My emphasis.

10 Ibid., p. 15.

11 Ibid., p. 18.

12 Ibid., p. 18.

13 Ibid., pp. 391–8.

14 Ibid., p. 17.

15 *Leviathan*, I, 13.

16 It is true that certain States reject this dyarchy, but the motive for this refusal seems to me to be less one of fear than a will to independence.

Select Bibliography

Bachrach, Peter and Baratz, Morton S., *Power and Poverty: Theory and Practice*, New York: Oxford University Press, 1970.

Barry, Brian (ed.), *Power and Political Theory: Some European Perspectives*, London: Wiley, 1976.

Bell, Roderick, Edwards, David V. and Wagner, R. Harrison (eds), *Political Power: A Reader in Theory and Research*, New York: The Free Press, 1969.

Benn, Stanley, 'Power', in Paul Edwards (ed.), *Encyclopedia of Philosophy*, VI, New York: The Free Press, 1967, pp. 424–7.

Blau, Peter M., *Exchange and Power in Social Life*, New York: Wiley, 1964.

Connolly, William E., *The Terms of Political Discourse*, 2nd edn, Oxford: Martin Robertson, 1983, chapter 3.

Dahl, Robert A., 'The Concept of Power', *Behavioural Science*, 2, 1957, pp. 201–15.

——'A critique of the ruling elite model', *American Political Science Review*, 52, 1958, pp. 463–9.

——*Who Governs? Democracy and Power in an American City*, New Haven, Conn. and London: Yale University Press, 1961.

——*Modern Political Analysis*, 4th edn, Englewood Cliffs, NJ: Prentice Hall, 1984.

Debnam, Geoffrey, *The Analysis of Power: A Realist Approach*, London: Macmillan, 1984.

Emerson, Richard M., 'Power-dependence-relations', *American Sociological Review*, 27, 1962, pp. 31–41.

Etzioni, Amitai, *A Comparative Analysis of Complex Organizations*, New York: The Free Press, 1961.

Gamson, William, *Power and Discontent*, Homewood, Ill.: The Dorsey Press, 1968.

Gaventa, John, *Power and Powerlessness: Quiescence and Rebellion in an Appalachian Valley*, Oxford: Clarendon, 1980.

Gerth, H. H. and Mills, C. W. (eds), *From Max Weber: Essays in Sociology*, London: Routledge and Kegan Paul, 1948.

Giddens, Anthony, '"Power" in the recent writings of Talcott Parsons', *Sociology* 2, 1968, pp. 257–72.

Hunter, Floyd, *Community Power Structure: A Study of Decision Makers*, New York: Anchor, 1963.

——*Community Power Succession: Atlanta's Policy-Makers Revisited*, Chapel Hill, NC: University of North Carolina, 1980.

Jones, Allan, 'Power politics', in David V. Edwards, *International Political Analysis: Readings*, New York: Holt, Rinehart and Winston, 1970, pp. 207–25.

Lasswell, Harold, *Politics: Who Gets What, When, How*, New York: Meridian Books, 1958.

——and Kaplan, Abraham, *Power and Society*, New Haven: Yale University Press, 1950.

Luhmann, Niklas, *Macht*, Stuttgart: Ferdinand Enke, 1975.

Lukes, Steven, *Power: A Radical View*, London: Macmillan, 1974.

——*Essays in Social Theory*, New York: Columbia University Press and London: Macmillan, 1977.

——'Power and authority', in T. Bottomore and R. Nisbet (eds), *History of Sociological Analysis*, London: Heinemann and New York: Basic Books, 1979, pp. 631–76.

March, James G., 'The power of power', in David Easton (ed.), *Varieties of Political Theory*, Englewood Cliffs, NJ.: Prentice-Hall, 1966, pp. 30–70.

Martin, Roderick, *The Sociology of Power*, London: Routledge and Kegan Paul, 1977.

Mills, C. Wright, *The Power Elite*, New York: Oxford University Press, 1956.

——*Power, Politics and People*, New York: Oxford University Press, 1963.

Morgenthau, Hans J., *Scientific Man vs Power Politics*, Chicago: University of Chicago Press, 1965.

Nagel, Jack H., *The Descriptive Analysis of Power*, New Haven, Conn. and London: Yale University Press, 1975.

Oppenheim, Felix E., '"Power" revisited', *Journal of Politics*, 40, 1978, pp. 589–608.

Parsons, Talcott, *Politics and Social Structure*, New York: The Free Press, 1969.

Partridge, P. H., 'Some notes on the concept of power', *Political Studies*, 11 June 1963, pp. 107–25.

Polsby, Nelson W., *Community Power and Political Theory*, New Haven, Conn. and London: Yale University Press, 1963. 2nd edn, subtitled *A Further Look at Problems of Evidence and Inference*, published 1980.

Riker, William H., 'Some ambiguities in the notion of power', *American Political Science Review*, 58, 1964, pp. 341–9.

Rothchild, K. W. (ed.), *Power in Economics: Selected Readings*, Harmondsworth: Penguin, 1971.

Schattschneider, E. E., *The Semi-Sovereign People: A Realist's View of Democracy in America*, New York: Holt, Rinehart and Winston, 1960.

Simon, Herbert, 'Notes on the observation and measurement of power', *Journal of Politics*, 15, 1953, pp. 500–16.

White, D. M. 'Power and intentions', *American Political Science Review*, 65, 1971, pp. 749–59.
——'The problem of power', *British Journal of Political Science*, 2, 1972, pp. 479–90.
——*The Concept of Power*, Morristown, NJ: General Learning Press, 1976.
Wrong, Denis H., *Power: Its Forms, Bases and Uses*, Oxford: Blackwell, 1979.

Index